Yale
University

THE CAMPUS GUIDE

Yale
University

SECOND EDITION

AN ARCHITECTURAL TOUR BY

Patrick L. Pinnell

FOREWORD BY

Linda Koch Lorimer

PRINCETON ARCHITECTURAL PRESS

NEW YORK

Published by
Princeton Architectural Press
37 East Seventh Street
New York, New York 10003

Visit our website at www.papress.com.

Series Editor: Jan Cigliano Hartman
PAP Editor: Dan Simon
Layout, second edition: Bree Anne Apperley
Mapmaker: Tom Gastel

Special thanks to: Sara Bader, Janet Behning, Nicola Bednarek Brower,
Fannie Bushin, Megan Carey, Carina Cha, Andrea Chlad,
Russell Fernandez, Will Foster, Jan Haux, Diane Levinson,
Jennifer Lippert, Jacob Moore, Gina Morrow, Katharine Myers,
Margaret Rogalski, Elana Schenkler, Sara Stemen, Andrew Stepanian
Paul Wagner, and Joseph Weston of Princeton Architectural Press
—Kevin C. Lippert, publisher

Library of Congress Cataloging-in-Publication Data

Pinnell, Patrick, 1949–
Yale University / an architectural tour by Patrick L. Pinnell; foreword by
Linda Koch Lorimer. — 2nd ed.
p. cm. — (The campus guide)
Includes bibliographical references and index.
ISBN 978-1-61689-064-3 (pbk.)
1. Yale University—Guidebooks. 2. Yale University—Buildings. 3.
Yale University—Buildings—Pictorial works. 4. Yale University—
Buildings—History. I. Title.
LD6338.P55 2012
378.746'8—dc23
                                                          2011046816

CONTENTS

HOW TO USE THIS GUIDE

This guide is intended for architects, visitors, alumni, and students who wish to have an insider's look at the most historic and interesting buildings on campus and around the city of New Haven, from traditional architecture by James Gamble Rogers and John Russell Pope to Louis Kahn's Center for British Art, Paul Rudolph Hall, and Eero Saarinen's Ingalls Rink.

    The book is divided into ten walks covering the major areas of the campus. Each walk, or chapter, comprises an introductory section that describes the history of the area, with a three-dimensional map and a list of the buildings, followed by entries on each building (or cluster of buildings). Each building is discussed in its historical context, recounting the evolution of the university.

Visitors are welcome to tour the main campus of the University:

Further information from:
Yale Mead Visitor Center
149 Elm Street
Open: Mon.–Fri. 9AM–4:30PM, Sat.–Sun. 11AM–4PM
203-432-2300
www.yale.edu/visitor

Patrick Pinnell provides us with a treasure trove of historic and architectural information about Yale University. With this second edition, the first-time visitor to Yale will be introduced in detail to the campus, and alumni will delight in the new and restored architectural dimensions of their alma mater. The late Yale historian George Pierson claimed:

> Yale is at once a tradition
> A company of scholars
> A society of friends.

This volume shows how the University's architecture contributes to the truth of this statement. It also supports the remark of Yale's late president, A. Whitney Griswold, who maintained, "A great university should look at architecture as a way of expressing itself."

Yale has been fortunate in the architecture it has fostered. Since 1717, when it relocated to New Haven, the University has evolved into a living textbook of architectural styles and tastes. Today, the Yale campus in New Haven stretches over two miles in length and encompasses nearly three hundred structures. Although those of us who are part of the modern Yale are dedicated to the primary missions of research and teaching, we also see the stewardship of our architectural heritage as an important responsibility.

When the first edition of this guide was published in 1999, Yale was embarking on one of the most ambitious building programs in its history. Since then, we have completed the renovation of more than four million square feet of space, including comprehensive renovations of all of Yale's twelve undergraduate residential colleges and careful restoration of some of Yale's modern classics, including Eero Saarinen's Ingalls Rink and Paul Rudolph's Art & Architecture Building (now Rudolph Hall). It may be that Yale has made one of the greatest investments in historic preservation of any institution in our country during the last decade.

In addition, we have added to the treasury of Yale architecture in the last decade through the construction of new facilities. Among them are Cesar Pelli's Malone Engineering Center, a modern research center that complements the neighboring nineteenth-century structures, and Kroon Hall, the new home for the School of Forestry & Environmental Studies, both of which set a standard for sustainability that will serve us well into the future. The medical campus, which includes Yale's first design by Frank Gehry, has also expanded in the last decade.

These accomplishments are a result of investing over $4 billion in renewal and expansion of the campus facilities. But we are poised, as always, to look ahead with commitments to have every new structure meet at least LEED Gold standard and to embark, when resources permit, on the construction of two new residential colleges so that additional young people can have the opportunity to experience a Yale College education. A future edition of this guide will properly introduce the colleges and Yale's new 136-acre West Campus, which is located seven miles toward New York and is fast becoming a hub of scientific and medical science innovation, with art and conservation activities on the drawing board as well.

We hope that this campus guide will provide you with a thoughtful history and commentary about Yale's three centuries of campus planning while offering insights into the academic aspiration that helped shape the buildings of Yale. The guide also reveals much about the evolution of the University, its educational philosophy, and its relationship to New Haven, the city that has been Yale's home for almost all of its 310-year history.

We are grateful to Princeton Architectural Press for mounting this publication and to its author Patrick Pinnell for his continuing interest in Yale.

Linda Koch Lorimer
Vice President of the University

The Yale University campus, if certainly beautiful in places, odd, or just interestingly old in others, often seems inscrutable and inward-turning. Its architectural expression tends toward the reserved. To a surprising degree it presents this impression to the first-time visitor and leaves it with the campus veteran. The latter has learned how to navigate the place, and discovered some of its less visible interests or pleasures, yet does not always have any clear conception of the overall campus, much less of how

East Rock

it got to be as it is. Part, but only part, of the hiddenness that characterizes the campus comes from the fact that many of the buildings surround and draw their life from courtyards almost invisible to the street. That is a literal inscrutability, easily enough comprehended even if not penetrated. More puzzling are the many instances of mysterious building behaviors out in plain sight. The flamboyantly occult boxes of secret societies are dotted around the campus, and strange juxtapositions and asymmetries where the obvious importance of some building, one thinks, would usually have produced clear order around it; why does Harkness Tower rise so abruptly on its Branford College corner, for instance, and peer so obviously off-center into the Old Campus? Then there are the many instances of vistas and paths started and brought up short; the pleasant little walkway down Library Street, between Branford and Jonathan Edwards colleges, centers on Dwight Hall but leads up to a blank wall, with no window, much less an entrance, to fulfill the vista's promise. The question inevitably arises, what happened?

The fact that there is an answer to this question is the first step in understanding the inscrutabilities offered by such single puzzles and individual buildings. Something happened. There is a story to be found out and unfolded, an answer usually involving the relationships of groups of buildings on campus and in the city of New Haven—and of course it is really the story of the people who conceived, paid for, built, and used them—that explains the blankness, hiddenness, or conversely the place and direction of openness. Yale's buildings are interdependent to a very high degree, even (or especially) when they are built in contrasting architectural styles. This is the shared fact underlying many of the diverse ways in which the campus is problematic, hard to "read." Place-based relationships, especially in old places like Yale, have the odd property of often being hard to pick up when in the place, because old forces have gone away or new structures arrived to disguise old situations; but also of being almost impossible to pick up at a distance from the place, however good the maps and documents available. The first responsibility of this guide is to relate a building's conception and life to the campus overall, and second to discuss the building's physical properties. The premise is that that explanation usually will be of common interest to most people who are reading this campus architectural guide—visitors, planners and architects, staff and faculty, administration, students and alumni, historians—and will do much to make other information on use, technics, appearance, patronage, and designer hang together more coherently.

All but the last of the guide's ten walks are organized as a tour; each walk begins with a history sketch that discusses a Yale theme suggested by the buildings in that area. While not pretending to be systematically chronological—the campus is too complexly layered to make that possible— some effort has gone into sequencing the information in the history sketches so that, read first to last, they accumulate in a way that gives an impression of overall University history. A certain amount of information has necessarily been repeated in different sketches and in the entries for individual buildings, in the hope of addressing the interests of those who wish to find out about a single building, and of those who are looking for a larger picture. This book should be understood as an architectural guide that offers some history, in other words, rather than a history of Yale narrated by means of buildings.

That notwithstanding, there are a certain few things about the history of Yale's development and geographic situation that underlie the University's buildings, singly and collectively, now and in the past. These can be quickly named and described, though they are complex, nuanced, and ramifying, and a full account of them is far beyond this book's scope.[1] It is critical to appreciate that Yale is Puritan in its origin, and New Haven the town thought of itself as the defiant, leading demonstration of Puritan ideals. This may seem of only the most distant relevance today, long centuries of change after the New Haven Colony's foundation in 1638 and the College's origin in 1701. But an argument can be made that, well past the time anyone might have referred to the opinions of John Davenport, New Haven's minister-

founder, or thought about points of theological doctrine in the course of making College decisions, certain patterns of construing the world and of institutional behavior in response, patterns that originated in Puritanism,

Old Brick Row and New Haven Green, 1856, drawn and published by Barber & Punderson

continued to operate. Foremost of these was the habit of interpreting the world, and therefore determining the College's physical form, according to the theological doctrine of typology.

Differences between theological and architectural usages of the term bear explanation. Typology as a concept in architectural theory and practice was current from the eighteenth to the early twentieth centuries; it was mostly dumped when modernist theory condemned it as insufficiently open to innovation, and then returned in somewhat debased form after the 1960s. In its pragmatic contemporary understanding it says this to architects: given a certain sort of building use—fire station, factory, farmhouse—study of previous examples will show you a similarity of basic organization despite superficial changes of style and material, and you may then save time and gain reliability by employing that organizational structure to imprint your own new design. As most often employed it is a utilitarian procedure that regards the past simply as a useful resource to be mined for the benefit of the present; time really only moves forward.

Typology as idea and doctrine was not original to Puritan belief but is much older, dating to the apostle Paul and the early centuries of Christianity. It makes a wider, more powerful, and far more complicated assertion, particularly relative to past and present events, than does the concept of architectural typology. God, according to this view, has foreordained the world from beginning to end, from inception and Edenic fall to final redemption, and done so in a way that tells human beings about it if they pay close attention. Patterns repeat; an event, a set of people, a scene, or a type can be seen not only as itself, but also and equally the fulfillment of an earlier prefiguration and the anticipation of a fulfillment to come. Cycles of fall and redemption continually supersede and destroy, then prophesy each other, even as time moves toward ultimate closure. Most importantly, of course, types in the Bible's Old Testament foreshadowed those in its New, the New Law fulfilling but also abolishing the Old. But the process did not end with the establishment of Christianity. The convictions that God minutely watched over every present moment, and that He provided types that made legible the foreordained cycles leading to ultimate redemption, held a powerful grip on the Puritan imagination.

*First Yale College, reconstruction drawing by Theodore Diedricksen Jr. (*Beginnings of Yale, *1916)*

Yale College in the late 1870s: The repetitive-type buildings of the Old Brick Row at the moment they began to be replaced by the block-edge buildings that became the Old Campus

Strong circumstantial evidence exists to suggest that Davenport and his followers, when looking for a site to plant their colony, recognized, in the landscape of East and West Rocks and the pattern of rivers around what would become New Haven, a recurring biblical type, that of the Israelite's encampment in the wilderness, Solomon's Temple, and other figurations of community. The founders affirmed their recognition of the type and literalized it on the ground with the unusually perfect geometry of the town's famous Nine Square Plan. In so doing, they likely followed an illustration in one of the many books of the time that analyzed and illustrated such biblical ideal settlements, perhaps Juan Bautista Villalpando's of 1596–1604 for the Temple of Jerusalem rebuilt, according to the vision of Ezekiel, in a nine-square pattern. New Haven, then, was established with a physical form and system of governance that were consciously typological; Minister Davenport and his followers, wrote Cotton Mather of Boston, "did all that was possible, to render the Renowned Church of New Haven, like the New Jerusalem."[2]

This is a long way of getting around to explaining that at Yale there has been a remarkable persistence in repeating certain building patterns in the campus's spatial organization. There has also long and often been in evidence a deep conviction of the special chosenness of the place and the community that are Yale, an insistence (appearing like snobbery to some outsiders or, to others, especially from New York or Boston, to be maddeningly contrary to social and economic facts) that it is central and not peripheral, a model to be followed rather than a provincial emulator of metropolitan ideas and forms. The repetition is best characterized as theologically, not architecturally, typological in mindset, that is to say, not originating in mere usefulness, unthinking conservatism, or simple reverence for the past, but instead out of the sense that each recurrence may resemble the one before but really destroys and re-creates it. This is a seemingly subtle difference, until one realizes that it licenses not only repetition in the Yard of the Old Brick Row but also—equally so—the demolition of the Row and its replacement by the perimeter block dormitories of the Old Campus. Typological thought, confident of underlying continuity, recognizes the necessity and desirability of transformation under new circumstances. Similarly Yale's historical sense of uniqueness and centrality, of being a self-forming community which need not pay much attention to opinions from elsewhere, except to look back occasionally and check who is following, looks very much like an attitude inherited—typologically transformed—from the New Haven of Davenport, the Collegiate School of Abraham Pierson, and the Yale College of Thomas Clap. In its truest form it is not really arrogance or willful ignorance, but, rightly or wrongly, a sense of higher communal mission.

Fundamentally the way to see into Yale's hiddenness is to see it with the place's fondness for continuities, for types and relations of types, in mind. Looking at an individual building, seeing only its particular beauty or peculiar quirkiness, will certainly gain one something, but the greater fascinations of the whole will almost certainly never become visible. Look for repetition (and also for attempted repetition, partly frustrated; there is a good bit of that around) and buildings will begin to adhere to each other in the mind's eye, begin to cluster into constellations of meaning. Yale is one of the world's most interesting and architecturally significant campuses, one to be studied, studied again, and studied yet again, and valued for the revelation of human patterns it records and may yet anticipate.

WALK ONE: THE OLD CAMPUS AND
NEW HAVEN GREEN

> Radical though it be, the work here illustrated is dedicated to a cause
> conservative in the best sense of the word. At no point does it involve denial
> of the elemental law and order inherent in all great architecture; rather it
> is a declaration of love for the spirit of that law and order, and a reverential
> recognition of the elements that made its ancient letter in its time vital
> and beautiful.
> —Frank Lloyd Wright, *In the Cause of Architecture* (1908)

The first impression of three centuries of Yale architecture is one of
remarkable growth, variety, and change. Certainly that impression is
accurate, but it disguises an even more remarkable continuity, a persistence in
what can be thought of as architectural behavior, which must be given equal
attention in a survey of the diverse buildings. Yale has been both praised and
criticized for being a conservative institution, in general and sometimes in its
architecture, even as its innovations are noted—in architecture and aesthetics,
for example, Yale established North America's first college art gallery and
first school of art, and constructed some of the world's most compelling
modern buildings—but too often the deep history and true complexity of
the relation of new and old, the interdependence of the perceived radical and
perceived conservative, at Yale and in New Haven, go unnoticed.

If a form of scriptural interpretation—a typology of sorts—filtered
the ways New Haven and then Yale understood and characterized the
relationships of scripture and the world; if a variety of forces threatened its
standing and hence perhaps caused it to be more tenaciously held; and if
the effects of that doctrine were intensified by an in-between geographic
situation; then a reflexive basis appears for some of the continuities Yale's
buildings manifest over time. The institution's attempt to maintain a basic
set of forms associated with the creation and maintenance of a community
(whether as an end in itself or as a means is moot), both with and against the
various forces of change coming from its own growth and from its context,
provides a useful way to structure an account of the complex history of New
Haven–Yale relations. Seeing the school's architectural history in this way
also helps to make succinct sense of what is at first encounter a bewildering
variety of events, inventions, and directions.

It is well established that the Puritans who founded the New Haven
Colony in 1638, especially minister John Davenport, intended almost
from the outset that it have a college. Puritanism was functionally and
etymologically a radical branch of English Protestantism; "radical" or "from
the root" properly describes its desire to return to the pure faith and simple

forms of early Christianity. New England Puritans manifested that belief directly in architecture with a new building type, the meetinghouse, "the only original architectural invention of the English colonies," according to one historian. Yet, while new, it was at the same time radically conservative in that it was intended as a re-creation of the earliest Christian assembly halls; that is its paradox to our eyes. The colonists had no doubt that the preservation of the purifying new-and-old religion that had been their reason for emigration was dependent upon a scripture-studying laity guided by a learned, vigilant ministry. The invention of the meetinghouse proves their appreciation of the notion that the preservation of the religion was inseparable from the building forms in which it occurred. The buildings for a college might well be considered to further the process of practicing a purifying religion, not only in terms of builders' traditions or utility but with an alertness to the typological conditioning certainly present at their origin.

From its belated foundation in 1701 until its definitive establishment in New Haven in 1717, education within the Collegiate School occurred in the wooden houses of its successive minister rectors in shore towns between New Haven and the mouth of the Connecticut River, as well as in Milford, south of New Haven and up the river to Wethersfield, close to Hartford. Their parlors held the school's library, while the ministers' wives took care of food in the characteristic kitchen ells at the rear. The local meetinghouse was the symbolic center of the College's life, though not its daily focus. The situation once in New Haven was in some ways larger but not much different organizationally. The wooden first Yale College House was essentially one house multiplied by three—three standard center-chimney, center-hall houses put together end to end, enlarged a little at one end for the sake of a library and hall, with a big kitchen ell jutting out at the same end. The premise was that the people of Yale constituted a household, larger than other New Haven households, but still providing the same domestic services of shelter and sustenance. The significant difference in New Haven, though, was the utter clarity of the local spatial situation; the broad front of the communal College House fronted and helped define the space of the square Green, in the center of which stood the square meetinghouse in which students, faculty, and other citizens worshiped on Sunday. To say that Yale shared that focus with New Haven is somewhat deceptive, since the College was not only in but a participating entity of the town.

That unified communal system, visually expressed and visually reinforced, became less clear with the construction of Connecticut Hall in 1750–53. It was set further back from the Green than the wooden College, making ambivalent the sense of full participation. Then with the first Yale Chapel of 1761–63, steepled but near enough to being square as a traditional meetinghouse, and the introduction of College services, President Clap removed any ambiguity. New Haven was giving indications of crypto-Episcopal theological unreliability, and Yale wished to reserve its right to withdraw for the sake of constructing its own community. Still, its buildings—now two in type, a dormitory and an assembly building, recognizably kin in that they were the same heights and built of the same brick, and used the same windows—acknowledged and fronted the public Green. In the same period, on the side away from the Green, a separate dining Commons began the gradual move of certain functions, previously integrated into the two college building types, into their own independent structures in the backyard of the College.

With the Trumbull Plan of 1792, Yale turned the two types into prototypes. The institution now began to grow in two different ways. Most obviously, it expanded gradually by alternating construction of a dormitory-type with that of an assembly-type, by 1836 accumulating the eight-building array called the Brick Row. The mind-set of this system, note, is exactly the same as that which in 1717 produced the first Yale College building by multiplying a standard house-type. Meanwhile the College also grew by the proliferation of more experimental types out back. The rear of the College Yard became the place not only for the privies and coal storage, but also for strongbox structures housing new activities of functional and symbolic significance; the Cabinet of 1819 displayed an expensive, prestigious mineralogical collection, and the Trumbull Gallery of 1832 established a similar status for art. Meanwhile too, the factory system, housed in buildings confusingly like those of the Row, was emerging in New Haven.

Between 1842 and 1846, the school mustered a large financial effort to construct its first structure designed as a library; the Old Library, now Dwight Hall, was placed in the rear of the Yard, not in the Brick Row. This move signaled a 180-degree turnaround of Yale's orientation, away from symbolic participation in the realm of the New Haven Green, which held the Connecticut Capitol, on which Yale relied ever less for financial support, and Center Church, with which Yale's relationship was ever less exclusive. The library, built in the type-form of a Gothic chapel, definitively displaced the memory of the New Haven meetinghouse. Yale began to look upon New Haven more or less as just the source for the utilitarian services it did not itself provide, and as entertainment. In the same year the Library started construction, Commons closed down, and for the rest of the century Yale men ate in other designated commons or dispersed to New Haven restaurants and little free-floating clubs. The Fence went up on three sides of the College, really a wall of perching men looking out on the city, and High Street and the Library were pushed through basically as fire engine access.

The 1860s saw Yale seriously consider moving away from its center city location. Instead it simply knocked down the Row and reinvented its dormitory type as an urban fortification wall, retaining for the most part the internal organization of the Row dorms but changing the orientation to recognize the Library and the interior of the campus as their focus. The Sheffield Scientific School was founded and prospered in this period, a counter institution within Yale that not only acknowledged the importance of contemporary industrial society but also, in that it proceeded on the European model of a student body housed in the town rather than the English model of a dormitory-based college, acted as an irritant reminding Yale of how far it had moved from its New Haven affiliations. What unity a burgeoning Yale could claim in the last decades of the nineteenth century was due more to its athletic teams than to any common experience of daily life, a curriculum, or a shared history.

A drive to rectify the confusion of realms began as the bicentennial celebration of 1901 approached. By fits and starts Yale reinvented itself, bringing its students back onto campus for eating, sleeping, and study, and accumulated a physical structure that enabled it to return to its root purpose of shaping a knowable small community of common purpose and symbolism. Bingham and McClellan Halls, on this walk, were respectively the programmatic and the stylistic last steps toward the *College of Memory* of Walk Three.

1. Rector Abraham Pierson Statue
Launt Thompson, sculptor, 1874

Yale's statues speak. Not only do they say who they honor and in what fashion, but also, more subtly, they speak volumes in what can be called the body language of statues—placement and orientation. The *Rector Pierson*, Yale's first public sculpture, is one of several statues with a sort of Flying Dutchman history of appearing at different places around the campus over time and saying subtly different things at each appearance. Pierson's first post in 1874 was beside the newly built School of Art (Street Hall, 1864–66), staring sternly out from the campus toward Chapel Street and implicitly announcing to the public that this suspicious stuff, "art," did indeed have some spiritual worth. Vanderbilt Hall's construction in 1894 displaced the statue, and it found its new site and thus its new message here in the enclave of the Old Campus. Turned away from the street, indeed from the whole outer world, it was to speak only to the elect within a campus newly closed off from the surrounding city.

"Hank Statue," the student nickname derived from the Latin inscription on its base ("Hanc Statuam…"), commemorates Rector Abraham Pierson (1646–1707). Pierson presided over the first six years of an institution not yet called Yale (it was the Collegiate School) and not yet in New Haven (it taught its lessons in locations near the mouth of the Connecticut River, within a neutral zone between the rival colonies of Hartford and New Haven). Pierson was the son of the Reverend Abraham Pierson Sr., founder in 1644 of the shore town of Branford, Connecticut, and a staunch supporter of New Haven founder John Davenport's strict theological orthodoxy. Pierson Jr., Harvard College, Class of 1668, preached for twenty-two years (1673–99) in Newark, New Jersey, a town founded by secessionist New Haveners intent on preserving the old ways of Puritanism after their colony's forced unification with theologically more liberal Hartford. His leadership of the infant college was successful, despite the considerable additional responsibilities he undertook as a local minister, and his sudden death was a setback for the school. Ten years and much travail ensued before it found a permanent home, and shortly after its permanent name, in New Haven.

Judged as art, the 1874 sculpture by Launt Thompson (1833–1894) is not in a league with the best of the filial-piety colonial ancestors in bronze with which Gilded Age Americans began to stock their cities, like Saint-Gaudens's swashbuckling *Puritan* of 1884, up the road in Springfield. But Thompson's stern, quiet figure was apparently appreciated two generations later by James Gamble Rogers, architect of Harkness Tower on the other side of High Street. Stand on the busy sidewalk in front of the Pierson statue and note how exactly the large

arch at the base of the Tower frames the sculpture in front of it; Gamble Rogers, himself something of a swashbuckling individualist within traditional architectural styles, here offers an appropriately deferential, campus-unifying compliment to the rector and his sculptor.

Another copy of the statue is in Clinton, Connecticut, within the constellation of sites at which the Collegiate School was conducted. There it is paired with another effigy by Thompson, of Charles Morgan, donor of both Pierson copies.

Rector Abraham Pierson Statue

2. Connecticut Hall, Old Brick Row, and Nathan Hale Statue

Connecticut Hall
President Thomas Clap, Francis Letort, and Thomas Bills, 1753
Nathan Hale Statue
Bela Lyon Pratt, sculptor, 1913

Time was when Yale built great, plain, brick halls like Connecticut Hall in the reflexive way the ancient Greeks built temples at Paestum. There *was* variation, but it was subtle, visible only to those initiated into the system. From 1750 until just after the Civil War, Yale men built them, and lived, studied, and played in them, in a succession of buildings that asks for biblical rhetoric: "And South Middle College begat South College, and South College begat North Middle." The assembly became the fabled Old Brick Row, a vanished Yale from whose days Connecticut Hall alone is left to tell the tale.

Connecticut, more often known in the days of the Row as South Middle College, was built in 1750–53 with funds cobbled together from a lottery, the Connecticut Assembly, and proceeds from the sale of a French ship captured in a hot interval of the long-lasting, on-and-off English and French struggle for North America. President Thomas Clap's was the guiding intelligence for the fundraising and the design, the latter of which owed much to Harvard's Massachusetts Hall of 1718–20. Francis Letort and Thomas Bills carried out construction of the 40-by-100-foot structure, setting it well back from the street, behind the long wooden barracks of the original Yale College building of 1717–18. (Long since torn down; see Bingham Hall.)

The internal organization followed the tradition of English college buildings, with stacks of rooms paired around a central stairhall in a manner later called the "entryway system." (It is a dormitory design strategy that is intrinsically inferior for watchfulness and control to the "hall system" of long central corridors, favored in the twentieth century generally and for women's dormitories in particular.) As built, each room had a larger, shared sleeping space and two tiny, four-by-five-foot, individual study and prayer booths. These latter, along with recitation rooms, were the key spaces of a Puritan education. (At Harvard, students were charged for the use of a study but not for a bedchamber.) Daylight for reading was indispensable, so Connecticut Hall's original big sash windows often had partition walls set right behind them, apportioning light and air for a study on one side, sleeping space on the other. The puzzling pairs of smaller windows in the middle of the building's long facades came out of this same internal arrangement; each served one student study's need for light on the pages of a book or a Bible.

Nathan Hale Statue

Connecticut Hall was the first of five nearly identical 64-student halls, which Yale built as the College grew, in 1793–94, 1801, 1820, and 1835, in a line broadside to the New Haven Green like so many brick men-o'-war. The dormitories alternated with other, similar-sized brick boxes, turned perpendicular to the Green and equipped with steeples, which housed chapels, classrooms, and office space. These too were built at intervals as needed, in 1761–63, 1803–4, and 1824. It was a formula for college growth at once functional, practical in its tuition-based cash flow implications, and visually powerful. The Brick Row was regarded as the "Mother Plan" of American colleges as new institutions were founded across the expanding country in the nineteenth century.[1]

The Old Brick Row, open to the city and looking too much like a "factory of men," gave way after 1870 to a new Yale made up of stone buildings focused inward on green courtyards, turned away from the gritty reality of industrial New Haven. Saving only Connecticut, all of it was torn down by the time of the College's Bicentennial celebration in 1901. A couple of twentieth-century campaigns have transformed Connecticut from a dormitory into a working monument to Yale's history. The building's center has been hollowed to make a high meeting room, plain yet proportioned like a banquet house, now the scene of University-wide faculty meetings. Student rooms are now faculty offices and seminar rooms equipped with Windsor chairs and calligraphically incised slate plaques commemorating famous occupants. There is no trace of the tiny individual study-boxes once fundamental to a Yale education, but sitting on one of Connecticut's wide slate sills, within the thickness of the old brick walls, looking out the small-paned window sash at the Old Campus outside, it is still possible to sense something of the simultaneous power and tenderness that went into building the Row.

At the northeast corner of Connecticut Hall stands a statue representing a fettered, open-collared Nathan Hale, Class of 1773, as he utters his famous patriotic regret just before being hanged as a spy by the British. (It previously stood at the center of the east facade, facing toward the Green.) The American sculptor Bela Lyon Pratt (1867–1917) in 1898 imagined a Hale who, though more

romantically modeled, made a fitting pair with the Abraham Pierson statue set up
on the Campus a generation before. If the Pierson statue represents the spiritual
scholar-teacher, Pratt gave Yale its heroic, team-player student. Pratt's statue was
finally erected on the campus in September 1913. Another copy of the statue stands
at the entrance to the Central Intelligence Agency in Langley, Virginia. For those
interested in related statues, there is an 1890 Hale bronze by Frederick MacMonnies
(1863–1937) in New York's City Hall Park, and a study for it rests on the main stair
landing of Woodbridge Hall, the University's chief administration building.

3. Dwight Hall (Old Library) and Theodore Dwight Woolsey Statue

Dwight Hall
Henry Austin, architect, 1846
Woolsey Statue
John Ferguson Weir, sculptor, 1896

Dwight Hall, as it is now used and named, appears to be an moderately early
Gothic Revival (1840s) place of worship, its small-scaled elements and dry profiles
revealing the architect's sources in books rather than direct experience of the style.
The symmetrical composition is rooted in Federal-era classicism, even though Henry
Austin (1804–1891) used proportions and details culled from such publications
as Augustus Charles Pugin's *Specimens of Gothic Architecture* to distance the
building unmistakably from the solid, unstylized boxes of the Old Brick Row. Austin's
brownstone building is dark in multiple senses, its dreamy otherworldliness in
contrast with the barnlike colonial directness of Connecticut Hall, the only surviving
building of the Row.[2]

But Dwight Chapel was not built to be a chapel. It was conceived as Yale
College's first purpose-built library, the College's own in the middle section, three
student literary societies' private book collections in the wings. Austin's structure
was placed well behind the Row in what was then the backyard of the College, in
the company of privies and woodsheds. From the building's deliberate distancing of
itself, stylistically and physically, from the main line of College buildings, much can be
gleaned about both the utilitarian and the "self-image" concerns of Yale of that time.

By the early nineteenth century, with the pioneer manufacturing success of Eli
Whitney and others, the city increasingly made its living in the factory, a building
type relatively new to America and often built of brick. As more factories sprung up,
attracting as they did a population of workers often rural or foreign in origin, Yale men
became less enchanted with the College's aging brick boxes, which bore more than
a passing resemblance to the new intruders. Yale scientist Benjamin Silliman tried
to justify the Row structures as "manufactories, not indeed of cotton and wool,

but of mind," but that spin attempt went nowhere fast. By the 1830s the College clearly had an image problem.

Nonetheless, in 1835 Yale obdurately built its last Connecticut Hall clone, Divinity College, a dormitory marking the north end and limit of the system. The last possible site in the Row was a gap where a steepled library should have been built. The book collections belonging to the College and its student organizations clearly needed to be brought together out of the various rooms and corners in which they were cached; here was the opportunity to give them the single building that dignity and utility demanded. By the time serious discussion and fund-raising began in the late 1830s, even Yale had to recognize the need for a change in its time-honored system of Row-type structures. In 1838 Harvard had begun construction of its new library, Gore Hall, in a Gothic design that owed something, though perhaps not quite enough, to King's College Chapel in Cambridge, England. A. J. Davis, a New York architect with strong New Haven ties, had already completed a library for newly founded New York University in a similar style, and had still other projects in hand. Gothic was in the air.

But if it seemed a bad fit to jam an odd library peg into the last hole in the Row, license to build elsewhere, and in a different style if desired, came from another direction altogether. The Library had to be made safe from fire, coal-burning in particular. Fire is an age-old librarian's concern, from the burning of Alexandria on down. In New Haven that perennial concern would have been heightened not only by recent disastrous fires in the city in 1836 and 1837, but by the fact that new heating technology was just coming into use. Stimulated by the increasing scarcity and expense of wood, citizens and Yale students were learning how to burn coal, a fuel that had first been sold in the city in 1827. (Some at first did not believe that "rock" could provide heat; when coal was first used in a local hotel, "many persons went to see it burn, and the *faithless* were made to *believe*.") If the Yale Fire Marshal of the 1990s had halogen-lamp worries, imagine the trepidation of the College administration at the introduction of coal into all the old fireplaces, which, room by room, were then the only source of heat in student rooms and classrooms alike. Imagine in particular the anxieties of any librarian about a building sandwiched tightly between two large collections of student-tended fires (called dormitories), and one motive for putting the new building elsewhere becomes very apparent.

The location chosen, then, had the advantages of freeing the new building from awkward juxtaposition of architectural styles and of minimizing the likelihood of flames jumping from nearby buildings. It also allowed a breadth for the structure that let the different libraries—Yale College's, and those of the Linonian, Calliope, and Brothers-in-Unity societies—have visible identities and more daylight. The concern about fire remained strong enough that the building as constructed had no heating whatever, and a plan that featured load-bearing masonry firewalls cutting each segment off from its adjacent neighbors (hence the five separate entrances still

Woolsey Statue

visible today). Construction began in 1842 but proceeded by fits and starts due to finances; the College even used the threat of fire to try to set one under donors. "That Yale College should have existed one hundred and forty years," went one appeal, "with no other accommodations for books, than small chambers and mere attic apartments, quite insecure against the ravages of fire, is a fact, both surprising and humiliating."

The items Yale moved into the Library after 1844 included a diverse collection of ancestral busts, coins, art, stuffed animals, geological specimens, and four Chinese scrolls eulogizing George Washington, as well as books. The Library was not so much a place of scholarly research (our contemporary assumption) as a *Wunderkammer* of evidence for God's providence.[3] Thus when collection after collection subsequently moved out of the Library into its own building—the art into Street Hall in 1867, the scientific specimens into the first Peabody Museum in 1873–76, the books to Sterling Library in 1930—and the building converted in 1931 to become Dwight Hall and chapel, it was not so much that it was turned into a religious structure; religion, rather, was the only thing left behind. The organ and colored glass windows now in the chapel, ratifying its status, long postdate the original construction of the building. Since 1931 the building has sheltered and taken its name from Dwight Hall, the center for Yale's volunteer social-outreach programs, as well as other University religious and charitable organizations.

Confusingly enough, the statue directly in front of Dwight Hall represents neither one of the Dwights who was a Yale president; the seated figure memorializes Theodore Dwight Woolsey (1801–1889), Professor of Greek and President 1846–71. Woolsey was at least related to the Dwights (he was a nephew of the senior Timothy Dwight), but he is commemorated here in a statue, unveiled in 1896, for his presidency and, presumably, because he was a major donor to the original construction of the building. The sculptor, John Ferguson Weir (1841–1926), was the first director of the School of Art and is better known to history for his paintings (stylistically, half Wright of Derby and half Piranesi) of dark, dramatic industrial interior scenes. Weir's bronze Woolsey is more contemplative than the tight-jawed visionary

Augustus Saint-Gaudens portrayed in the marble bust, dating from the mid-1870s, which long watched over the Woolsey Hall entrance foyer and is now in the Yale Art Gallery. Saint-Gaudens's Woolsey is the president who, with his students, came under siege in Connecticut Hall by a mob with cannons one evening in 1854; Weir's is the Woolsey who helped set in motion the demise of the Old Brick Row and the retreat of Yale from the outside world.

Seen from the sidewalk directly in front of the statue, Woolsey's introspective face is precisely sheltered by the Gothic arch of the Dwight Hall facade behind him. Higher up, just below the copper roofs of the octagonal towers at the four major corners of the Old Library, grotesque heads grimace down at the Campus. In the first decade of the new century, plans have been floated to move Dwight Hall, the student-run public service organization, out of the building and down to 143 Elm Street, facing the Green. As of this writing the idea is on hold.

4. Farnam Hall, Durfee Hall, and Battell Chapel

Farnam Hall
Russell Sturgis Jr., 1870
Durfee Hall
Russell Sturgis Jr., 1871
Battell Chapel
Russell Sturgis Jr., 1876

The year before the end of the Civil War, a diverse group of men, holding in common deep pockets and an interest in the Yale of the future, stepped forward with donations for new buildings. The year 1864 marked the gifts that resulted in the Art School (Street Hall) in 1866, two dormitories (Durfee and Farnam Halls) by 1871, and the third chapel (Battell) in Yale's history by 1876. These four buildings indicated new directions the College took in the post–Civil War years— in gifts to the institution, in its relationship to New Haven, and in its ways of memorializing itself.

New York architect Russell Sturgis Jr. (1838–1909) designed Farnam and Durfee almost simultaneously, and Battell Chapel not many years after. It is possible that what to our eyes today seems a subtly but definitely disjointed relationship among the three buildings—most obviously the way the Chapel's main entrance dumps out unceremoniously into the end wall of Durfee—was intended by Sturgis. He was an early and ardent American proponent of the version of Gothic Revival architecture advanced by the English critic John Ruskin (1819–1900), and the tight-packed Yale juxtaposition bears considerable site-plan resemblance to Oxford's 1866 Keble College Chapel and its two flanking dorms, designed by Ruskin sympathizer William Butterfield.

Farnam Hall

One of Sturgis's intentions certainly needs no guessing to discover; the three structures together made an elegant but tough bastion of the corner of College and Elm, unmistakable evidence of Yale's decision to wall its life off from the city. The dormitories turned their entrances and living areas in to the College block, setting in motion the change of thinking that would eventually lead to this area being called not the "College Green" or "Yard," as formerly, but the "Campus." To make way for Durfee, limited space dictated knocking down the newest dormitory of the Brick Row, Divinity College (1836), an extravagant, donor-alienating move of a sort to which the Yale Corporation was not normally given. That this was the course adopted indicated the force of purpose behind the enclosure movement. Clearing space for Farnam required demolition only of the venerable Second President's House (1799), used since 1847 as a laboratory by the small, displaceable Department of Philosophy and the Arts, seed germ of both the Graduate School and the Sheffield Scientific School. The Campus strategy would prove to be almost as visually formidable, practical, and economical for its day as the Row had been in its.

Farnam, in brick and a variety of stones, and Durfee, in stone, are four-story structures based on the same time-honored entryway system used in Connecticut Hall six generations before. They got their (original numbers) twenty bedrooms and ten common rooms per floor in different ways; Farnam, built first, experimentally split its floors down the middle, each suite's rooms all facing the same way, in or out, while Durfee reverted to the traditional Trumbull Plan of the Row dorms, with all bedrooms located on the outside face and all common rooms on the Campus face. Either way, the new standard-size dorm increment was eighty beds, up from the

Battell Chapel

Brick Row's usual sixty-four. For all the drastic change in overall strategy, Yale's reflex method held true; evolve a type, then perpetuate it.

Farnam is the more interesting building of the pair, indeed having only one rival, the Center for British Art, for the title of most tectonically didactic building on campus; lintels, column shafts and bases, and all other components of the facade are made of different kinds of brick and stone chosen according to the hardness and other characteristics appropriate to the placement and function of the piece in question. Like the Kahn-designed building, Farnam grades the size of its structural elements from ground to sky, stepping its floors slightly inward as it rises. Durfee is less complex. Still didactic in its sorting-out of materials, like the contrast of smooth, floor-indicating belt courses with random rough ashlar walls, it is saved from pompousness by lighthearted polychrome window arches, by cautious experimentalism in iron window supports, and most of all by the positively goofy corner colonnettes and tourelles, the frozen-in-stone skyrockets at the major corners of the facade. When it opened, Durfee was claimed by the College seniors as theirs, not only (perhaps) because it was equipped with the fireplaces Farnam lacked and gentlemen liked, but because the multiple tall chimneys for those fireplaces, in combination with the stylish corner features, gave the building a high-hatted jauntiness, all too soon to vanish under student wear and black grit in the New Haven air. From being at first the focus of upper-classmen's living, with the annual secret-society ritual of Tap Day in front of Durfee, the two buildings slid into being "Dirty Durfee" and "Filthy Farnam." Since the 1920s they have been freshman dorms; architect Edward Larrabee Barnes renovated them in the mid-1970s, using funds originally intended for two new colleges.

The school wedged Battell Chapel into the corner defined by Farnam and Durfee not long after their completion. From the outset the school's object in building it was not only to shelter faithful in worship but to profess faith in Yale itself. Battell was to "provide a memorial hall–a family gathering place–which might be open to all the children of this prolific alma mater on days of academic festivity." Forty stained-glass windows memorialize Yale luminaries in light, and plaques, tablets, and inscribed quotations line the interior. Yale discontinued required morning chapel in the 1920s, but, besides the religious services that daily continue in the building, a sense abides of Battell as the University's moral hub. Architect J. C. Cady enlarged it in 1893, and Herbert S. Newman restored its astonishingly bright polychrome interior in the late 1980s. On the exterior, note how Sturgis wrapped the Chapel in a blind Gothic arcade screen, straight out of Ruskin's 1853 *Stones of Venice*, presumably to distinguish it from Farnam and Durfee.

Farnam, Durfee, and Battell were among the first Yale buildings to be named for individual donors rather than function ("Old Chapel"), location ("South Middle"), or legislative funding ("Connecticut Hall"). These buildings forecast the new post–Civil War funding pattern, in which it was to the concentrated wealth of individuals or families, rather than to state government or collective small-scale donations, that Yale would look for its building patronage.

5. Lawrance Hall, Welch Hall, and Phelps Hall

Lawrance Hall
Russell Sturgis Jr., 1886
Welch Hall
Bruce Price, 1891
Phelps Hall
Charles Coolidge Haight, 1896

The events that produced Durfee and Farnam Halls and Battell Chapel had been set in motion in the mid-1860s, during the last years of Theodore Dwight Woolsey's presidency. Woolsey's successor, Noah Porter, took office in 1871. His term saw Yale build much, but most of the new architecture was instigated by and for the non-College components of the institution: Timothy Dwight almost single-handedly saved the Divinity School and built it a new cluster of chapel, library, and dormitories (1869–81); the banker George Peabody installed his nephew, Othniel Marsh, in a new, grand natural history museum (1873–76); and the trustees of the semi-independent Sheffield Scientific School embarked on a protracted expansion campaign (1872 and after). To be fair, Porter watched over the installation of basic new infrastructure while in office, including steam heat lines connecting Campus buildings to a central boiler, and sewer lines and indoor plumbing fitted into existing buildings; but only late in an administration lasting fifteen years, until 1886, did any new architecture appear on the central Yale block.

Under the pressure of a slowly increasing undergraduate population, Yale called Durfee and Farnam's architect out of retirement to design another dormitory. Russell Sturgis Jr. (1838–1909), starting in 1880, had traded his drafting board for a writing table, and he would go on to become one of the country's leading critics and historians of art. Lawrance Hall, completed in 1886, was his swan song. Lawrance's basic module (entryway stair on the Campus side only, common room on that side, two bedrooms facing the street) nearly duplicated that of Durfee (1871). The elevations are thinner, more vertical, and fussier than those of its elder brothers, with neither the quiet probity of Farnam nor the jauntiness of Durfee.

Timothy Dwight, grandson and namesake of the first Yale president, succeeded Porter in 1886. Dwight immediately recommended the process of turning the campus block into an enclosed quadrangle and Yale, legally and administratively, into a genuine university. His immediate priorities were to build a vastly enlarged, research-oriented University Library, of which Chittenden Hall in 1888 was to be the first installment, and a new classroom building, Osborn Hall (see Bingham Hall), started the same year. While still following the plan to line the outside of the College block with a wall of buildings, tearing down the Brick Row to form an idyllic green quadrangle inside, both structures softened the hard outside wall by having entrances on the street side as well as on the protected interior. Osborn's was a great curving mouth at the corner of Chapel and College, which, though it displaced the much loved Fence, still acquired great student and public affection.

Osborn's architect, Bruce Price (1843–1903), was next called on to design the first new dormitory of the Dwight years, Welch Hall of 1891. It plugged, but not completely, the College Street frontage remaining between Osborn and Lawrance, leaving one gap for a fence and gate on the south toward Osborn, and another, larger one intended for a gateway building, on its north. The ambivalence toward further enclosure for the College block did not end there; as Welch was constructed, there was still another way into the Campus by way of a vaulted

Lawrance Hall

passage directly through its center. The passage entrance, now closed, and the stairs leading to it, are still visible on College Street. No doubt a good part of this openness was specified by the donor, who gave the building in honor of his father, a former mayor of New Haven. But beyond that fortuitous

Welch Hall

circumstance, it is clear that by the early 1890s President Dwight was attempting to create a kind of urbanistic halfway covenant in which the dividing walls between Yale and New Haven would definitely exist but be more permeable curtain than armored barrier. Price was an inventive jackdaw of an architect, eclectic but with a gift for making striking, often abstractly geometric forms. He is best known to history for his houses for Pierre Lorillard in Tuxedo Park, New Jersey, interesting in their own right and for their influence on the young Frank Lloyd Wright. Perhaps as a consequence of reactions to the demonstrative character of Osborn, brownstone Welch is one of his quieter designs. It cannot be called either Gothic or classical, though it refers to both styles, and it certainly pays homage to Durfee in its elevations and to Farnam in its plan, reinstituting, but now with fireplaces, the nontraditional one-sided suite arrangement of the early, more experimental Sturgis dormitory.

Phelps Archway (properly, Phelps Hall) filled the gap between Welch and Lawrance in 1896. Yale's habits die even harder than its buildings: when the new dormitory (Welch) was built, adjacent land was left open in anticipation of future classroom and office needs (Phelps); this is just how the Old Brick Row grew for generations. Phelps's architect was New Yorker Charles Coolidge Haight (1841–1917), dubbed by a later critic "Peacemaker" for his ability to design structures that resolved clashes between discordant neighbors. The task of reconciling Lawrance on one side with Welch on the other was not his toughest job, but still one must admire the smoothness with which Haight pulled it off. Even more than arching the transition from one side to the other, Phelps's corner towers venerate the Old Library (Dwight Hall), which it now faced across open ground that had been newly cleared by demolition of the Brick Row. The building thus also attempted to broker a certain sort of peace across human as well as architectural generations, despite its involvement in demolition of the Row, a peace that the man in whose name the building was donated would likely have approved. W. W. Phelps, BA 1860, had been a leader of the "Young Yale" movement in the 1870s, advocating modern management for the University and a secular Yale Corporation, exactly the kinds of reform Dwight instituted in his administration. Haight's crisp, abstract Gothic tower has for decades been home to the Classics Department.

6. New Haven Green

Center Church
Asher Benjamin and Ithiel Town, 1815
United Church
Ebenezer Johnson and David Hoadley, 1815
Trinity Church
Ithiel Town, 1814

Outside Phelps Gate and straight across College Street, the New Haven Green slopes gradually down under a canopy of trees to Temple Street and its three churches, then levels and opens out to the business buildings of Church Street. The renovated Green has a kind of rough-around-the-edges splendor, which, truth be told, has been its condition as often as not since it was laid out as the central unit of New Haven's Nine-Square Plan sometime between 1638 and 1641. For all the aspirations loaded into that startlingly pure geometry—the best evidence indicates it was conceived by its Puritan founders as a Type of the camp of the Tribes of Israel in the Wilderness—the young Colony's English builders took a couple of trial and error decades figuring out how to deal with the different materials and more extreme weather of New England, which meant that even significant buildings began to look bad almost from the day of completion. Thus however aspiring and originally four-square the first meeting house put up, approximately in the center of the square, in 1640, it very soon became a maintenance problem and had to be replaced altogether in 1670. The development of the Green and its buildings is commensurate with that beginning, a Jacobethan play turned urban history, featuring a mix of clowns and cows with the high drama of political and religious rivalries, of squalor with ceremony. The Green of the present day is really the result of a series of post-Revolution campaigns to bring physical dignity to New Haven, the two most notable led by James Hillhouse (1754–1832), a landowner, developer, U.S. senator, and Treasurer of Yale for a half century. The first effort removed the weeds and stones of the didactically decayed ("Remember, Man…") Puritan graveyard behind what is now the Center Church site, while the second planted the elms, which in their glory decades made New Haven by consensus a beautiful city, and in their longer decades of Dutch Elm Disease made it by similar consensus a decrepit one.

The three present-day churches went up almost simultaneously, shortly after Hillhouse's efforts began to take hold; they are the results of a paroxysm of competition among two Congregational groups and an Episcopalian one, between 1812 and 1815. The three buildings have compound origins in published drawings from abroad, consultations with non–New Haven architects, and talented local builder-designers. Center Church, properly First Congregational, is the legal

Phelps Hall

Center Church

descendant of the 1640 meetinghouse and probably occupies its site. Asher P. Benjamin (1773–1845) sent down a design from Boston, which was put up in 1812–14 by the studious and inventive Ithiel Town (1784–1844). Like most major New England churches of the era, it was based on James Gibbs's 1721–26 St. Martin-in-the-Fields, London; the allegiance to the well-tried type, while strange to sensibilities that wonder why a Revolution made so little difference, was characteristic of the time and, most certainly, of New Haven. Further proof of that lies immediately north in the United Congregational Church of 1812–15, which is still another St. Martin type-variant, concocted from a slightly different mix of the same sorts of sources worked together by the builder, David Hoadley (1774–1839). Both churches have hovering saucer-dome vaults inside, not a St. Martin feature, and both make knowing, visually smart variations on aspects of the mutual model. For

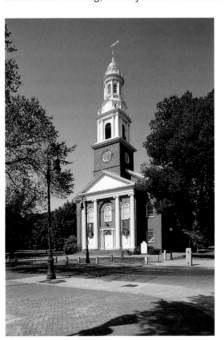

United Church

example, where the London church's portico order is Corinthian, Town's Center Church porch is in the heavier, lower Doric but compensates with a taller, delicate steeple and spire. In his version of the same features, Hoadley sought a gentler and more contained effect, with Ionic portico half-columns pushed back into the brick volume behind, and a tower that follows Gibbs's closely up through its third stage but then replaces the model's spire with the rounded closure of a tempietto dome. Town and Hoadley earned the commemorative tablets in their respective buildings' vestibules.

Both men went on to design notable works in the area, Hoadley

Trinity Church

the Philosophical Building (1819) at Yale, Town on the Green again, and elsewhere in New Haven as well as nationally. Town's timesharing temple for the Connecticut co-Capitol (1827–31) stood on the Green between Phelps Hall and Center Church until it was torn down by New Haven in a fit of pique over losing the state government entirely to Hartford, later in the nineteenth century. While just beginning work on Center Church, Town was also commissioned by New Haven Episcopalians to do Trinity Church (1813–14), its appearance on the Green neatly symbolizing the push of the former Church of England into power-sharing in Connecticut. Much altered over the years, Town's Trinity is still of architectural interest as one of the earliest Gothic Revival buildings in America. Immediately to its south on Chapel Street occurred the 1854 killing that precipitated an armed siege of Yale. Indeed, the design of the fence around the Green, by the local builder Nahum Hayward around 1846, is evidence of not only abstract civic pride but a residuum of the mid-nineteenth-century town-gown problems culminating in that murder. Its granite piers and cast-iron rails are handsome, nearly immovable let alone throwable, and definitely unsittable. It is a design in contrast with the homely yet well-loved Yale Fence, which stood across College Street. The Fence's wooden rails, from 1833 until its demise, afforded Yale men not only a good perch to survey the town, but also, on occasion, easy conversion to weaponry and fuel for fires.

7. Bingham Hall and plaques for Yale College, the Fence, and Osborn Hall

Bingham Hall
Walter B. Chambers, 1928

Bingham Hall, of 1928, is the latest and least Yale-looking structure to occupy this corner on which Yale began. Surprisingly enough its collegiate Gothic design came from the same architect, Walter B. Chambers of New York, who three years earlier designed McClellan in neo-Georgian style. Bingham has a certain quiet quirkiness

Bingham Hall

in the entry hall under the tower on the Old Campus side, which shows off a bit of 1920s picture-palace terra-cotta zip, as do the gargoyles atop the tower. As built, the building housed an odd mix of uses: dorm rooms, club rooms, a library high in the tower, and, least likely of all, an astronomical observatory with a copper-covered dome (removed in a 1990s renovation).

Yale College Plaque

Two plaques low on the east face of Bingham's tower mark this corner as the deepest dig spot in Yale-New Haven archeology. Reverential in bronze, the smaller tablet reminds those having Latin and a memory for their Virgil that this was "the cradle of our race" (*gentis cunabula nostrae*), location of the first Yale College building of 1717–18. Set into the wall to the left of the "cradle" tablet is a bas-relief rendition of an old photograph of the Fence, student worthies atop it, the Old Brick Row behind. At Yale the term "the Fence" refers to *the* Fence, the unpainted wooden two- or three-rung affair that rimmed the College Yard after 1833, gradually supplanted by the

The Fence

accumulation of perimeter-block, non-street-facing dormitories after the U.S. Civil War, and had its last stand–or sit–here in 1888. In its prime, the four undergraduate classes each had its own jealously guarded Fence section, seniors holding down the hot corner at York and Chapel, just in front of where the old wooden College had been. Yale had several fences before the Fence, of the more formal, expensive, vertical-picket variety, and afterward lots of even more expensive stone walls with elegant wrought-iron gates; none gained the cheap, post-and-round-rail Fence's astonishing centrality to Yale life.

That a rail fence, unlike a picket one, could be used as a seat was just the pragmatic precondition to why the Fence acquired such psychological magic. Students quickly discovered after the Fence's erection that it was interesting both to see and to be seen there. It was a place to pause and pose. The Fence's gratifying emotional grip probably took even stronger hold when its social status was reinforced by the advent of photography. From the 1840s on, those easy power-poses and blustery class groupings were recorded to intensify their memory. Like a half-comprehending medieval reenactment of a Roman rite, pictures of athletic team captains are still taken on an embalmed section of the Fence kept in Payne Whitney Gymnasium.

Between the death of the Fence in 1888 and the construction in 1926–28 of the current placeholder, Bingham Hall, there was a building here that won Yale's affection but lost out to urban policy and good taste. Bruce Price's Osborn Hall was demolished after only thirty years–"I know thee not, old man"–because its boisterous style did not comport well with Yale's self-image after its bicentennial (see Vanderbilt Hall). It also was too open to New Haven; its grand entry was too inviting and its location at the city's busiest corner made it acoustically untenable as a classroom building in pre-air-conditioning days. Function provided the excuse that taste desired, and Osborn is memorialized in a stone bas-relief at the northwest corner of Bingham's Old Campus face.

8. Vanderbilt Hall and the Gold Coast
Charles Coolidge Haight, 1894

A little under a quarter century after Farnam and Durfee prophesied the certain, if not immediate, death of the Old Brick Row, Vanderbilt in 1894 was concretely the beginning of the end. South College of 1793–94 (Union Hall) and the First Chapel of 1761–63 went down to make way for it. Their destruction also marked the symbolic end of the expectation that the life of a Yale student was one of relatively egalitarian near-austerity. Rooms in the Row could be rendered comfortable, old photographs show, personalized a bit with the odd piece of antique furniture, but they all were really just better or worse versions of the same low-ceilinged academic cell. With its steam heat and mantled fireplaces, up-to-the-minute plumbing, and wainscoted living rooms, Vanderbilt aimed to bring the College's economic elite back on Campus by competing with the Gold Coast of posh private dormitories that, after the Civil War, had grown up on the other side of Chapel Street from the Campus. (Warner Hall at 1044 Chapel Street, 1892, is a surviving example.)

This Yale dormitory was a minor but characteristic member of the family of buildings financed by the *folie-a-batir*-infected children and grandchildren of Commodore Cornelius Vanderbilt of New York City, and is kin to the Vanderbilt country houses in Newport, Rhode Island; Hyde Park, New York; and Asheville, North Carolina. All these showcased historical styles and rich materials, and also held the absolute latest in technical conveniences; Vanderbilt's innovations in heating and plumbing were tied into a new campuswide system run from a boiler house where the main courtyard of Branford College is now. The dormitory memorializes William H. Vanderbilt (1870–1892), who died of typhoid fever in his junior year at Yale. His parents donated the building, and his father, Cornelius Vanderbilt II (1843–1899), was given an honorary MA at the commencement of 1894. Frederick W. Vanderbilt, William's uncle and Cornelius's younger brother, least flamboyant of the family and an 1875 graduate of Sheffield Scientific School, would later give Yale the wherewithal to construct dorms forming the core of Silliman College.

Vanderbilt was the first of many Yale buildings Charles Coolidge Haight (1841–1917) of New York designed. Yale, one imagines, might well have been a kind of consolation prize to Haight, who in the year Vanderbilt was completed lost to Charles Follen McKim the commission for Columbia University's new Morningside Heights campus. Haight was left to deliver his dated Gothic up the Vanderbilt-run railroad to more conservative New Haven. The dormitory's location presented Haight with

Vanderbilt Hall

campus design problems something like the conversational challenges of a dinner-party guest seated between Emily Dickinson and Teddy Roosevelt. On one side, Street Hall was witty but withdrawn, and looked even quieter by contrast with the exuberant, grinning maw of Osborn Hall (demolished; see Bingham Hall entry) on the other. The architect here earned his "Peacemaker" nickname; giving Vanderbilt a U-shape around a street-side carriage court, he effectively separated the incompatible neighbors while creating an elegant new front for, and gateway into, the Campus. The two facades ending the U on Chapel are cleverly treated so that the building's considerable thickness appears as thin gable-ends, more compatible with Street Hall's entry porch. In-the-know New Yorkers seeing the dormitory would, despite its style, have immediately recognized its likeness to some of the clubs, luxury apartment houses, and swank group dwellings of Manhattan.

9. Street Hall
Peter B. Wight, 1866; renovation: Ennead Architects, 2012

While Yale has long claimed the distinction of having had the first college or university art gallery in North America—the Trumbull Gallery opened in 1832 on a site just north of the Woolsey Statue—the works displayed in it were valued less as art and more as didactic examples of patriotism and filial piety. Trumbull's paintings were historical machines that commemorated Washington and the Revolution, and the College's collection ran to eighteenth-century portraits of Yale officers and donors. The impetus for what today would be recognized as a museum and art school came from this building's donor, Augustus Russell Street (1791–1866), a wealthy New Haven resident and Yale graduate who took his family to live and travel in Europe for five years in the mid-1840s. (The experience abroad left Street appalled at the American diplomatic corps' language abilities, and so he eventually established a professorship of Modern Languages at Yale.)

But other American problems confronted Street, his wife, and three daughters soon after their return to New Haven from Europe. The March 1854 murder of a

New Haven barkeeper, allegedly by a Yale student—a low point in a worsening spiral of class- and ethnic-based town-gown troubles (see Woolsey Statue)—took place at the corner of Chapel and Temple streets, literally at their doorstep. The family then moved a block away into the security of the New Haven House Hotel, at the corner of Chapel and College, where the Taft now stands. Yale-New Haven relations continued unevenly; 1858 saw another low point—the death of a New Haven fireman, allegedly at the hands of a student—as well as a promising high one—an art loan exhibition and lectures, attended by town and gown alike, in the new Alumni Hall on campus (see Lanman-Wright Hall). Street seemingly concluded that Yale's and New Haven's, indeed America's, problems could be at least mitigated by exposure to the level of art he and his family had seen in Europe. As bad luck would have it, all three of Street's daughters died young. Thus it was both the town-gown situation and his and his wife's sorrow that lay behind Street's 1864 offer to the Yale Corporation to fund a School of Art and erect a building to house it. He was quite explicit about what mattered to him. The building was to be at the corner of Chapel and High streets (thereby balancing and recalling Alumni Hall and the art exhibition there), and it was to have "one front with entrance on Chapel Street, and another entrance on the college grounds": townspeople and students were to have separate but equal access to art. When he died, Street's 1866 will gave additional money, stipulating that the School was "for the admission of pupils of both sexes…it being among the objects of this gift to provide, for those desiring to pursue either of the fine arts as a profession, the means of instruction and improvement, and to awaken a taste for, and appreciation of, the fine arts, among the undergraduates of the college, and others."

An Art Council established by the Corporation selected Peter B. Wight (1838–1925) as architect, a logical enough choice, since in 1865 Wight was just finishing construction of the National Academy of Design in New York. Wight was part of a group calling itself the Association for the Advancement of Truth in Art (it included Russell Sturgis, who would design Farnam, Durfee, Battell, and Lawrance Halls), and vocally espousing the aesthetic ideas of John Ruskin. The Ruskin-inspired Oxford Museum of 1855–60 provided Wight with an appropriate model. Street's basement held drawing and modeling rooms; the ground floor had studios, classrooms, and a library; and the windowless upper floor had two large skylit galleries and

Street Hall

wide corridors for exhibitions. The original plan was an asymmetrical pinwheel of a protofunctionalist sort. The masonry components are differentiated according to structural place and function. As with the Oxford building and the National Academy, the stonecutters were encouraged to produce their own designs for closely observed botanical column capitals; this was in the best Ruskinian rhetorical tradition of Truth in Nature coming from and producing Truth in Art. Wight tried mightily, but did not succeed in convincing Yale to top the building's corner octagonal turrets with high conical roofs.

Profits from admission fees for an early, highly successful exhibition were used to buy plaster casts of classical sculpture, a number of which survived to be incorporated in Paul Rudolph's Art & Architecture Building. Street Hall and A&A have been seen as sharing much that was more important than the casts. Nearly a century separates the two buildings but, said the great modernist art historian Sir Nikolaus Pevsner in a biting dedication (Rudolph present, November 1963), in Street's naive expectation of social improvement by individual betterment through art, rather than by hardheaded social and structural functionality, A&A's artistic excess and probable social failure lay implicit. Street Hall was renovated extensively by Ennead Architects in 2010–12.

10. Linsly-Chittenden Hall

Chittenden Hall
Josiah Cleaveland Cady, 1890
Linsly Hall
Charles Coolidge Haight, 1907

"Linsly-Chitt" counts as one building on Yale's maps and schedule-sheets today, but in origin it is two very different structures, artfully but forcibly joined. Even additional smoothing over in a late 1990s renovation does not serve to disguise the fact that Yale here started in one direction but then swerved off in another.

Round-arched Chittenden Hall, to the south, was created in 1888 by J. C. Cady (1837–1919), its architect, and the newly appointed President Timothy Dwight, as the first installment toward a grand new University Library, which would eventually stretch up High Street along most of the west side of the Old Campus. It was to be an outward sign signifying the spiritual and organizational transformation of Yale from a college—an institution centered on teaching a defined closed curriculum to a body of undergraduates—into a university, a place in which research of all sorts, and graduate and professional studies, held equal status. At Yale, that transformation was more protracted and complex than at many American schools, precisely because of the age and strength of tradition in the College. It was the major thrust of the Dwight presidency.

Cady was trained in New York by an expatriate German practitioner of the *Rundbogenstil*, the round-arched style in which the state institutions of Bavaria and Prussia were built or rebuilt from the 1830s forward. German universities set the standards to which American ones aspired. Dwight himself had been at Bonn and

Chittenden Hall

Berlin in 1856–58. The implications of the use of *Rundbogenstil* would have been clear enough: centralized administrative authority, disciplinary specialization, equal recognition of science and technology with the humanities. Cady's earlier Yale buildings were exactly in that spirit, but for just those reasons tending to decenter the traditional discipline-and-piety formulae of the College. North Sheffield Hall, 1872–73, designed as the Sheffield Scientific School's first new building, was a tough brick cube whose overt Prussianism stood for different things than the Ruskinian Farnam Hall, built for the College at nearly the same time. (Watson Hall, built by Cady in 1894–95 as the Sheffield Chemical Laboratory, survives and gives a good feel of *Rundbogenstil* heft.)

While two renovations have disguised or destroyed much of the original building, enough of the space and decorative program survive to reveal the original feel of Chittenden Library's main reading room. Above the corner fireplace is a bronze plaque noting Simeon B. Chittenden's donation in memory of his daughter; plaster relief heads of the world's great authors once looked down at the bent heads of students studying their works. The glory of the room is a Tiffany window explaining in elliptical nineteenth-century allegories the purpose of a university library; while Art and Music stand to the side, Science and Religion meet and gesture in the middle, presided over—or is it refereed?—by Love.

Linsly Hall

By early in the twentieth century it was clear that Cady's full plan would never be carried through. While many of Dwight's organizational reforms had been implemented, resistance to demolishing the old College Library (Dwight Hall) had hardened after the all-too-symbolic loss of the Old Brick Row and the College Fence. Yet Arthur Twining Hadley, Dwight's successor, was faced with a dire need for further library expansion. "The increasing number and variety of…researchers… has rendered the old-fashioned departmental library inadequate," he wrote. "The university library has to meet these needs, and to meet them on a large scale." By this time it was almost inevitable that, faced with a gap as problematic as that between Chittenden and the Old Library, the veteran peacemaker of Yale, Charles Coolidge Haight, would be called on as architect rather than Cady. Haight responded with Linsly Hall of 1906–07. As with his two earlier Campus buildings (Phelps Hall and Vanderbilt Hall), corner octagonal towers disguise the difficult junctures with earlier structures, and proportions and materials accomplish what in the computer era would be called a pretty good morph between Chittenden and Dwight. Linsly's interiors are notable for their hardwearing but elegant materials, particularly for some excellent Guastavino tile vaults in the Old Campus–side entry stair.

With the opening of Sterling Library in 1930, Yale renovated Linsly-Chittenden to accommodate classrooms and faculty offices. A 1998 renovation brought those uses up to date, added a new High Street entrance, and found additional room to expand within the existing structure. Goody-Clancy Architects, of Boston, lifted a dormer straight from Henry Hobson Richardson's Sever Hall at Harvard to bring light to new spaces in Chittenden's roof.

11. McClellan Hall

Walter B. Chambers, 1925

In 1901, ensconced in elegant new digs in Woodbridge Hall, Yale's administrators heaved a sigh of relief at having almost completely destroyed the Old Brick Row, just in the nick of time to celebrate the University's bicentennial, regretting only that overly nostalgic alumni had kept them from finishing the job. A long generation later,

McClellan Hall

another administration ironically enough found itself much criticized for building a new Brick Row box of a dormitory. McClellan Hall was erected in 1924–25, not so much because the University had a real shortage of appropriate housing (though it did; hundreds of undergraduates lived in boarding houses on Wall and Crown streets), but because the surviving Brick Row building, Connecticut Hall, was perceived to be in need of balance. Vanderbilt Hall in 1894 had set up not only a new gateway into the Campus from Chapel Street but also, by extension from that gateway, a new orientation for the Old Campus. It defined a new axis between the commercial world of Chapel and soon-to-come University expansion to the north (the Bicentennial Buildings). Still later, with the work in the 1920s on what would become the Cross Campus, that axis was felt to have increased significance; to the architects and administrators of the day it made the Old Campus feel like a boat, prow at Vanderbilt, with Connecticut like a revered but absent-minded old uncle who insists on sitting off the beam. Hence, they added McClellan for balance.

The building's architect, Walter B. Chambers of New York, also designer of Bingham Hall, borrowed the gambrel-roofed massing of Connecticut Hall, then wrapped it in prettier, more delicate details. Connecticut's windows march in constant rhythm; McClellan's are irregular. Its rooftop dormers do not coincide with the entryway doors below. In short, it is a fussy design. The forty-six beds provided by the building did little to help the College's major shortage, and McClellan's location, squashed tightly up against busy Linsly-Chittenden, has left generations of occupants of those beds to live life in a brick fishbowl. The axis, and access, to the Cross Campus, which was McClellan's reason for being, has never managed to make its way through Durfee Hall and past the defenses of the traffic engineers watching over Elm Street.

12. Lanman-Wright Memorial Hall
William Adams Delano, 1912

Lanman-Wright Hall, a dormitory and the home of Yale Station's mailboxes (long the main link students had with the wider world), was one of the last buildings added to the Old Campus. (Bingham Hall, which went up in 1928, was the last.) Built in 1912, Lanman-Wright replaced the examination and reading rooms of A. J. Davis's castellated 1851–53 Alumni Hall (see Skull and Bones). Lanman-Wright was one of the earlier Yale buildings remodeled or built new by William Adams Delano (1874–1960) and Chester Holmes Aldrich (1871–1940), New York architects. Delano & Aldrich contributed a wide variety of buildings to the Yale campus over a twenty-year span, including Lanman-Wright, William L. Harkness Hall on the Cross Campus, Sterling Chemistry Lab on Science Hill, and the Divinity School. The architects are best known for their Long Island country houses for the socially prominent, but compiled a large and diverse body of other work besides, including

Lanman–Wright Memorial Hall

the first buildings of LaGuardia Airport and Delano's 1949–52 renovation of the White House.

The eclectic styling of Delano & Aldrich's buildings distracts from their shared characteristics of intricate if unobtrusive spatial arrangements, well-thought-out if quiet detailing, and, in urban buildings, the sophistication of relationships to the street. Lanman-Wright unfortunately is not up to their usual standard in any of those three areas. While the building succeeded in packing a large number of student rooms atop the working half-basement of Yale Station, and more or less disguised the large volume with some intricate roofline manipulation, the numbers were gained at the expense of a cavernous courtyard, notoriously dark during the long months of winter, and an abrupt relationship with High Street. The brownstone detailing is laconic and sometimes just plain bad, with field-sawn stones cut illogically to fit what seem to have been precut window jambs. Generic escutcheon-bearing lions on the courtyard side soften the building's visual spareness only a little. Still, it must be acknowledged that the raised courtyard has some social virtues and that the building's height and gable-ends make for an appropriately strong corner at Elm and High streets. Certainly James Gamble Rogers thought so, since he three times echoed Lanman-Wright's massing on the other corners of the intersection, in Saybrook, Trumbull, and Berkeley colleges.

WALK TWO: THE ARTS AREA

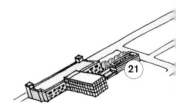

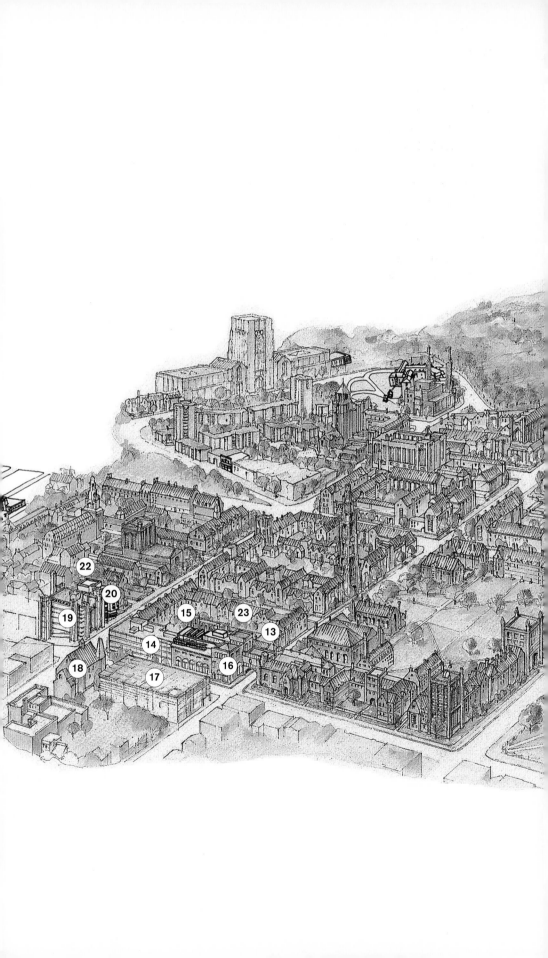

[In a democracy] the number of consumers increases, but the opulent and
fastidious consumers become more scarce…the productions of artists are
more numerous, but the merit of each production is diminished.
                              —Alexis de Tocqueville, *Democracy in America* (1839)

The taste of youth for secrecy, for ceremonies, for imposing words, is
extraordinary; and frequently bespeaks a certain depth of character. In those
years, we wish to feel our whole nature seized and moved, even though it be
but vaguely and darkly. The youth who happens to have lofty aspirations and
forecastings thinks that secrets yield him much, that he must depend on
secrets, and effect much by means of them.
                              —Johann Wolfgang von Goethe, *Wilhelm Meister's Apprenticeship*
                                     (1796, translation by Thomas Carlyle, 1824)[1]

At the southwest corner of the Old Campus and for a block or two beyond,
the buildings jam tightly against one another with a density and intricacy
of relation, or nonrelation, not approached elsewhere on campus. Most
of these places are for public display of art or drama or for professional
instruction in the arts; three house self-perpetuating societies of different
degrees of openness to the world; others, originally built for selective social
gathering, now shelter the public arts. The conjunction of art buildings with
fraternities and secret societies may be a matter of chance—though that is
not for certain—but the juxtaposition in any case brings out the point that,
at Yale, pursuit of the goal of individual development has been more than
usually linked to group endeavor, group development, and secret instruction.
The origins of Skull and Bones and of Yale's first cautious embrace of "Art"
share the same moment in time, as well as a degree of impetus from the
Romantic movement. Understanding this can aid deeper understanding
of the buildings on this walk, and also perhaps something more of the
Yale graduates, participants in these institutions, who have gone on to play
prominent roles in American finance, politics, art, and drama.

The Trumbull Gallery, forerunner of the School of Art, opened on
October 25, 1832, the same academic year in which a group of undergraduates
led by William H. Russell, fresh back from a year of study in Germany,
formed Skull and Bones. John Trumbull's paintings chiefly celebrated
patriotic themes, the record of his life's work commemorating the events and
self-sacrificing heroes of the Revolution. The aim of Russell and his brethren
of the Class of 1833 was *Bildung,* the achievement of a self-knowledge,
despite life's shortness, which would redound for the betterment of society;

on the model of Goethe's *Wilhelm Meister,* the search for personal identity (overseen by a benevolent secret society) is caught up in the drive to establish or refound group, and ultimately national, cultural identity. Trumbull's work is an early form of the Romantic paradox of individual heroism being both the expression of and a force for the advancement of nationhood. The Yale secret societies, whatever else one might say of them, operate on the overtly Romantic proposition that discovery of an inner, individual self corresponds with, and furthers, the aim of forming an ideal community. By the 1830s, the decade of Andrew Jackson and Alexis de Tocqueville, Yale (like America) was steadily expanding and diversifying, and the problem at hand increasingly centered on how to form a community from a collection of individualistic, unhierarchized strangers. In New Haven, art and enlightened brotherhoods were seen as two sometimes overlapping answers to one question. Art, as defined by an elite recognizable by high individual accomplishment, was to provide social glue within a democratic society.

Augustus Street explicitly connected art with the cause of social harmony in his early-1860s donations to establish the School of Fine Arts (see Street Hall), thus carrying Trumbull's proposition a step further. One suspects that Daniel C. Gilman (Yale's Librarian and Skull and Bones, Class of 1852), who in 1858 instigated an annual series of public art exhibitions that led up to Street's gifts, quite agreed. Thus while the School, like the Trumbull Gallery before it, was the first collegiate institution of its type in America, it should be recognized that the founding of the gallery and the school were motivated by a belief that art provides a stabilizing and unifying force, which paradoxically grows out of the disciplined development of individual talent. This nineteenth-century notion is at odds with the prevailing twentieth-century idea that artistic expression is most valuable when excitingly destabilizing. Yale was pioneering in the foundation of its art collection and artistic instruction, but its motives should be understood as coming from the earlier sort of idea about the role of art.

But this is only to say that, on into this century, Yale's attitude has been simply a more intense version of that of American society as a whole. Judging from what the country has built over the last decades of this century, the museum seems to be the last building type people generally can muster enthusiasm enough to pay for. Art, and the buildings that house it, are accepted to the degree that they stimulate without demanding control, are supported as long as they simultaneously provide a sense of newness and a sense of heightened connection to other people, to defining and understanding groups both past and present. Louis Kahn's design for the Yale Center for British Art is remarkable in this regard, for it is as challenging as any visitor wants it to be, no more but certainly no less.

Compared with museums, art schools are less certain of support, because what they are supposed to do is much less clear, both to potential supporters and no less so to their own students and faculty, though this is seldom discussed. Does the encouragement of individuality, of the task of finding individually expressive forms and content, finally connect people more strongly or help drive them apart? Is not the idea of teaching individuality a paradox in the first place, and an elitist, paternalistic one to boot—perhaps just another kind of secret society mentality? Is it the role of art in general, and architecture in particular, to prop things up or tip shaky things over? Paul Rudolph's design for the Art & Architecture Building, fondly called simply A&A, is probably the clearest built statement of these dilemmas that can, or should, be made. For better and worse simultaneously, as such it sums up more than a century and a half of the questions implicit in its own programmatic content and the pursuits within the buildings around it.

13. Skull and Bones, Alumni Hall Towers, and Hidden Gardens
Skull and Bones architect unknown, 1856

Alumni Hall
Alexander Jackson Davis, 1853

Yale's version of the Great Sphinx, "Bones," has brooded on High Street since 1856, first in date and still *primus inter pares* of the secret (now "senior") society tombs on campus. The basic organizational facts of Skull and Bones's history are readily enough found out. Since its inception by a group of fifteen seniors in 1832–33, the Russell Trust Association (its legal name; it is not in a legal sense part of the University, though the two historically have had, to say the least, interlocking directorates) has "tapped" fifteen new members in the spring of their junior years. The group meets in its hall Thursday and Sunday nights through their senior year, in turn selecting and tapping the next fifteen. Beyond basics, the fog gets very thick very quickly. Those tapped into Bones down the decades have included future presidents of Yale (galore) and the United States (three), and names central to the workings of Wall Street, the CIA, and even the Library of Congress. Rumors about the society–its origins, its rituals, occult puppet-mastering of Yale, the country, the universe–of the sort that used to be whispered mostly among awestruck freshmen, can now be found at conspiracy-discussion sites on the internet. If Bones listens at all to that, it never answers.

After carrying on operations in rented rooms for a couple of decades, the society built the first part of its present structure in 1856, when the block was mostly occupied by large, single- or two-family houses and stables. Seen from High Street, the left-hand block was the first building, its door in the center where there is now a window. A second piece was added onto the rear in 1883, then, Yale's typological conservatism at work, the original chunk was faithfully duplicated in another expansion in 1903. A new entrance was put between the new and old "testaments," or wings. The architect of the original wing is usually said to be Henry Austin (1804–1891), and very occasionally A. J. Davis (1803–1892), but neither Austin's nor Davis's archives contain drawings for it. Both architects did work in the area at the time, and both their oeuvres contain examples of comparable brownstone-built romantic gloom. Overall proportions and the face-bedding of the stonework, as well as the bluntness of the Egypto-Doric detailing would suggest Austin, but on the other hand, when Davis's Alumni Hall (1853) was demolished in 1911 to make way for Wright Hall, Bones carted the stonework of its twin Gothic towers down High Street. Re-erected behind the tomb, they have presided over a hidden garden since 1918. Whether this was an act of filial architectural piety cannot be known until the Russell Trust cracks open its vaults.

But more important than knowing the architect's identity is noting that the Sphinx resonates both backward and forward with other Yale buildings. John Trumbull moved his patriotic painting collection into the skylit, almost windowless box of the Trumbull Gallery (see Yale Art Gallery and Woodbridge Hall) in October 1832, the fall of Skull and Bones's first year of existence, and was buried in its basement on his death in 1843. Whether or not there is a causal link, the similarity of form and purpose is striking; inside a sepulchre, mysterious processes take promising but uninitiated

Skull and Bones

young men through a *Lehrjahre* of self-discovery and group bonding. Trumbull and Yale intended to inculcate patriotism by exposing students to art. Whatever rituals go on in Bones, they have certainly manufactured generations of individuals who took the song and saying "For God, for Country, and for Yale" seriously.

14. Yale University Art Gallery
Louis I. Kahn, 1953; renovation, Polshek Partnership Architects, 2006

The buildings of Louis I. Kahn are notoriously hard for nonarchitects to understand. What is this one but a box housing a spectacular art collection? The short answer is that this is a building of deceptive obviousness, one that, like some of the best work it houses, speaks quietly with a depth appreciated through repeated encounters. An early twenty-first-century renovation has brought it back, after a half century of hard and sometimes unsympathetic use, so that its originality and brilliance can be appreciated. It now serves as the centerpiece of Yale's outstanding amalgam of art museum buildings and collections. The Yale Art Gallery is free and open to the public.

In fairness, it took even perceptive architects and clients a good long time to begin to appreciate Kahn; the Art Gallery commission came only in January 1951, as he neared his fiftieth birthday. "Loonie Lou" was known for his inspiring teaching and poetic, if often elliptical, discussions of the meaning of architecture. Newly inaugurated Yale president A. Whitney Griswold entrusted him with the commission on the recommendation of George Howe, the patrician Philadelphian heading Yale's architecture program. Kahn's building was dedicated in November 1953 and immediately recognized as paradoxical. While it was the first Modern structure on Yale's central campus, its utterly blank four-story brick facade on Chapel Street and its deep, elaborate, concrete ceilings showed an interest in exploring the expressive powers of density and weight, a departure from the desire for lightness so great as to suggest flight, which characterized Modernist theory and practice of the day. In Kahn's career, this building marked the beginning of his search to combine "silence and light," as he put it, of monumentality and grace, of creating buildings that could evoke a deep sense of place and time without recourse to historical styling. The Gallery is significant in its own right, but also as one of the turning points in the universal sea-change in building design that occurred in the twenty years after its opening. The Yale Center for British Art of 1977, by Kahn across Chapel Street, is one of the culminations of that movement.

It was a very near thing that Kahn's Gallery happened at all. Other architects were seriously considered for the commission, and, even after the design was set, Yale had to represent the building to the Federal Office of Defense Mobilization as a "Design Laboratory" to obtain the steel to begin construction (in June 1952) during the Korean War. Earlier still was the odd chain of stalls and misfires that accumulated over forty years: the stillborn 1911 attempt to make a Skull and

Yale University Art Gallery

Bones courtyard (see Art Gallery Courtyard); truncation of the Old Art Gallery's build-out in 1928; termination of work on a design by Philip L. Goodwin, who had built the Museum of Modern Art in New York City, due to Pearl Harbor; finally Goodwin's 1950 resignation of the commission, ostensibly because of health, more likely due to Griswold's imposition of a tight budget. But in the end it did happen, and the Gallery became the first of a number of buildings that has made Yale and New Haven a destination of architectural pilgrimages from around the world.

Kahn's building takes its basic massing from the 1928 Swartwout design, retaining a recessed center-block entrance, though sliding circulation off to one side rather than allowing it to proceed straight up to the courtyard. Swartwout's service dock on York Street was retained, but the west face of the Gallery was pulled back to make a narrow courtyard, emulating the moats of the colleges on the same street and allowing light into the basement level. Kahn regarded subsequent alterations to the Gallery, not by his hand, as vandalism, and they precipitated his departure from teaching at Yale. These, it is good to report, have been removed in the 2006 renovation.

In 1974–76, after Kahn's death, Herbert S. Newman succeeded in putting a much-needed large auditorium, accessed from the Kahn building, underneath the Weir Hall-Art Gallery courtyard without harming either the Gallery or the courtyard and its old elm trees.

15. Art Gallery Courtyard and Weir Hall

Weir Hall
Tracy & Swartwout, 1912; Everett V. Meeks, 1924

Skull and Bones hit the high water mark of its architectural ambitions in 1912, when George Douglas Miller, a Bones alum of the Class of 1870, having bought up almost the rest of the block (he seems briefly to have lived there earlier) and filled up its center with a great plateau of earth, ran out of money in the course of building an Oxfordesque cloister for the society (Tracy & Swartwout Architects). Or so the story goes. Clearly the society could have finished the job if it had wanted. Whatever its reasons, Bones settled for the secret garden over the eastern wall and the rebuilt towers. The incomplete building, its courtyard, and the rest of the Miller property passed to Yale in 1912. Everett Meeks, head of the Architecture program within the School of Fine Arts, finished the structure to be used by his students, with funding from Edward S. Harkness. It was named Weir Hall in 1924 to honor the long-serving director of the School of Fine Arts, John Ferguson Weir (1841–1926). Ever flippant toward age and authority, frank about their own behavior after long nights "en charrette," and also somewhat aware of the deeper history of the site, the architecture students called it Weird Hall. A bronze plaque set into a central windowsill reads:

THE ORIGINAL PART OF WEIR HALL, PURCHASED BY YALE UNIVERSITY IN 1912, WAS BEGUN IN 1911 BY GEORGE DOUGLAS MILLER, B.A, 1870, IN PARTIAL FULFILLMENT OF HIS VISION "TO BUILD, IN THE HEART OF NEW HAVEN, A REPLICA OF AN OXFORD QUADRANGLE."

~

IN ACCORDANCE WITH HIS WISHES, THIS TABLET HAS BEEN ERECTED TO COMMEMORATE HIS ONLY SON, SAMUEL MILLER (1881–1883), WHO WAS BORN AND DIED ON THESE PREMISES.

Evarts Tracy (1868–1929) and Egarton Swartwout (1870–1943), Yale college graduates in 1890 and 1891, respectively, were young veterans of the McKim, Mead & White office in New York City when Miller commissioned them. Tracy and Swartwout were near contemporaries of James Gamble Rogers (1867–1947, BA 1889), and like him and many of their peers of this era, could pull off well-planned, stylistically creditable buildings in whatever garb the client or context indicated; most found it useful to be able to design academically accurate versions of Gothic, in addition to Free Renaissance and

Weir Hall

other forms of classicism. Here, scrupulously following the "vision" of Miller, they designed not just a generic English quadrangle but something quite close to a replica of Magdalen College (1474). The angled, oddly truncated tower on the west is an incomplete version of (what more appropriate?) Founder's Tower, Magdalen's original gateway, and the windows and crenellations on Weir mirror those on the Founder's Tower range.

Among others important to the later history of Yale building, Eero Saarinen (BFA 1934) received his architectural education here. Philip Johnson taught in Weir; how much, one wonders, do Kline Biology Tower's round mechanical systems "servant spaces" owe to Bones's empty Gothic towers, how much to Johnson's association with Louis Kahn? Kahn taught in this building from 1947 until 1953, when the architecture studios moved across the courtyard to the Kahn-designed Art Gallery. The complexly beautiful raised courtyard then found itself behind still another inscrutable wall, now Kahn's building on Chapel Street rather than Skull and Bones's on High. The Schools of Art and Architecture still return to Miller's courtyard every spring for the hopeful rituals of commencement.

The Art Gallery courtyard may be reached through the Gallery or, irregularly at other times, seemingly at the whimsy of University security, by way of a passage, gateway, and stair between Skull and Bones and Jonathan Edwards College.

16. Old Art Gallery and High Street Bridge

Old Art Gallery
Tracy & Swartwout, 1928

The Old Art Gallery (OAG) was, and is after renovation, an intriguing puzzle of a building. As originally constructed it was an intricate assembly of large and small, high and low spaces, with dimly daylit whispering galleries, seemingly conceived to challenge conventional ideas about necessary relationships between architectural style and spatial sophistication. Behind sculpturally enriched thick walls, alluding to the architectural history of northern Italy and southern France, lay a cleanly functional spatial organization for a set of galleries, offices, and classrooms. The building, and the spiraling assembly with Weir Hall (sharing the courtyard) and Street Hall (connected by a bridge; see Walk One), opened in October 1928. The overall group was strikingly similar in plan to another school of art, Walter Gropius's pioneering Modernist Bauhaus, at Dessau, Germany, opened in December 1926. Despite its historicist masonry, OAG conceded nothing to the glassy Bauhaus in its complex interlocking of rooms and functions.

Weir, founding director of the School of Fine Arts, a quiet but enormously persistent man, had overseen the art collections and the programs in painting and sculpture in Street Hall, across High Street on the Old Campus, through decades

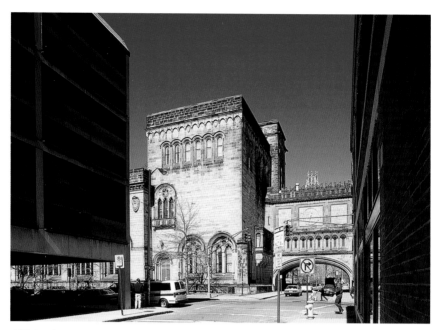

Old Art Gallery

of polite indifference and benign neglect on the part of the University. But by 1910, as the end of his forty-four years of obduracy at Yale (1869–1913) approached, his work was clearly paying off. Yale College students were not only interested in art, but by then had sufficient latitude in degree requirements actually to take classes. Weir lived to see expansion of the art school building, but of a leapfrog sort, into the hall named in his honor in 1924, rather than onto the site, just across High from Street, he had anticipated.

Weir died shortly after, in 1926. In April of that year Edward S. Harkness, who had previously funded Weir Hall's completion, agreed to pay for a new Art Gallery, located where Weir had anticipated but of a size beyond the old man's fondest dreams. Tracy & Swartwout, New York architects, proposed a design that would occupy the whole of the property acquired by George D. Miller (see Art Gallery Courtyard), stretching on Chapel from High Street to York, and finishing off the elevated garden with a library for the School of Fine Arts. It was never built. Of that design, one of two symmetrical wings was built and opened in 1928. If the design had been entirely built, the two wings would have flanked a grand central hall, featuring Professor Weir's plaster casts, and a staircase sweeping with opera-house grandeur up to the hidden courtyard. It remains to be discovered why things did not proceed further.

Evarts Tracy, BA 1890, and Egarton Swartwout, BA 1891, headed a firm with a national reputation. They won the competition for the Missouri State Capitol in 1912 and built the National Baptist Church in Washington, DC, in 1922–33. Freely vigorous in many styles, the firm's work was characterized by a clever use of siting and modeling, and a flare for dramatic silhouettes. Here, exemplifying these traits, the gallery bridge over High Street is a model of eclectic scenography, the all-time favorite photographers' frame for Harkness Tower.

Inside OAG, the large gallery parallel to Chapel Street is one of Yale's great rooms. In the floor at its northeast corner, easily missed, is a dark stone slab with an inscription. It commemorates the painter and patriot John Trumbull, whose gift of paintings to Yale essentially founded the college's art collection. The third burial place of Trumbull and his wife lie below. The architects depicted the Trumbull Gallery (John and Sarah's first resting place was beneath it, in the middle of what is now the Old Campus, straight down from Trumbull's painting of George Washington) in a bas-relief halfway up the Chapel Street elevation. Tracy & Swartwout also put a dimensionally correct (30 feet by 60 feet) gallery recalling it on top of the bridge leading back to Street Hall (their second burial spot). The faithful old stone plaque noting the Trumbulls' presence has followed their mortal remains' journey as invisible pendants to the Washington portrait as Yale moved it around.

The early twenty-first-century renovation of the OAG and the High Street bridge tied them much more integrally to the Kahn Gallery on the west and Street Hall on the east. The Art History department having moved over into the Loria Center on York Street, the offices and classrooms it formerly required were mostly unsuitable for gallery space, and gave way to a flexible variety of exhibition galleries connected by a much more understandable circulation system. The whispering gallery vaults just outside the elevators were saved, fortunately; the offices of Vincent Scully and other eminent Yale art historians were not. Something of the original spatial inventiveness returns, though, in the character of the renovated complex, even if many original rooms gave up the ghost. A new stair, for example, winds its way upward with glorious inefficiency to a large gallery, skylit by dimpled wavelike diffusers, atop the massive tower at the northwest corner of Chapel and High streets. Even more striking are a set of new galleries added above the former top level and a

Yale Center for British Art

south-facing outdoor terrace hidden behind the stone parapet of the original Chapel Street facade. The views from the latter—of New Haven and its landscape out to the horizon, of the whole of Yale's arts district, set in the city—are breathtaking.

17. Yale Center for British Art
Louis I. Kahn, Pellecchia and Meyers, 1977

Tested against almost any standard, this is Yale's best building. It opened in April 1977, three years after the death of its designer, Louis I. Kahn (1901–1974), and some eleven years after Paul Mellon's gift to Yale of funds to acquire a site and endow a building to house his collection of British art and books. The Center for British Art (BAC) is a compact rectangular prism, 120 feet by 200 feet, four stories above grade and one below, lidded by a flat roof of skylights uniformly tiled in precast concrete coffers. It has such a quality of elegant reserve compared with the functional massing in his other works that one can infer Kahn believed that "reserve" was a positive in its own right, and a proper expression of the program and character of the institution—not only the BAC but Yale University. The exterior's not-quite-stern beauty depends on a discreet mutability, changes made by the sky on the mill-finish, pewter-like steel panels and subtly varied glazing, rather than on the drama of contrasted masses or cast shadows. The building requires most contemporary observers to lengthen their attention spans, to take the time to observe it as closely as a sailor does the weather and an ancient Greek did a temple's near-invisible curvatures.

It has often been remarked by critics and historians, Vincent Scully foremost among them, how the BAC complements and culminates the series of Yale galleries and art buildings on Chapel Street. But the BAC should also be understood as recalling another, vanished art building, the Trumbull Gallery, Yale's first, whose image is carved into a frieze-band on the Old Art Gallery across Chapel from where Kahn put the BAC entrance. Beyond its immediate contextual conversations— between Kahn and Rudolph, Kahn and the Old Art Gallery, Swartwout's Beaux-Arts old gallery (a style in which Kahn was also schooled), and between Kahn and his younger self in the Art Gallery—the BAC is a meditation on a particular building type long important at Yale, the veiled box or treasury.

In Kahn's building, as was the case in Trumbull's version of the type, exhibit spaces on an upper level draw light from the sky, while necessary but more mundane activities occupy the spaces at grade. Chapel Street's art buildings, then, together make up an *exemplum* of the tradition of individual creativity occurring simultaneously with the surprising continuity of old types reborn.

While the BAC is nearly symmetrical around an axis parallel with its long facade on Chapel Street, its entrance is on a diagonal from the northeast corner, askew by traditional standards. The placement reflects a complex design history, condensing

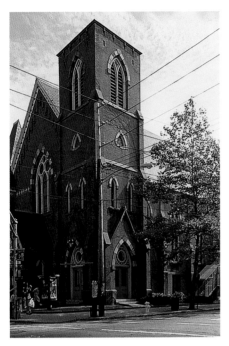

Yale Repertory Theater

larger and more articulated early projects with two entrances, one on High, one on Chapel, into the smaller, rhythmically integrated structure as built. The low, dark entry porch leads into the skylit and vertical entry court, which with the library court to the west, make up the pair of Rooms around which the building is structured. (Kahn liked to capitalize the terms, such as "Room," for his critical elements.) The interior feels generous but deliberately short of grand, and warm, a country-house effect intended by Kahn, Mellon, and Jules Prown, the Center's first director, as appropriate to the art in Mellon's collection—genre and sporting paintings, still lifes, and ancestral worthies.

With silver grayness outside and intimacy within, the Center exists in its own British weather and provides its own British refuge. It also prompts reflection, as Mellon intended, on Yale's English roots. It is as wrong to think those relations always placid as it is to regard the BAC as an easy building. Kahn's design has in it something of both Courtier conviction and Puritan fire, and so revisits the genesis of New England and Yale. The BAC is free and open to the public.

18. Yale Repertory Theater and Holcombe T. Green Jr. Hall, Yale School of Art

Yale Repertory Theater
Rufus G. Russell, 1871; Patricia V. Tetrault, 1975
Holcombe T. Green Jr. Hall, Yale School of Art (former Jewish Community Center) *Weinstein and Abramowitz, 1954; Deborah Berke, 2000*

For most of Yale and New Haven's time together, there has been nothing like a hard-built edge around a geographic entity (a campus), a border separating it from another entity (the town). The buildings at and near the corner of York and Chapel streets make a good demonstration of the longstanding fogginess of just where Yale begins and ends. Buildings and sites have passed from non-Yale ownership to Yale, sometimes vice-versa, and occasionally back again in both directions.

On the southeast corner, diagonally opposite Rudolph Hall, the Yale Repertory Theater has occupied since 1969 the structure put up and used by the Calvary Baptist Church from 1871 until 1966. Yale acquired the building, intending to tear it down to make way for a new Art Library connected to the BAC, but the Kahn building escalated in cost and plans for the Library were deferred, then shelved altogether. Always hungry for space, the Drama School was given use of the church temporarily and then on a permanent basis when it was clear that the BAC would not require the site. Patricia V. Tetrault (B.Arch. 1955) was the architect of the renovations for "The Rep." The designer of the original church was Rufus G. Russell (1823–1896), a New Haven architect trained in the office of Henry Austin. Russell periodically gained Yale or Yale-related commissions, such as West Divinity Hall of 1873–74 (see Calhoun College) and Warner Hall of 1892, opposite Vanderbilt Hall, built as an exclusive private dormitory. As Elizabeth Mills Brown notes in *New Haven: A Guide to Architecture and Urban Design* (1976), the decision to remove the church's steeple to secularize it is to be regretted; A&A's dramatic lift was better when it was not a solo performance.

The hand of Louis Kahn also brushed the former Jewish Community Center (JCC), a half block west at 1156 Chapel Street. While Charles H. Abramowitz (Yale's Sheffield Scientific School, B.Phil., 1914) and Jacob Weinstein (architect of the 1927 Langrock Building at York and Broadway) designed the Center, which opened in April 1954, Kahn was officially on board as a consultant. There is more than a passing similarity between 1156 Chapel Street's front facade and the west front of the Yale Art Gallery, dedicated in November 1953. Both allow the verticals of a mostly glass curtain wall to pass, uninterrupted by spandrels, up to a thin, flush roofline. More importantly, both buildings pull back from the street to make a moat, a form of building behavior that is understood around Yale to be not nearly as unfriendly as the term would indicate; the lower-level court is planted with flowering trees, giving something to the city while at the same time providing a measure of privacy for the moated buildings' lower-level spaces. The mature version of this civic tactic appears now, well treed, next to the BAC. After more than a decade of dereliction, the old JCC was bought by Yale in December 1996, renovated, and renamed Green Hall, a new home for the School of Art, with an Experimental Theater for the Drama School designed by New York architect Deborah Berke. The building puts the School of Art back in the role of mediator between town and university, a role envisioned for it by Augustus Street, its originator in 1864. (See Street Hall entry.)

19. Rudolph Hall

Paul Rudolph, 1963; renovation, Gwathmey Siegel Architects, 2008

The Art & Architecture Building, usually called A&A and now named Rudolph Hall, is Yale's most famous, admired, hated, and reviled building. So many legends have grown up around it that, just to begin with, it is perhaps useful to give a basic

Rudolph Hall

factual accounting. In 1958 the School of Fine Arts, as it had been called since it was started in 1866, was reorganized as the School of Art and Architecture. It was headed by a new dean, with Paul Rudolph (1918–1997) as the first Chairman of the Department of Architecture. Rudolph served from February 1958 until May 1965. A&A was designed in his offices on High Street, work commencing in 1959, the School moving in for the fall term of 1963, the building finally dedicated in November 1963. It survived a major fire in the early morning hours of June 14, 1969.

The building's so-called survival of the 1969 fire must be qualified, and that is where facts end and sermons of various flavors take over. A&A was an international media star and pilgrimage point even as it was being built, while its architect was portrayed as the man destined to fuse the authenticity of the American roots of Modern architecture (read, Frank Lloyd Wright) with the sophistication of later European Modern masters (read, Le Corbusier). Besides those America-is-now-stage-center, cryptopatriotic undertones (Abstract Expressionism had been making the same claim for American painting in the years just before), A&A symbolized the counterattack of architecture understood as art, pursued by determinedly individual knights-errant, against architecture understood as a technical means to a social end, best pursued by collaborating techno-nerds or specialists. "Let's face it,"

Rudolph said, "architects were never meant to design together…architecture is a personal effort, and the fewer people coming between you and your work the better." Rudolph could have offered no more direct challenge to his own Harvard mentor, Walter Gropius.

The building began by most accounts to lose its aura not long after it was put into service, and Rudolph's personal status began to decline accordingly. The debunking began from the platform at A&A's dedication, when the architectural historian Sir Nikolaus Pevsner obliquely but unmistakably took the building to task for its excessive self-expression. Pevsner questioned whether any building of quality can result without the give and take between a client and an architect—and at A&A there was none, since Rudolph, not Yale, acted as client. Architect and client aside, certainly it shortly became apparent to its users that the building had functional and technical shortcomings as dramatic as its exhilarating play of light, vistas, and structure, and furthermore that the bad aspects were often directly linked to the good. Rudolph left Yale in mid-1965. Whether or not the fire of 1969 was deliberate, the event became an emblem for one generation's rejection of another's values, forms, and politics. In the late 1990s, unsurprisingly, A&A became a touchstone as a new generation reexamined the architect's possible role as expressive artist.

With the demolition of a rabbit warren of painter's studios on the fourth and fifth floors, following the School of Art's move over to the former Jewish Community Center across Chapel Street, these floors have been restored to something like their condition in 1963. From the A&A roof terrace there is a good view of the pair of red hills, East and West Rocks, and the harbor, which all together edge the flat-bottomed bowl of New Haven topography. From there can also be seen Rudolph's 1962–66 Crawford Manor, an elderly housing project four blocks away at the corner of Park Street and North Frontage Road, the closest of the several other Rudolph-designed buildings in New Haven.

The two corners that begin and end the southern edge of Yale's historic core—Chapel and College streets on the Green, and A&A's Chapel and York streets at the edge of the Nine Squares—have a dubious shared history of carrying important, characterful, yet loved and hated buildings. The buildings there have been attacked often by students and sometimes by townspeople, and occasionally killed by administrators. The original Yale College building and Osborn Hall, at the former corner, and A&A on the other, mark extremes of Yale's architectural and human behavior.

20. Jeffrey H. Loria Center for the History of Art
Gwathmey Siegel Architects, 2008 (LEED Gold)

If Paul Rudolph was correct in asserting that "architects were never meant to design together…architecture is a personal effort, and the fewer people coming between you and your work the better," then Charles Gwathmey (1938–2009) started off in a less-than-ideal situation while designing the new building adjacent to Rudolph Hall, formerly known as A&A or Art & Architecture, now dedicated as the Jeffrey H. Loria Center for the History of Art. The whole architectural world was watching, it seemed, as he felt his way through the design. Gwathmey, a Rudolph student himself, had the benefit and the burden of many other people trying to referee an architectural wrestling match on what was a very tight site in the first place.

It would be wrong to think of Gwathmey's contest as being against Rudolph. Instead, his old teacher's ghost was one of many figures, living and dead, kibitzing in the space between Gwathmey and his work. Rudolph's was not even the most august of the attending ghosts since, as with Rudolph's A&A, Frank Lloyd Wright and Le Corbusier were both also present and attempting to wrest control. Wright was basically an architect of houses who occasionally designed larger buildings that were still fundamentally domestic in scale and organization; Le Corbusier was a gesturing juggler of geometric weights, light and pretty-colored ones in his early career, heroically heavy ones later on. In A&A, Corbusian influences more visibly controlled the final result; Rudolph made monuments even of his houses. In the Loria Center, Gwathmey's own career-long success in sculpting houses seems to have tipped the balance of the match-up in favor of what is finally, surprisingly, a building whose character is domestic.

Seen together as a Wöllflinian pairing in the classic dark-lecture-hall-side-by-side slide comparison, Rudolph Hall and Loria bring out each other's qualities. The former's front door is up a long set of heroic steps, like a capitol or a museum (and Rudolph rather thought of it as both), while the latter's is at ground level in a little single-story mass like an upside-down backyard washtub. The windows in Rudolph Hall are just glass stretched to fill in between the horizontal and vertical concrete volumes, quite different from Loria's, which are differently sized rectangles cut out of the sculpted vertical blocks, curving and angled, making up the zinc-clad building proper. The former strategy is monumental, the latter house-like. Loria's silhouette does not pierce the skyline; the old A&A does so with high drama. Instead of the upthrusting mass Rudolph plants so firmly at the intersection of York and Chapel, Loria carries a thin limestone corner floating a couple of stories in the air, like a flimsy shield protecting an outsized example of the beach houses for which

Gwathmey, with the same family of forms, gained fame in the 1960s. In the end, Loria makes us realize how delicately conceived and balanced A&A/Rudolph Hall is, for all its weightiness.

Along with designing Loria, Gwathmey's firm renovated A&A, now officially called Rudolph Hall.

Rudolph Hall, left; Jeffrey H. Loria Center for the History of Art, right

The spatial brilliance of the older building is now again visible, while other aspects of its original state have been selectively restored; the eye-popping original orange carpets are back, but not the cargo netting that was supposed to serve as window shades.

The Loria Center houses the Department of the History of Art, relocated from what was long known in the arts-area vernacular as "across the street," in Street Hall and the Old Art Gallery. It is a good place in which to pursue sorting the "anxiety of influence," as the English Department's Harold Bloom described the processes by which artists (or cultures) define themselves. The historians working in Loria could do far worse than parsing their own place. Gwathmey's match with the figures and forces tugging at the design makes for a fascinating study, resulting in his implicit reminder to all that while both Loria and Rudolph Hall contain offices and classrooms, the activities taught in each are fundamentally different in nature. Art history is a scholarly discipline and so deserves an in-house protective privacy, while architecture is a public art and ought to take a stand on what exactly that responsibility means.

21. 32–36 Edgewood and Howe Street Garage
KieranTimberlake, 2007 and 2008 (LEED Platinum)

At the edges of the Yale campus, eras have been characterized historically by an increasingly impacted bunching-up of buildings on one side of some street thought of as marking a hard boundary between New Haven and Yale. Then a Yale building crosses the line and a breakout occurs. In the arts area, Yale occupied various buildings with a concentration focused on the corner of York and Chapel streets. Deborah Berke's Green Hall renovation of 2000 led to thinking about a BAC annex on Crown, a block deeper into the city to the south, and a renovation for a temporary A&A facility on the same street. The big step away from York and Chapel, though, comes with fraternal triplet buildings housing studio and gallery functions that, variously light on their feet, jumped into a single block of the Dwight-Edgewood neighborhood. All came from the Philadelphia firm KieranTimberlake, which during that decade also became Yale's architects of choice in the steady march of renovations of the undergraduate colleges.

Whether they learned their lesson in quirky, contextual Philadelphia or picked up some tricks from James Gamble Rogers in the course of the renovations, the result is a distinctly different set of behaviors on the parts of three buildings conceived together to put a lot of new space into a typologically and stylistically diverse old neighborhood, here in a zone transitioning between retail and residential character. For decades, the block was asphalt-carpeted at its center with a medley of parking lots that occasionally broke out to the sidewalks; whatever their other virtues, the new buildings at least ameliorate that situation even if they reflect a country still, in

36 Edgewood

32 Edgewood

Howe Street Garage

the early twenty-first century, being weaned off its parking addiction.

The Howe Street Garage puts what is ostensibly retail space on most of the sidewalk level, then proposes a graphic-design solution to the ubiquitous urban problem of how to make a parking deck facade "interesting." Philadelphia has a record of pioneering the use of such flattish graphics to address urban situations, with the work of the Venturis, Romaldo Giurgola, and others. Here on Howe, KieranTimberlake's four-story minimalist diagonal spreads of dark rectangular cards, with the shop front base, make an overall impression strangely like that of the nearby chunky, four-story, rectangular, dark-paneled BAC. In their similarity, KieranTimberlake's building seems to wear a sort of amusing Louis Kahn Halloween costume.

22. York Street–Fraternity Row

202 York Street - Yale Daily News
Adams & Prentice, 1932
204 York Street - Beta Theta Pi
James Gamble Rogers, 1927
210 York Street - Wolf's Head Society; Phelps Association
Bertram G. Goodhue, 1924
212 York Street - Zeta Psi
E. V. Meeks, 1929
222 York Street - University Theater and Drama School
Blackall Clapp & Whittemore, 1926; James Gamble Rogers, 1931
224 York Street - Psi Upsilon
James Gamble Rogers, 1928
232 York Street - Delta Kappa Epsilon
James Gamble Rogers, 1930
205 Park Street - Drama School Annex
Delano & Aldrich, 1930
211 Park Street - Chi Psi
H. Herbert Wheeler, 1929
215 Park Street - Alpha Delta Phi
James Gamble Rogers, 1931
217 Park Street - Phi Gamma Delta; Vernon Hall
James Gamble Rogers, 1932

The University and its fraternities in the late 1920s and early 1930s wrapped this stone, timber, and slate village around the Wolf's Head secret society of 1924. For a brief span, the ensemble was a center of Jazz Age glamor at Yale. On the north, the Drama School, which opened in 1925, drew the New York theatrical world to teach, scout, and occasionally perform. On the south, the *Yale Daily News* luxuriated in digs supplied by Henry Luce, of *Time* magazine prose and profits. Looped between and leading through the block to Park Street, the fraternities provided hammer-beamed dining halls and cozy rathskellers to their initiates.

Yale's building program of the 1920s and 1930s caused this cluster to come into being, then effectively killed it. First, the construction of Sterling Library and the Cross Campus displaced the *News* and the frats; then Yale's consulting architect,

Yale Daily News

James Gamble Rogers, created an overall plan for these blocks, and the refugee organizations hired architects (most often Rogers himself) and built their individual bits. Then, in 1928, the University adopted the system of residential colleges, which effectively gave every undergraduate the dining halls and club rooms that had been the new fraternities' attraction. That decision, coupled with Black Friday on Wall Street in 1929, meant that the fraternities were as dead as a raccoon coat even if they did not immediately know it. Many leased their buildings to Yale or sold out. The ones that hung on saw a false renaissance in the tweeds, khakis, and white bucks of the 1950s and early 1960s, but that ended in the Age of Aquarius. Since the 1970s the buildings have mostly housed outposts of the schools of drama, art, and architecture.

This ensemble of buildings hangs together in a relaxed yet coherent way, simply from their architects' awareness of how they are seen from the sidewalk and

Wolf's Head Society; Phelps Association

collectively. They echo each other in form and materials, but are never identical. Inside, they are wonders of spatial inventiveness, unexpected rooms, varied levels, and amusing circulation paths, which, despite the historical trappings, would likely have been admired by Adolf Loos as examples of *Raumplan* organization.

University Theater and Drama School

Meanwhile, the *News*'s 1932 Briton Haddon Memorial by Adams & Prentice (Adams was a classmate of Henry Luce in 1920; T. Merrill Prentice, PhB 1921) has been renovated. The University Theater and Drama School over the years has proven serviceable, though even a remedial 1931 facelift by Rogers did not give Blackall, Clapp & Whittemore's 1925–26 structure the signs of life inside that are the *sine qua non* of urbane theater buildings. It contributes least to Fraternity Row. Wolf's Head, a romantically ruinous English Cotswold manor on steroids, contributes most; Bertram Goodhue (1869–1924) was always more willing than James Gamble Rogers to pull the picturesque stops out all the way.

23. Jonathan Edwards College

James Gamble Rogers, 1932;
renovation, Herbert S. Newman and Partners, 2008

All ten original Yale College colleges put into service between 1933 and 1940 came equipped with an abundance of facilities for living, work, and play, as well as a sense of age, of elements pulled together, given a patina by time. Only in Silliman, largest of the colleges, and in Jonathan Edwards (JE), the smallest, was there much more than a trace of authenticity to that sense. From the standpoint of what it hints at in the historical palimpsest of its site, JE is the most interesting of the colleges, because much of its quirky complexity came about as necessary solutions to real problems. The land on which the college stands was one of Yale's earliest property acquisitions across High Street, a program that began under duress in 1858 but accelerated after the Civil War with pressures to broaden the College's curriculum and modernize its provision of water, heat, and electricity. There was also a complex real estate dance later on, involving Skull and Bones, Yale, and the School of Art, which partly filled up the block out toward Chapel and York streets.

The long and short of it was that by the late 1920s, when the decision was made to go to a college system, the site designated for JE was hemmed in and irregular, and demanded the incorporation of existing structures. Rogers responded

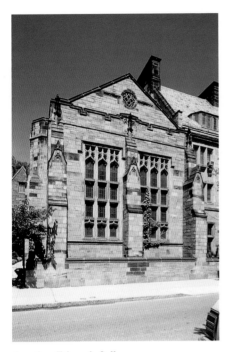

Jonathan Edwards College

cleverly, placing the dining hall to get morning and midday light (while at the same time avoiding an impolitic stare at Skull and Bones), using the private master's house garden to alter the proportions of what would otherwise have been an excessively long courtyard, and a myriad of other small, thoughtful adjustments for the sake of light, privacy, and scenery in cramped quarters. The view back toward Harkness Tower from JE's dining hall entry is one of the great vistas (read, photo opportunities) on the campus. After the architecture program moved out to new quarters in the Art Gallery (keeping "their" view of Weir courtyard), Weir Hall became part of the college, adding still another quirk or two to the assembly.

WALK THREE: MEMORIAL QUADRANGLE AND THE WESTERN COLLEGES

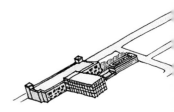

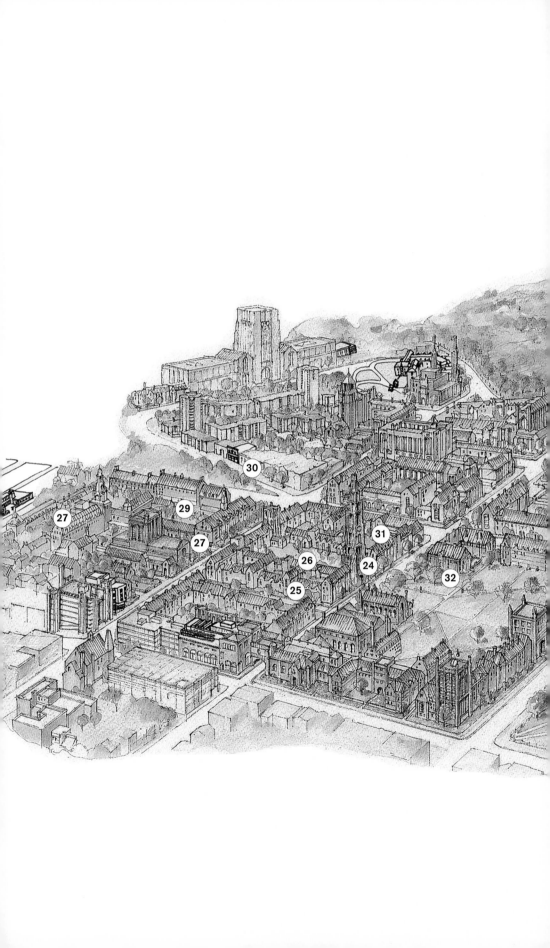

The forces that produced the Yale College colleges that are the principal stops on this walk—the forces that account for their existence and architectural character—can be understood by a brief account of two men whose money paid for most of what is seen here. The walk is less about patronage than it is about time and change, and the power of the idea that meaning and identity can be found and formed in the ritual act of returning to home.

The Yale from which the first man, John W. Sterling, earned a BA in 1864 had 632 students, the great majority of whom, 471, were in the College. The Class of 1864, in which Sterling had distinguished himself sufficiently to be among the fifteen tapped for Skull and Bones, was something like 130 in number; every member of the class knew him, and he them, by face, name, and accomplishments. They all had had their triumphs and tragedies in essentially the same course of study, and that curriculum—indeed Yale life in general—had been encountered in a small set of familiar buildings. While the number of these buildings had increased over the years after 1750, they remained unchanged in essential character. Sterling went on to a successful New York financial career as founder of Shearman & Sterling, advising the thunder-lizard Morgans, Harrimans, Stillmans, and the like of the Jurassic Age of Wall Street. He died in July 1918, leaving Yale an enormous bequest explicitly for building. The fall 1918 term enrolled 1,153 students in the College, out of 2,554 in the University. Not only had Yale quadrupled the student population, the students were scattered among eleven programs in dozens of buildings around the city.

Edward S. Harkness, the second man, received his BA in 1897. He was the younger half-brother of William L. Harkness, 1881, and Charles W. Harkness, 1883. All of them were immensely rich by dint of their father's early investment in John D. Rockefeller and the odd idea of a business in petroleum, an idea that grew to become the Standard Oil Company. Edward started his Yale career miserably. In the heyday of the dashing, athletic Yale Man, the male counterpart to the Gibson Girl, he was shy and overweight, came from Cleveland, and, with no one to show him the way over to the Gold Coast opposite Vanderbilt, had found digs in one of the rooming houses catering to students who were unsuccessful in vying for a spot on the under-dormitoried campus. The waste in this situation was noted by a savvy administrator; Edward was paired up with a future Bonesman for guidance and wound up happy with his undergraduate career. He was aware, however, of the likelihood of the "average men, like himself" getting lost in the balkanized diversity of an ever larger Yale.

By the time of the First World War, there was widespread sentiment that Yale needed to pull its physical plant together, not only for the sake of its students' lives, but also for the sake of understanding itself as a single entity, one community, however diverse. As old buildings and old coherences had vanished, and new programs and a welter of buildings arose, the College became surrounded by the components of a university. After years of reluctance, the Yale Corporation in 1887 declared the ensemble Yale University. The task then, put simply, was for the University to discover ways to return to being a tight-knit place, collective though competitive, with buildings that fostered that. So in the period between 1919 and 1940, Yale thoroughly remade itself both organizationally and physically. Fueled by the Sterling bequest and ongoing gifts from the Harkness family, an immense construction program produced ten undergraduate colleges, each originally housing a body of students almost exactly the size of John Sterling's Class of 1864. Operating on a common basis of shared, university-provided classes and resources, each college was different. But all were assembled from architectural forms drawn from the memory of old Yale (quite literally) or from a kind of invented memory of what old Yale should have been. All were christened with old names, encouraged to see themselves as ancestral exemplars, and expected to develop a sense of being a double-affiliated community—contemporary college with University and contemporary college with old Yale College. The complexity and promise of modern life would not be ignored, but absorbed and integrated in conscious and unconscious ways.

Of course everyone involved—donors, architects, faculty, and students—knew on one level that this was, and is, all just a set of elaborate architectural games played out around green courtyards. That knowledge seems not to have prevented the buildings from accomplishing the intended purpose, more serious than mere stylistic nostalgia, of making a knowable Yale of small but long continuities. It is not coincidence that Bart Giamatti, Yale president from 1978 to 1986, could write about another serious game, baseball:

> That is why it breaks my heart, that game. It breaks my heart because it was meant to. Because it was meant to foster in me again the illusion that there was something abiding, some pattern and some impulse that could come together to make a reality that would resist the corrosion, and because after it had fostered again that most hungered-for illusion, the game was meant to stop and betray precisely what it promised. Now, of course there are those who learn after the first few times. They grow out of sports, and there are others who are born with the wisdom to know that nothing lasts. These are the truly tough among us, the ones who can live without illusion or without

even the hope of illusion. But I am not that grown up or up to date. I am a simpler creature, tied to more primitive patterns and cycles. I need to think something lasts forever, and it might as well be that state of being that is a game. It might as well be that, in a green field, in the sun.

What Giamatti describes applies equally to the college of memory, of a hope for more primitive patterns and cycles, which Yale has often sought to make for and of itself.

24. Harkness Memorial Tower and Memorial Gate

Harkness Memorial Tower
James Gamble Rogers, 1921
Memorial Gate
Samuel Yellin, craftsman and metalsmith

Sterling Library and Harkness Memorial Tower, both designed by James Gamble Rogers, are respectively the functional and emblematic axes around which Yale University turns. By the time the Tower, the first of that pair, was completed in 1921, Yale was stretching out north to new buildings on Science Hill, south to the newly developing Medical School. The new structure immediately assumed its intended roles of central marker and symbolic pivot. Its craggy silhouette is distinctive, more like a beacon-rock piece of badlands geology or stalagmite than a church steeple or generic Oxbridgian campus bell tower. Visible and audible (its dinnertime carillon playing Pavlov to College appetites) from one end of the campus to the other, Harkness was built to remind the people of Yale that, for all their diverse bustle, they are in one community.

The Tower is the most prominent feature of the building complex put into service as the Memorial Quadrangle in 1921, then in 1933 converted into Branford and Saybrook colleges. The "Memorial" was not only to Stephen V. Harkness, a silent partner in John D. Rockefeller's Standard Oil enterprises, and to the dead of the World War, but to all sorts of things, activities, and persons associated with Yale history. In contrast to the inscriptional reticence of earlier buildings, the Quadrangle was everywhere systematically laden with Yale names, sculpted Yale faces, leaded Yale windows. On the main blocks the references are by and large to people and events, while on the Tower, Yale rises upward by graduated stages into idealist apotheosis; from the ground-level war memorial chapel, to effigies of eight of the University's "most eminent sons," to representations of Life, Progress, War, Death, Peace, Prosperity, Effort, Order, Justice, Truth, Freedom, and Courage.[1] Along the

Harkness Memorial Tower

founder John Davenport, was vicar before his emigration to America's Boston. English architectural historian Sarah Whittingham suggests that there may have been some contemporary inspiration from the much less well-known design for the Wills Memorial Building and Tower, by the architect Sir George Oatley, in Bristol, England; Oatley and Rogers were acquaintances. Neither, however, exhibits the adroit vertical integration, the seamless slow dissolve from ground to sky, shown off by Harkness Tower. While Rogers may well have started out from Boston and Bristol, or even Princeton, his goal of making an architectural emblem for a place means his standards were really such things as Karl Friedrich Schinkel's 1813 painting *Gotischer Dom am Wasser* or Turner's views of Fonthill Abbey.

Rogers could not have found a more sympathetic collaborator than the master metalsmith Samuel Yellin (1885–1940) of Philadelphia. The Polish-born craftsman made wrought iron and other metals into impossibly graceful and rhythmic shapes. The Memorial Gate beside Harkness Tower is one of the masterworks among his pieces around the Memorial Quadrangle and the campus. Yellin often said, "I was born with a hammer in my hand"; certainly here and elsewhere around Yale he commanded it in work that complemented Rogers's own strong sense of what the nature of materials could bring to the feel of a place.

25. Memorial Quadrangle, St. George Plaque, and Library Walk

Memorial Quadrangle
James Gamble Rogers, 1921
Yale University Landscape Plan
Beatrix Jones Farrand, 1920s

South on High Street from Harkness Tower extends a range of Branford College, which shows off one of James Gamble Rogers's many clever ways of yoking functionalism and faux age to deal with the design problems in the 1916–21 Memorial Quadrangle commission. As it came to him, the program was a starkly divided one. It specified the desire for a single grand symbolic element, the Memorial Tower, then the need for a large number of small-scale elements, dorm rooms for 630 students, with almost nothing middle-sized in between to help the problem of giving variety and, as well, visual linkage between large and small. (Dining halls, masters' houses, and other midsize elements came into the program only with the conversion to two colleges in 1933.) Rogers's scheme, accepted in March 1917, laid out the student rooms to frame seven courtyards—one very small, three small, two medium, one large—and graded the framing ranges from low on the south side (Library Walk) to high on the north side (Elm Street). This allowed sunlight penetration and gave one kind of variety. Rogers then modeled the basic framing masses in ways that further broke them down for small-scale variety; he also artfully grouped elements together to stand up against Harkness Tower and other towers, respectful but not dwarfed by them. This range provides a clear instance of how he did it all; here, the mass-modeling tactic was to make the thing look as though it were once a large basilica that then got made into condos. The big-scale buttresses tie a ground-floor set of rooms (made from a former "side aisle") together with second- and third-floor rooms (made from an earlier "nave" space), which share the tracery of former large nave windows.

The dry "moats" and their low walls are another tactic, at once functional and historically referential, which Rogers introduced in the Quadrangle and then summoned again in his subsequent Yale work. With them, daylight could be introduced into the basement service rooms and, since they were conceived as always filled with ivy, flowers, and trees, privacy could better be afforded to ground-floor residents and the interest of color and greenery given to passersby. The moats were a very urban creation, giving something positive to Yale and to the streets of New Haven, especially as planted by the landscape architect Beatrix Jones Farrand (1872–1959). Whether out of lack of understanding or lack of maintenance money, or both, not nearly enough of Jones's handiwork is still in evidence—she designed not only the Quadrangle moats, but the plantings of many college courtyards as well.

Where the High Street range turns the corner westward into pedestrian Library Walk, down behind some usually undertended bushes in the moat, is the Memorial Quadrangle cornerstone. The cornerstone was laid on October 8, 1917, the anniversary of the 1717 raising of the first New Haven collegiate building's timber

frame. Visible below it, a small tip of the hat to the real history of the site, is a miscellany of masonry chunks from buildings demolished to make room for the Quadrangle, among them the first Peabody Museum and the first Yale gymnasium. A little further along, the vault bricks in the Pierpont Gateway into Branford allegedly come from the Old Brick Row.

Further west, a buttress supports a multistory bay window, exhibiting a stone carved with a scene of St. George killing a fiery dragon. This may be still another recycling of Yale materials, ambiguously stated, even more vaguely interpreted. The carving is very close to the site of the

St. George Plaque

first Yale Gymnasium (1859–1917), one of the buildings torn down to make way for the Quadrangle. The need for a formal gymnasium began to be felt when, following turf-war conflicts between students and New Haven firemen, and the murder and riot of 1854 (see Street Hall and Walk One entries), a city ordinance banned football on the Green. Blood ran bad even away from the Green, and a firehouse located near the corner of High and Library from the early 1840s (perhaps as a safety measure against fire in the Yale Library) proved to be a flashpoint. On February 8, 1858, a fight between firemen stationed there and a group of students, members of the "Crocodiles" eating club, resulted in the shooting death of one of the firemen. No trial was ever held. The Yale faculty apparently decided that it preferred the risk of fire to the certainty of more trouble, and acquired the engine house from a willing City. Yale replaced it with the (Old) Gym, its first building west of High Street. So back to the stone St. George and his victim: is this Justice finally visited on a Crocodile, or a young Yale hero killing a fire-beast, or possibly James Gamble Rogers squelching the obnoxious fire and smoke of the coal-fired university heating plant, also very close by, also torn down for the Quadrangle?

The removal of the firehouse was one of many acts Yale undertook to disentangle the school from the city in the period between 1860 and 1970. Another such effort was the closure of Library Walk to traffic in the mid-1920s; it is hard to realize that Model Ts once putt-putted through what is now the walk fronted by JE and Branford. Yale gained this quiet stretch of green in a trade for New Haven being allowed to enlarge Grove Street and swing Tower Parkway around the Yale Central Power Plant—the new steam-generating monster, which in 1918 replaced its demolished and possibly allegorized predecessor.

26. Branford College
James Gamble Rogers, 1933;
renovation: Perry, Dean, Rogers & Partners, 2000

In a hiccupy series of negotiations between 1928 and 1930, Yale was persuaded that it should adopt the student living arrangement called the "college plan." More important still, Edward S. Harkness, who had been one of its advocates all along but felt maltreated by the University, was repersuaded to fund this transformation of the campus. James Gamble Rogers, eventual architect of eight of the first ten colleges, became the driving force in the affair, and it would not be inaccurate to say that at Yale in the 1920s and 1930s the architectural vision, supported by a very well-heeled donor-client, dragged administrative and curricular change along in its wake.

The first seven colleges opened on September 25, 1933, some built from scratch, some renovations, some hybrids of new construction and old. Branford and its nonidentical twin, Saybrook, were created by adding new dining halls,

Branford College

common rooms, libraries, and masters' houses to the partitioned Memorial
Quadrangle, which had opened in 1921 as housing for the senior class. Rogers
preferred to design his Yale buildings to look like respectful renovations even when
newly built, so the opportunity to renovate some of his own simulated renovations
must really have delighted him.

Loyal Saybrugians will disagree, but Branford seems to have gotten the bigger
and better side of the partitioned wishbone. Not only does the latter technically have
ownership of Harkness Tower and three of the four smallest, sunniest, and most
picturesque of the Memorial Quadrangle courtyards, it also has the largest. Two
ranges of Saybrook and its dining hall look into the Great Court, but the turf and the
name are Branford's.

Rogers's Branford, both the initial work and the renovations, is of very high-quality
design and workmanship. Authentic materials are of the highest quality; artificial
materials usually look old but work better than the genuine article. The roof "slates,"
for example, which show off particularly well in the three small courtyards, are a
man-made composite. The sheer quality of the construction is what let Branford
and its contemporary Yale buildings mostly survive the period of deliberate deferred
maintenance in the 1980s, and maintain their dignity despite frequent slipshod
repairs in recent years, in particular the often badly executed, poorly color-matched
masonry repointing. All four Branford courtyards are worth not only a quick glimpse
and a snapshot, but close study to understand the high degree of calculation
that Rogers used to achieve the deceptively easy charm and livability. (The three
south courtyards are named, east to west, Linonia, Calliope, and Brothers-in-Unity,

after early Yale literary societies; Branford commemorates the town east of New
Haven, toward the mouth of the Connecticut River, in which a group of ministers
met in 1701 to found the Collegiate School.)

Branford's dining hall is one of Yale's most glorious rooms, with natural lighting
as spectacular as that of Beinecke Library, but more varied. With two long, high
walls of golden-tinted glass facing east and west, it manages to be cheerful almost
no matter how dark the day or how dense the essay due dates. Since it is on the
second floor, its views are over the York Street traffic on one side and at a better
angle across to Harkness Tower on the other. The moiré of mullions and silhouetted
moving figures, outlined by a sunset seen *through* the dining hall from Branford
Court at suppertime, is magical.

27. Pierson Walkway and Pierson College

Pierson College
James Gamble Rogers, 1932; renovation: KieranTimberlake Architects, 2004

Pierson and Davenport colleges are Siamese twins, possessing their own
distinctive buildings but not quite fully separated from each other, hence always
a little more rivalrous in their mutual relations than in those with other colleges.
Pierson's dining hall backs up to Davenport's rear courtyard, while a stroll down
Pierson Walkway to the College's entry tower is often accompanied by the sound
of dishes clinking as Davenporters dine. Even the two colleges' names have
something of a covert, built-in competition to them: who was responsible, really,
for getting Yale going? John Davenport, founder of New Haven Colony, who was
determined that it would have a college? Or Abraham Pierson, the Collegiate
School's first rector? The architect of both colleges, designed together in 1930
and built 1931–32, was once again James Gamble Rogers, a man known to like
a good joke.

Whatever the degree of döppelganger play intended between Pierson
and Davenport, it was certainly less important to the overall conception of the
colleges than were two urban design mandates set up by Yale. The administration

decided it was highly desirable to
give Davenport a strong sense of
connection eastward, back across
York Street toward the Old Campus.
In the other direction, west toward
Park Street, it was equally desirable
to present a sympathetic but firm
campus edge to the houses and
apartment buildings of the Dwight-

Pierson College

Pierson courtyard, so-called "Slave Quarters"

Edgewood neighborhood. Trouble could have arisen from the fact that Yale presented Rogers with a site too narrow for two colleges on the east, and seemingly too wide for a nonoppressive institutional wall on the west. The architect managed not just to sidestep the problems but use them as a stimulus to smart, unusual, and quite unforced architectural forms and placements.

Pierson allows Davenport to occupy all but a few feet of the York Street side of the site, but makes those few feet really count by filling them with a stone and iron gateway much showier than Davenport's nearby low-key entrance. The gate is at the tip of a long trunk of Pierson space nosed out nearly the length of a football field from the college's great court. To make sure the connection is unmistakable, Rogers placed a tower, unusually tall for a college, to signal the main courtyard entrance as one walks down Pierson Walk. (For whatever reason, the tower seems based on that of Independence Hall in Philadelphia, dating from 1753.) The courtyard and its major buildings are another of the architect's deceptively easygoing bravura performances. From relative formality at the north, with the entry tower and the Park Street gatehouse making a cross axis in front of the symmetrical common room and set-back dining hall facade, the courtyard telescopes down, divides, and becomes asymmetrical and house-scaled at the south, where the master's house courtyard and the picturesque Slave Quarters (so-called) stand. The breadth and formality allow for the higher dorm ranges necessary to get in all the required rooms, while the smaller pieces make a sympathetic fit with the scale of pre-existing Fraternity Row to the south.

It is well worth a stroll out either of Pierson's two back gates—one by the dining hall, the other by the master's house—to take in the expanse of the Park Street facade. It is more than five hundred feet of frontage, broken into sections that provide variety and interest to passersby while clearly announcing that Yale proper begins at this line of buildings, iron fences, and brick walls. It is not accidental that the southern gate is topped with a tower and aligns exactly with Edgewood Avenue, projecting a guarded welcome out into the city.

28. Dwight-Edgewood Neighborhood, St. Thomas More Chapel, and Thomas E. Golden Jr. Center

St. Thomas More Chapel
Office of Douglas Orr, 1938
Thomas E. Golden Jr. Center
Pelli Clarke Pelli, 2008

On the other side of Park Street from Davenport College begins the Dwight-Edgewood neighborhood. It is named for two of its principal streets and began to develop in the post–Civil War years as a mixed neighborhood of light manufacturing, housing, and notable churches. From the late nineteenth century, at least, when Yale workers, faculty, and graduate students no longer felt compelled to live close by the University–thanks to the convenience of street cars and the popularization of bicycles–the Dwight-Edgewood neighborhood was one they favored. Even when a household had no immediate connection to Yale, no one failed to miss the bands of undergrads who swarmed through the neighborhood to and from Saturday baseball and football games in the parks to the west, an ebb and flow that began after the Civil War and had its highest tides after completion of the Yale Bowl in 1914.

Among the residents of Dwight-Edgewood, one deserves special mention, for his Yale connections and also for the part he played in setting the direction of forces that fundamentally reshaped New Haven and many other cities. Robert Moses (1888–1981), the urban planner, politician, and power broker, was born in a house

(now lost to urban renewal) at 83 Dwight Street, son of a prosperous Jewish department store owner and his strong-willed wife. The family moved to Fifth Avenue when Moses was quite young, but his imagination had been caught by Yale and he returned to become a member of the Class of 1909. He made a reputation by mounting an unthinkable challenge to Walter Camp, the patriarch of Yale and American football, over support of other, "minor" sports. Later in his career, Moses not only challenged but used or rolled right over men, families and organizations far more powerful than Camp in the course of enormously expanding the park,

St. Thomas More Chapel

bridge, and highway systems in all directions from New York City. Moses pioneered the use of automobile-centered infrastructure and land-use patterns to change the shape of cities and the lives of Americans. The mixed results attending that crusade are quite visible in New Haven, not least in the free-fire zone, cleared but never used for Route 34, which marks the south edge of Dwight-Edgewood.

The neighborhood contains a fascinating representative array of building types dating from the early nineteenth century on. Charles Moore, when dean at the School of Architecture, in 1966 gutted and rehabbed an unpretentious little Elm Street house for himself in a sheetrock and plywood homage to Sir John Soane's house in London. A walk around will turn up the evidence of many other architectural "interventions" in the area, some by Yalies, some not. Certainly the walkability, the porches and trees, and the variety and adaptability of the various types made the neighborhood in the 1960s and 1970s instructive for the generation of Yale Architecture graduates who went on to form the core of the neovernacular and New Urbanism movements.

St. Thomas More Chapel, in Dwight-Edgewood and serving both Yale and the neighborhood, is one structure worth note. It was designed by the office of Douglas Orr in 1938 and has a kind of Scandinavian tempering of traditional masonry with a modernist sense of light and abstraction, visible especially in the interior. (Orr, BFA 1919, MFA 1927, became the architect or associated architect of many Yale buildings.) Around the corner from More House at 344 Elm is the senior society tomb of Manuscript, 1962–63, designed by King-lui Wu (1918–2002). It is a match in scale and elegant reserve to the crisp little Greek Revival houses of the area, and its interior shows off Wu's extraordinary command of natural lighting.

Immediately south of the 1938 St. Thomas More Chapel, César Pelli and his associates replaced a generic small commercial building with a tight cluster of interconnected structures, forming a central courtyard that faces across Park Street to one of the back entrances of Pierson College. The cluster is almost, but not quite, a cloister. Pelli was clearly thinking about the way that, in the classic, standardized planning of medieval Cistercian (in particular) monasteries, subsidiary specialized buildings—chapter house, refectory, and so on—were grouped around a courtyard to the side of the church, but he did not want to make a new, condensed version of that model. The Pelli firm has a long history of designing buildings informed by type and history, but never taking them literally. The most literal-minded decision here was to face the new buildings in brick closely matching that of the Chapel so as to subtly unify the complex.

The Thomas E. Golden Jr. Center expansion allows the Catholic Church at Yale to serve a wider variety of purposes, both religious and secular, more easily. It has a round, chapter-house-like meditation room, seminar rooms and lecture hall, and a recreation room. There is also some commercial space on Park Street.

The whole ensemble is an urbane understatement, deferential to its surroundings.

Emblematic of that is the flat-topped limestone campanile, a material standing out from all the red brick around it, but then tucked back in the entry courtyard so as not to compete with the striking profile of the Chapel's lead spire and angels.

29. Davenport College

James Gamble Rogers, 1932; renovation: KieranTimberlake, 2005

If Pierson College shows off James Gamble Rogers's cleverness in urbanism and site planning, its nonidentical twin, Davenport, demonstrates the architect's ability to use stylistic sleight of hand to mitigate architectural problems. At the same time, this college allows one to see how much Rogers relied on a sort of genetic memory of the building types in which Yale had housed itself since its New Haven beginnings. What follows, then, is an attempt to describe Davenport and to further indicate how it illustrates Rogers's methods in designing within the Yale context in general.

While Davenport residents and the public seem to find interest and humor in the famously two-faced (Gothic on one side, Georgian on the other) York Street range, many architects are outraged by it. And it is not only those whose sympathies are modernist; traditional-minded designers get equally livid. The former group wants the programmatic contents and structure inside Rogers's package to be forthrightly displayed on the outside, while the latter wants the package wrapper to have its own integrity, please: Gothic, Georgian, modern, almost no matter what so long as it is consistent. Rogers did not like having his hands tied in either of those ways. He was nothing if not pragmatic, and therefore decided that in some cases the most effective bang for the available buck came from playing the architectural elements in Vicinity X in harmony, sometimes from playing those in Vicinity Y off against each other. Style,

Davenport College

programmatic expression, and structure were simply good, useful tools, a means to an end. All were to be mastered, but not mistaken for purposes in themselves.

So Rogers equipped the east facade of Davenport with the height, materials, moats, stone-mullioned bay windows and leaded casements, and general rhythms of the Memorial Quadrangle across York, simply because the new whole was then more than the sum of the two facing buildings. Together, they effectively controlled the character of a third element, the street between them. Not that the two buildings are identical; the Quadrangle was just built too expensively to copy, and besides, the Davenport facade had a different list of secondary jobs to do, like making sure its entry was dignified and visible without competing with the Pierson Walk gateway.

Once away from York and into the Davenport courtyards, the problem changed. There was one principal design fact with which Rogers had to deal, and it was of his own making. In the interest of creating the requisite quantity of student suites, efficiently, economically, and with the best sunlight management, Rogers made the ruthlessly clear decision to achieve the bulk of necessary rooms by placing a massive, repetitive, 550-foot-long block along the north edge of the site. His problem therefore became how to soften that bold, necessary, but too utilitarian move; basically, how now to assert *difference* where on York Street he had asserted *similarity*. The break of the college into two courtyards, and all the small-scale elements and level changes at the base of that long slab block, and the various acts of urbanistic legerdemain in which other University towers are magically drawn into Davenport vistas (the one east to Branford's Wrexham Tower from the narrow upper terrace of the larger courtyard is really good) are all in the interest of disguise and distraction. Utility and practicality are utterly necessary, Rogers implies, but left untreated their results are just too stern. Hence the eminently civil, Virginian, Doric colonnade, which draws attention upon entry to the college. Direct quotations from famous buildings help out too; the rear facade of the entry gate is unmistakably a version of Boston's Old State House, lantern tower and unicorns included. (Is the courtyard's hidden joke a renewal of the rivalry between Thomas Jefferson and John Adams?)

But there was a historical as well as a utilitarian origin to the too-long block of student rooms. The north range of Davenport is composed of three-room suites, a common room with fireplace facing one side of the range, a pair of bedrooms facing the other. Not only is this internal arrangement like that of Durfee Hall from 1871, it is identical to what John Trumbull drew up in 1792 for what would become the dormitory blocks of the Old Brick Row. Rogers's eight entryways worth of such units in the range, four stories high, are really four blocks of the Row re-created and pushed together. Rogers employed type-thinking, a common recurrence at Yale. The picturesque arrangement of other college elements to soften the factory-like result, the overlay of architectural allusions, is an attempt to find the appropriate twentieth-century version, the antitype, to the Yale Row type.

30. York Street and Broadway

Arnold Hall
Herbert S. Newman & Partners, 2007
29–45 Broadway
Hammond Beeby Rupert Ainge Architects and Judith DiMaio, 2001
Off-Broadway Theater
Christopher Williams Architect

The short run of shopfronts at the southwest corner of York Street and Broadway is the remnant of a concentration (rivaling Chapel Street's) of small stores and services. Some were and are upscale, some decidedly not, and the area is more interesting for the mix. The variety was the result of this corner being in essence a town gate, the place where since the late eighteenth century all the different sorts of traffic—local, regional, industrial, commercial—coming in on Elm, Whalley, and Broadway converged to enter the central Nine Squares of New Haven.

On York Street, above the ground-floor shopfronts' self-conscious and discrete respectability, decades of ad-hoc adaptation have made a fascinating architectural palimpsest. Once-posh townhouses have had layers added and subtracted, and bright signs adjoin the large windows of tailoring workrooms dating from before electric lights. J. Press Clothiers, almost the last survivor of its gentlemen's tailor species, moved here from Chapel Street in 1908. On the corner is the 1927 Langrock Building, by Jacob Weinstein (later one of the architects of the old Jewish Community Center), a New Haven merchant's valiant attempt to keep his architectural tailoring up to the standards of the Memorial Quadrangle across the street. On Broadway, in one of those anonymous nineteenth-century brick buildings that continue to provide the cheap, adaptable space that cities really need, Tyco Copy and the Yankee Doodle soldiered on to provide two fundamental fuels of academic life, paper and hamburger. The Doodle, owned and worked by one family since midcentury, had a classic sign and vintage fittings to go along with the food. Sadly, it marched off into history in January 2008.

In the 1990s the University's real estate arm aimed to upgrade the stock of storefront space available on the Broadway retail strip, making available square footages of space and lengths of frontage that might be attractive to national retailers. It was part of a trend to strengthen businesses surrounding the campus and bring in clientele for local businesses, even if that meant abandonment of longstanding

29–45 Broadway

traditions. The most visible example of Yale's shift in focus was the decision in January 1996 to award the lease of the building that housed the venerable Yale Co-op, part of the Stiles and Morse colleges complex, to the large retail bookseller Barnes & Noble. The Co-op, a century-plus-old student-run institution, moved downtown and eventually died. With flagship retail space as the anchor, in effect, for a stretch of businesses as tightly managed as those in any suburban mall, it became possible to entice characteristically suburban retailers to come into downtown New Haven. Tom Beeby, a principal of Hammond Beeby Rupert Ainge Architects in Chicago and a former dean of the Yale School of Architecture, enlisted Judith DiMaio, then a faculty member at the school, to design the western third of the tripartite Broadway facade, while Beeby's firm designed the other two parts. In actuality all three retail spaces are under one roof, with centralized mechanical systems. Completed in 2001, the building is a chunky structure, as deep as it is wide, but manages visually—just barely—to hang onto the nostalgic sense of Broadway as a diverse collection of buildings and small businesses.

Opposite, across the neatened-up triangle of parking where Broadway and Elm diverge, Yale filled the gap between the corner building at Elm and Park streets and another early twentieth-century commercial building on Elm, further east, with the four-story Robert M. Arnold Hall, designed by Newman Architects. It is an annex to James Gamble Rogers's Davenport College, connected back into its main body both by gateway and by tunnel. Gates on Elm Street still manage to allow three thousand square feet of retail space below three stories of student rooms. It's an urbanistically smart building, with hints of Connecticut Hall in its appearance, and a protected courtyard between Arnold Hall and the northern range of Davenport. The lintels and sills of the second- and third-story windows are oddly elongated, but that is a quibble; the building is good enough in its city-sense, and in simply doing its job of providing shops and rooms, it does not need to do much in the way of look-at-me architecture.

31. Saybrook College
James Gamble Rogers, 1933; renovation: Perry, Dean, Rogers & Partners

Saybrook College has both its street entrances facing north onto busy Elm Street. Because Rogers gradually increased the height of the Memorial Quadrangle buildings, south to north, to capture the sun in the courtyards, the Elm Street range is high, five stories under a steep roof for most of its breadth, as well as wide, filling as it does the entire 300-foot-plus width of the block from York to High streets. As always, the architect developed a variety of interesting tactics to tailor an initial massing strategy for a better fit with its local circumstances. For example, the ground-floor rooms in the central section of the mass have an extra layer of stone screening, treated as a filled-in cloister, to give them at least a bit more visual privacy.

Saybrook College

The two entrances occur under little two-story projecting Jacobethan gatehouses, the only time Rogers used this motif at Yale, in what one suspects was an attempt to draw attention toward these quaint, cute pieces, and away from the large, rather dark, and strictly symmetrical whole.

The College's two main courtyards, Killingworth on the east and Saybrook on the west, are near mirror images in plan and massing, but have quite distinct airs about them. Killingworth feels quieter and sunnier, because it retains its grassy center and planting beds. Saybrook, the western court, has been stone-paved to its edges, has a decent-sized tree shading it from the south side, and opens through terrace and doorways into the common room and dining hall; it is darker, noisier, and more urban, a sense deepened by installation of the college basketball hoop ("the city game"). In keeping with the Memorial Quadrangle tradition, memorializing names, inscriptions, and bits of Yale commemorabilia are carved everywhere in both courts. In Killingworth, all entryways are named after Yale men whose names begin with *W*, either a Rogers witticism or the otherwise sobersided University naming committee getting a little giddy on the job.

At the southwest corner of Saybrook Court is the gateway leading into the College's third, smaller court, Wrexham. This one is a hidden gem, with a Doric

Saybrook College

arcade cloister on one side and the limestone complications of a tower on the other. There is in the conjunction Rogers's usual mix of pious reference and silliness, since the tower is loosely modeled on the one overlooking the churchyard in Wrexham, Wales, where Elihu Yale is buried, while the arcade is infested with little stone bulldogs dressed up in various sorts of College togs. It must have been one of the architect's own favorite places in the Quadrangle, and a plaque memorializing his contribution is in the wall there. The tower was intended to provide an asymmetrical balance to Harkness Tower for viewers in Branford Court, which it does, but its effect when encountered up close, looking up from its tiny courtyard, is altogether different and more appealing because less postcardish and deliberately "composed."

Saybrook's common room and dining hall, like Branford's, were made by carving out space within the walls of existing Memorial Quadrangle dormitory ranges a little over a decade after the complex opened. The two dining halls are different in character: daylit from east and west, Branford's feels classically balanced, while Saybrook's, its near-windowless north wall in radical contrast to south-facing bays and a dazzling myriad of banked casements, is romantically *chiaroscuro*.

32. Yale Station and Giamatti Bench

Yale Station, basement of Lanman-Wright Hall
United States Postal Service
Giamatti Bench
David Sellers, 1990

East along Elm Street from the gates of Saybrook, and on the same side of the street, is the stairway down into Yale Station. Still a strategic location despite the advent of email and cell phones, its entrance is identifiable even at a distance because of the attendant cluster of banners and sandwich boards. This was the location of the Yale telephone exchange and of the Postal Service branch serving the University from the time they moved across Elm from the old Berkeley Oval (see the tablets on the face of Berkeley College). Cheery, light, and clean, the current facility seems designed to avoid ever becoming the grunge-patinaed setting that, for several generations before the renovation, intensified the experience of the contents—letters, cookie package slips, draft notices, or, sometimes the best or the most awful of all possibilities, dumb emptiness—of the little brass and glass boxes stacked in their too-tight alcoves. Still, the oddity of a half-underground walk-through station is much to be preferred to standardized contemporary facilities designed principally to make interstate tractor-trailer mail trucks happy. The human design lesson here is powerful; with a corridor just wide enough for two close streams of people, in a place charged with the ties to an outside world, every half-second flash glance of a passing face offers a story to guess at.

Up and out the bank of stairs leading into the Old Campus, the sidewalk to the right leads back to the Abraham Pierson statue, where this book began. Diagonally right, another path aims toward Harkness Tower, and situated on a triangular eddy of grass to the right is a monument, in the form of an inscribed bench or *exedra*, dedicated to A. Bartlett "Bart" Giamatti (1938–1989). Giamatti would have liked it that both terms could be applied to his memorial. Commissioner of Major League Baseball at the end of his life, Bart loved the dugout benches of the sport as places of colorful language, professionalism, ritual, and fun. Earlier he had been a great

Giamatti Bench

teacher, a scholar of Renaissance literature, master of Ezra Stiles College, and from 1978 until 1986, the president of Yale. Giamatti knew a hawk from a handsaw, a Group W bench from an *exedra*, and moved easily among the different worlds that used those terms. David Sellers's design suffers a little from its placement, disengaged somehow in a way that Giamatti never was, but the contrast between the raw, squared-off, quarry-drilled back faces of the two granite blocks and the polished curve of inscribed seat makes the memorial not just a static object but an emblem of the processes of working stone. The inscribed quotation from Giamatti is explicitly also about process:

A LIBERAL EDUCATION IS AT THE HEART OF A CIVIL SOCIETY
AND AT THE HEART OF A LIBERAL EDUCATION IS THE ACT OF TEACHING

The gap between the two blocks has been explained as allegorizing the distance between student and teacher. At least for some, it also calls attention to the act of making, since a bench of the size and shape desired almost certainly had to be fabricated from more than one block of granite.

Giamatti, who can hardly be recalled without a cigarette in hand (sometimes two, in a characteristically self-ironic joke about the habit of smoking), would have enjoyed the fact that the Bench has become a refuge for the smokers now banned from university buildings.

WALK FOUR: STERLING LIBRARY, CROSS CAMPUS, AND NORTH GREEN

The Cross Campus is just that: two intersecting swathes of grass, each 450 feet long, through which every sort of student, faculty, and administrator crosses in the course of daily academic life. Grub Street (Blount Avenue), the walkway to Commons, traverses it; it is the place to take a last deep breath before diving down the rabbit hole into the surreal Cross Campus Library (now wholly transformed into the Bass Library) or the bleary intensities of the Law Library. The Cross Campus also marks a special place in the seasonal cycle of University life, since it is the greenroom where all students and faculty, College, graduate, and professional schools alike, assemble together for the procession across Elm Street into the Old Campus for the good-natured drama of Commencement. So taken for granted on high occasion or no occasion, the Cross Campus is surprisingly new to the life of Yale. It came into being in the late 1920s, in one of those perennial accommodations of grand vision and gritty reality that over time have given the campus its character as a series of partial, competing utopias. The tale of Cross Campus is exceptionally complex, even for Yale, but in broadest outline it has to do with the change of the institution from college to university, and the realization that this change in workings and psychology could only be made definitive by buildings and space. From our perspective it is hard to understand that the shift from college to university was much more than a nomenclature change, designed to reflect growth and the presence of a wider variety of class subjects. Embedded in the terminology shift, however, were conflicts of educational philosophy, turf wars between different areas of the campus, and reputations made and lost. Here it must suffice to say that the shift was long resisted, that Yale legally became a university in 1887, but that in order for legal fact to become psychological reality, the center of the institution had to be moved off the Old Campus. Yale College could not be mistaken for Yale University. That move took another four decades and more to be conceived and, more or less, completed, and that is what the Cross Campus and the buildings around it represent.

By the time the University name shift occurred, Yale was composed of any number of small satellite buildings and programs clustering loosely around two larger complexes, the College to the south and the Sheffield Scientific School buildings on the north. Two architectural moments were early predictors of how to make a coherent whole of this disparate collection; the College's Vanderbilt Hall of 1894, and the central university steam and power system that came along with it, and then the Bicentennial Buildings of 1901. The former unmistakably aimed a connecting axis in the general direction of Sheff, right through the center of poor surprised Durfee,

while the latter picked up that axis, provided a good reason for it with
Commons, then swung another connecting axis through the Memorial
Rotunda across to Sheffield's oldest building on the site now occupied
by Sterling-Sheffield-Strathcona (SSS) Tower. There, after 1901, matters
remained for a generation. If anything, the problem of unification became
even more complicated with the acquisition of Sachem's Wood in 1905
and the subsequent beginnings of Science Hill (see Walk Eight). Charles
Coolidge Haight, architect of Vanderbilt and other College and Sheff
buildings, as well as some of the earliest Science Hill structures, strove
always to suggest local linkages; but institutional rivalries made larger
ones difficult to contemplate.

By the closing months of World War I any number of forces were
militating for an overall reorganization of the University. To go along with
it, commissioned by a faction within the Yale Corporation, John Russell
Pope (1874–1937) in late 1919 proposed a sweeping overall vision for the
campus. The magnificent book with which he put forward the proposal
was called, blandly but significantly for those who understood what was at
stake, *University Architecture: Yale University A Plan for Its Future Building.*
Pope had the very unusual ability to design boldly, even ruthlessly, but
with enormous, taciturn reserve. Payne Whitney Gym later showed off his
architectural power at Yale, as did many buildings in Washington, including
the National Gallery of Art and the Jefferson Memorial, and the choice of
Pope to do a Yale plan was inspired. He observed that the University already
had two rudimentary organizing axes, Vanderbilt-Commons and Science
Hill-Sheff along Hillhouse Avenue, both axes more or less north-south.
First, Pope proposed, those two should be considerably pumped up, the
former blowing Durfee completely away and covering up Commons with
a tall-towered University Library, the latter blasting past Grove Street to a
new intersection with Wall Street. Wall Street was to be enlarged beyond
its wildest dreams, with a new University Gym at its head, a new square of
London-esque scale down at the intersection with Temple Street and the
extended Hillhouse. The three axes together made a giant, slashing urban
Z, a check mark hooking around the Green and the Grove Street Cemetery.
Between the clarity of the geometry and the unmissable bulk of the various
new buildings Pope thought should occupy prominent positions, never again
would anyone at Yale have been at a loss for how to navigate the campus.

The utter clarity of Pope's plan was both its power and a guarantee that
it would not be carried out as proposed. Even in the climate of reform that
held sway at the time, Pope's wholesale demolitions of existing serviceable
buildings and requisite acquisitions of New Haven real estate were just too
much. It was left to the canny, compromising, infinitely resourceful James

Gamble Rogers, who had already proven himself as a reinventor and flame-keeper of Yaleness in the Memorial Quadrangle, to be appointed consulting architect on a general plan (November 1920), and then gradually to rework Pope's basic notion into the Cross Campus of today. In February 1924 the *Alumni Weekly* announced the "Yale of the Future," showing drawings of the new University Library with a tower aligned not on Wall Street, as in the Pope plan, but midway between Wall and Elm, and for the first time began to refer to the green area at the intersection of axes as the Cross Campus. (Pope was bitterly disappointed but was consoled by a Yale honorary degree in 1924. He maintained cordial professional relations with Rogers, however, and came back to Yale for the Calhoun College and Payne Whitney Gymnasium commissions.)

The formal structure of Cross Campus thus determined, Rogers went on to participate in two other organizational struggles, the outcome of which made the Cross Campus into the activity center it became. First, he helped resist the idea that the Graduate School and the Law School could best pursue their operations in locations away from the center of campus; in putting the Law School and the Hall of Graduate Studies next to Sterling Library, Rogers made a powerful architectural ensemble and also guaranteed a greater concentration and diversity of human energy. Second, in a seemingly contradictory move that in fact resulted in a balance, Rogers lobbied heavily for the College Plan. Its adoption meant that the Old Campus could be occupied by freshmen, giving them a symbolic attachment to old Yale, but that the principal foci of undergraduate life would be dispersed in a loose constellation of colleges centered on Sterling Library and the Cross Campus.

Rogers's 1924 plan abandoned Pope's idea of extending Hillhouse through to Wall, and when Silliman was built in 1940 (ironically, by Pope's successor firm), it became clear that that method of tying the sciences into the campus was never going to be adopted. Rogers in 1924 did posit a major new university building across College to answer Sterling's stack tower, but, at the east end of the Cross Campus, no large building has come along to elbow out steadfast, off-center old 451 College Street. The Pope plan's incompletion has also meant that commencement processions, neatly formed up on the Cross Campus, must do a little skip-step jog, crossing Elm, to enter the Old Campus.

Domestic Tendencies in Yale Architecture

Yale buildings, unlike those of many other major American universities, do not feature much in the way of grandiose architectural elements, such as upper-floor rooms reached by wide outside stairs overseen by guardian statuary. It is not a place of *piano nobiles*, in which journeys to enlightenment are represented by allegorical mass processions up wide, high stairways. Nor does the absence of grand approaches and ceremonial entrances seem to be due to stylistic constraints, for Yale has buildings of all stylistic species and all behave similarly. All such building behavior intends to tell a viewer who he or she is with respect to the institution that erected the building, and to suggest the kind of place in which the institution lives. Yale's architectural rhetoric is mostly not of the public realm, but of the domestic and the private. The architecture of on-grade entrances into hidden communal courtyards in this century; the Fence, like that around a farmyard in the last century: these are drawn from the private realm. They are characteristic of houses extended yet houses nonetheless. The architectural rhetoric toward which Yale has gravitated over the decades is one that places students and faculty in a household. You are a family member, and you live essentially in private. This may not be either more oppressive or more liberating than being a public citizen, but it certainly subtly establishes the institution on a different basis.

The buildings on this walk show Yale's continued attraction to things domestic. The colleges around Sterling Library, which put masters' houses at the head and foot of the Cross Campus, and the unlikely preservation of small white houses around the Green by the University or groups associated with it, are directly domestic. So too is the Women's Table, paradoxically both a monument and, in its invocation of dining tables as well as tables of statistics on the number of women enrolled at Yale, a reminder of domesticity. The two New Haven buildings included here, the Public Library and the County Courthouse, make the same point by contrast as vest-pocket public monuments, which even in their modest scale speak in a way that, quite rightly, marks them as not Yale buildings.

All this is not to deny that Yale's architecture is indeed grand and quite undomestic in places. But it is so in a way that still makes it characteristically different from New Haven's public structures, and gives away an architectural mindset that has looked beyond the city for the psychological definition of where it lives. If anything, for example, the stack tower of Sterling Library is closer in form and effect to East and West Rocks than it is to the Courthouse or the old Post Office, and this is not accidental. When Yale began in the 1840s to build in the reddish brownstone of those Rocks, giving up on the Old Brick Row in good part because the Row's form and red-brick walls were too close to the look of factories, it was giving up affiliation with the local social order in favor of an independent association with local geology. By the 1920s even that was deemed too direct. In building the Memorial Quadrangle, Sterling Library, Trumbull, Berkeley, and other structures, James Gamble Rogers wanted geology and Yale's own history to come together. In choosing gold-brown seam-faced granite for the dominant material of the buildings, Rogers explained, "I determined at the start to endeavor to make the walls like the stone of some of the little islands between Saybrook and New London as they look in the afternoon when the sun shines on them. This, I felt, would give a warmth and cheerfulness that is so much needed during the season that the students are at New Haven." In short, the right place for Yale spiritually was felt to be not in New Haven but in the small seacoast towns, in the ministers' houses and meetinghouses, in which the Collegiate School was born and conducted classes from 1701 until 1717.

33. Sterling Memorial Library and the Women's Table

Sterling Memorial Library
James Gamble Rogers, 1930
Women's Table
Maya Lin, 1993

Sterling Library was the great weight that shifted Yale's center of physical and

Women's Table

psychological gravity from the Old Campus to Cross Campus. It was completed in 1930 after a protracted design history stretching more than a decade and involving the strongly held ideas of several prominent architects. It is also worthwhile to understand that James Gamble Rogers's imprint on the Yale campus—which was so large and is now so taken for granted—was neither predictable nor inevitable. Rogers made the most of receiving good luck from others' bad luck.

John W. Sterling, a New York lawyer long involved with Yale's finances and buildings, died July 5, 1918, leaving the University an enormous bequest for new construction. As luck would have it, Frank Miles Day (1861–1918), the Philadelphia architect who had been Yale's consulting architect and de facto campus planner since 1913, died a couple weeks before Sterling died. It was a time of tremendous unrest and change, and while the University had money for new buildings, it had no clear priorities for what to put in them or where they should go. Into this swirl a group of Yale Corporation members led by another New York lawyer, Frances P. Garvan, invited John Russell Pope, who produced the 1919 Plan. The full Corporation then designated the architects William Adams Delano (1874–1960), Paul Cret (1876–1945), and Bertram G. Goodhue (1869–1924) to report back on the merits of Pope's effort. As might be expected, their response, dated February 7, 1920, was in part supportive but in other ways a masterpiece of understated second-guessing; their most important demurral suggested that "the Library be placed where Mr. Pope places the gymnasium." Goodhue wound up with the Library commission, while James Gamble Rogers (1867–1947), on the strength of his work on the Memorial Quadrangle, was appointed to Day's old position of consulting architect in November 1920.

Goodhue worked away on a number of schemes, including one in the classical manner of the Bicentennial Buildings, while Rogers with the University librarian and the administration engaged in basic arguments over the size and placement of the building. When the Corporation published "The Yale of the Future" in January 1924, the various library drawings did not match each other, and, while Rogers's name was prominently featured in articles, Goodhue's was absent. Goodhue died on April 21, 1924, and his successor firm was not allowed to continue work on the Library. By May 1924, the commission formally was in Rogers's hands. He presented his own sketches in early 1925. Even so, the design was not settled until October 1927. Sterling Library in all its considerable glory finally opened in 1930.

The building remains astonishing, on a variety of levels. Perhaps most surprising, given the intricacy of its Gothic garb, is that it is a functionalist tour de force; books and paper movements are sorted out, rationalized, and mechanized to a fare-thee-well, the seam-face granite walls, stone vaults, and fairy castle roofline concealing advanced structural and mechanical systems. All the major interior spaces possess distinctive characters. Of the two original interior courtyards, the front one, associated with the Linonia and Brothers-in-Unity reading room, remains intact except for its plantings. (The rear courtyard has been redesigned and roofed over to a design by Shepley Bulfinch Richardson and Abbott, reopened as the Gilmore Music Library in 1998.) The Library has an enormous amount of ornament, a fact of considerable disgust to modern architects in 1930 (and now), but affording others an endless supply of amusement, instruction, and, some would contend, ideological propaganda. Throughout, the ornament and decoration are suited to the specified function of the spaces, right down to a bucket and mop for a janitor's closet.

The Women's Table, installed close to Sterling's main entrance in 1993, is in striking sympathy with it despite the change in artistic language to a mildly referential abstraction. Rogers and Maya Lin, its artist-architect (best known for the Vietnam Memorial in Washington, DC, designed when she was a Yale undergraduate in 1981), share a concern with marking place-ness and with geology. "Even my earliest work was influenced by geology and topology," Lin has written. "Interest in the land… make[s] me want to travel back in geologic time, to witness the shaping of the earth before man." The Women's Table is a journey back in time, contemplating in stone the Yale world in terms of its female student population; out from the focus of the elliptical granite table comes a thin but moving wash of water and a table of dates and numbers. In many senses it is a *tabula rasa* placed at Yale's front door, offering, magically, gentle criticism and affirmation. She invokes the family table, a familiar domestic image, but makes it new again with a new context.

34. Trumbull College

James Gamble Rogers, 1929 and 1933;
renovation: Goody Clancy Architects, 2006

South from Sterling Library on High Street is the master's house entrance of Trumbull College. Trumbull is named for Jonathan Trumbull, Connecticut's governor during the Revolution, and his artist-patriot son John. As was the Brick Row in its day, Trumbull has been denigrated for spareness, especially that of its brick-walled inner courtyards. In fact both the Row and Trumbull deserve high marks for their architectural and urbanistic intelligence.

Trumbull was reputedly James Gamble Rogers's favorite among his college designs, and only a little study suffices to make it clear why. It shows Rogers at his best not so much in the details and character of the components, though these are certainly among his more interesting and distinctive, as in his mastery of the urban chess game of anticipating the needs and forms of an expanding campus well into the future. To understand this, it is necessary first to look across Elm Street to the north face of Saybrook College, built 1917–21 as part of the Memorial Quadrangle; four gables, not equally spaced, punctuate the long facade. They are paired up at the ends of the block, leaving a long interval in the center, which, when they were built, corresponded with the width of the 1890–92 University Gymnasium

Trumbull College

then occupying the center of what would become Trumbull's block, across the street. The Saybrook gable ends predicted two new pairs of buildings bookending the old Gym, each pair with a narrow, south-facing court (now Potty Court and the master's house court) whose width corresponded with the gable-pairs interval. That in fact is what was built when Rogers, a decade later, was asked to design dormitories as part of the Sterling Library complex. A brief, odd period ensued, before the construction of Payne Whitney Gym and before the decision was made to adopt the college system with its dining halls, when the not-yet-named-Trumbull dorms were complete and flanked the great bulk of the older Gym, twice as high as the dining hall that replaced it.

Trumbull therefore is a palimpsest college, neither a true grafting-together of old and new buildings, like JE and Silliman, nor entirely of one moment, like Calhoun and Berkeley. Its components show themselves designed at different times and with different concerns, with the dorm ranges looking back across the street to the Memorial Quadrangle, the dining hall recognizing the enormous cliff of the Sterling Library stacks. The north face of the dining hall, one of Rogers's more original moments, adopts a byzantine verticality to deal with the striated, tall-buttressed mass looming opposite, over the lower volume of the Library's main reading room. The College, in short, manages to have its own distinct identity even as it both buffers Sterling from Elm Street and declares a connection across it to Saybrook, Branford, and Harkness Tower. Potty Court, westernmost of the College's courts, and nicknamed for the figure on the short south range, demonstrates how an unpromisingly proportioned space, of relatively unglamorous materials, can be made intriguing, entertaining, and workable by borrowed views (note how Saybrook's Wrexham Tower is brought in), carefully placed ornament, and smart landscaping (the side terraces, raised to seat height, invite socializing).

35. Berkeley College
James Gamble Rogers, 1933; renovation: KieranTimberlake, 1999

East on Elm Street from Trumbull, in the direction of the Green and on the other side of High Street, lies the front gate of Berkeley College. As he did with Trumbull's mimicry of Saybrook's gables, James Gamble Rogers in the early 1930s massed up this key corner to match the height and gable of Wright Hall (1912), opposite. That the two blocks of Elm Street between Broadway and the Green manage to have any sense at all of campus cross-connection, despite the river of traffic wheeling down them, is largely to be credited to Rogers's alignments of scale, building mass, and entrances across the street. (These two one-way blocks of Elm currently constitute a junior version of the Oak Street Connector, a glaring instance of imbalance, dangerous but unaccountably accepted as almost inevitable, between cars and pedestrians.)

Berkeley College

Berkeley's east face carries a scattering of ornamental reminders of earlier life and buildings on the site (so does the rest of the college). The Our Lady of the Telephone tablet marks this as the location of the first Yale telephone exchange, and a little further along are stone reminders of the shoeshine boys who spat and polished outside an earlier location of the Yale Station post office. These and other activities happened at the new hot corner of campus created by Yale's jump across Elm in the 1890s, with the University Gym on the site of Trumbull and the Berkeley Oval on the land now holding Berkeley. The Oval comprised a set of dormitory-office-classroom buildings (an earlier Berkeley, and White, Fayerweather, and Lampson Halls, and the little Round House containing the phone exchange) put up between 1893 and 1903, all to the design of Josiah Cleaveland Cady. As with all Cady buildings, they were solid and functional, but a rising tide of opinion held them not exactly elegant enough for Yale; Secretary of the University Anson Phelps Stokes wrote in 1911 that "the most unfortunate thing that ever happened to Yale architecturally was getting tied up…with the firm of Cady, Berg & See, a firm of… little architectural taste and ability." Despite such regrets, the university concocted elaborate schemes in the 1920s to save the Oval as part of the new Cross Campus. Had they been carried through, Berkeley College would have been, like Silliman, a hybrid of older and newer buildings. In the end Berkeley was deemed to be so close to Sterling that it had to be in architectural harmony with it, and so the college as we have it was built.

Berkeley is Yale's only two-part college, split across the Cross Campus axis into North Court, with the master's house and the slight majority of the dormitory suites, and South Court, with the dining hall and common rooms. Rogers was a notorious jokester, and there is an old legend that the college name was chosen not only because Bishop George Berkeley was an early patron of Yale but also because a miter, like the college, has front and back halves. The two U-shaped courts are connected underground by a north-south tunnel, which somehow manages to dodge past the east-west one between Sterling's nave and the Bass Library (formerly known as Cross Campus Library). The courts are the key to Berkeley's genial architectural character, both allowing southern sunlight in and providing low stone walls at the open ends of the Us to trap its warmth; Berkeleyites tend to be the last and the earliest outdoor sitters in the cycle of seasons. What with their cheerfully irrational swirl of brick with various kinds of stone masonry, some of it so horizontally proportioned as to look borrowed from Frank Lloyd Wright, the building walls fronting the courtyards aid the mood. Rogers provided two little pyramid-roofed garden pavilions, which once upon a time topped off the general Berkeley light-heartedness, but they were rudely and crudely claimed—the added concrete block walls inside often easily visible—as space for Cross Campus Library vents.

36. Calhoun College

John Russell Pope, 1932; renovation: Herbert S. Newman & Partners, 2009

Calhoun is the most compact of the twelve undergraduate residential colleges, containing its castellated mass within a 200-foot square surrounding a single multilevel courtyard. In character, it is a good deal more forthcoming than Pope often was, though still considerably less given to romantic detail than the colleges designed by James Gamble Rogers. Pope adopted the same iron-tinged granite used by Rogers on Berkeley for three exterior faces of the building, then switched to limestone for the Cross Campus face in order to match the slightly earlier W. L. Harkness Hall opposite, and again switched to a salmony brick informally laid and interspersed with black-burnt headers and stretchers for the courtyard walls. It is a refined, confident, and deliberately unshowy approach to linkages with the materials of neighboring buildings; much the same is true of its planning and massing decisions. For example, Calhoun and Berkeley faced a logistical problem

Calhoun College

with respect to locating service entrances, since both have four public frontages; Rogers and Pope coordinated a strategy of placing the dining halls on Elm Street and the kitchens and service areas on the Blount Avenue-Grub Street side. There, the self-serious theatrics of Porter Gateway adequately distract from the mundane coming and going of food and trash.

It is very hard to argue with anything about Calhoun, and at the same time hard to think of anything truly distinctive in a positive way—perhaps the closest thing to a quirk is the sudden drop in mass at the northeast corner for the master's house. Pope was an architect interested in timelessness and high quality. Calhoun got its share of both, but perhaps at the price of the blandness attaching to certain efforts to attain the ideal; in this, it is a Gothic cousin of Pope's Jefferson Memorial in Washington. Rogers and Pope cooperated well enough at Yale, but only one would have agreed with Sir Francis Bacon's adage that there is no beauty without a little strangeness in it. Pope, always the gentleman, would have politely demurred.

The odd footnote from a deeper historic perspective is that Calhoun occupies the site, indeed almost exactly the footprint, of one of the more strenuously angular of Yale buildings, the Divinity School complex put up by the second Timothy Dwight in 1869–74, mostly to designs by Richard Morris Hunt (1828–1895). It possessed five-story east and west dormitory ranges, a little like Farnam in massing but more given to points, props, and mansards in detail. The Divinity Library and Marquand Chapel stood in between, adjacent to each other, where Calhoun's common rooms and dining hall do now. When Delano & Aldrich added the Day Missions Library in 1911, where Calhoun's north range is, what resulted was Yale's first small enclosed courtyard, arguably evidence for the believability of the college plan when it was first proposed in the late 1920s. Pope held Delano partly accountable for the failure of Yale to adopt his 1919 campus plan, and Hunt by the 1920s was quite out of fashion. So there must have been for Pope a certain satisfaction—though he would never have acknowledged it—in seeing the old Divinity School knocked down in 1931 to make way for his Calhoun design. Delano by way of compensation was able to design, and Divinity to occupy, a splendid hilltop suburban retreat—or so it probably seemed at the time—far up Prospect Street.

37. Hendrie Hall, New Haven Free Public Library, and New Haven County Courthouse

Hendrie Hall
J. Cleaveland Cady, Cady, Berg and See, 1894 and 1900
New Haven Free Public Library
Cass Gilbert, 1908; Hardy Holzman Pfeiffer, 1990
New Haven County Courthouse
William H. Allen and Richard Williams, 1908

Hendrie Hall

A century ago, with construction of the University Gymnasium in 1890–92 on the site now occupied by the Trumbull College dining hall, and of Hendrie Hall in two installments, 1894 and 1900, for the law school, Yale showed that it believed that the future Elm Street would have a truly urban density. Both the Gymnasium and Hendrie were constructed as urban palazzo blocks with blank brick party walls on both sides, easily three times the height of the two-story late-eighteenth- and early-nineteenth-century houses they replaced on their respective blocks. E. E. Gandolfo's Gym is long gone, leaving only a handsome stone depiction on the first landing of Payne Whitney's main stair, but J. C. Cady's urbane, underappreciated Hendrie continues in solid service. It is a Tuscan block, symmetrical except where a side carriage entry passes through. Since the law school moved out of Hendrie to the center of the Yale campus in 1931, Hendrie has served as home to any number of Yale administrative offices and student organizations. Somehow, it has managed to retain a tattered dignity through it all; the

New Haven County Courthouse

second-floor front space, once the law library, is vestigially grand, and the cast-iron main stair is one of Yale's finest.

Cass Gilbert (1859–1934) remains among America's leading architects. He had just completed the New York Custom House in 1908 when he designed the New Haven Free Public Library, and would follow it with such diverse projects as the Woolworth Building in New York City (1911) and the U.S. Supreme Court Building in Washington, DC (1933–35). But the library is interesting in its own complexity, not simply because Gilbert designed it. It simultaneously pays homage to the United Church on the Green in front of it and to the four-columned, 1851–52 Trowbridge House, which it replaced. Perhaps precisely because Gilbert felt the tug of multiple responsibilities, the result seems a little fussy. (New York architects Hardy Holzman Pfeiffer completed the renovation and polychromatic postmodern addition in 1990.) Gilbert returned to New Haven in 1910 to author, with landscape architect Frederick Law Olmsted Jr., a comprehensive plan for New Haven. The city never adopted the scheme, and Gilbert's public library and 1918 Union Station proved to be anchors put down without the connecting chain to use them.

The New Haven County Courthouse is a contemporary of the Library, designed in 1909 by a New Haven architectural firm, Allen and Williams, and completed in 1914. The architects' inspiration was clearly St. George's Hall in Liverpool, England, constructed in 1841–56. Yet relative to its source, this building is smaller and less somber, reflecting the era's conviction that reformed, enlightened public institutions could indeed bring on the "civic improvement" the library, courthouse, and Gilbert-Olmsted plan envisioned. It was a moment that might have been New Haven's high water mark. The courthouse is a splendid building, whose formidably white exterior conceals a multicolored, multileveled set of spaces inside, never mind the indignity and implications of the metal detectors and surveillance through which all visitors must pass to see them. John Massey Rhind's *The Lawmaker* and *The Advocate* oversee the march up to the front door, while *Truth* and *Self-Denial* discreetly hang back around the corners.

38. Elm Street Houses

175 Elm Street, Elihu Society (Nicholas Callahan House)
1760s–1770s; Everett V. Meeks, 1911
155 Elm Street, Graduate Club (Jonathan Mix House)
possibly David Hoadley, 1799; R. Clipston Sturgis, 1902
149 Elm Street, Yale Mead Visitor Center (John Pierpont House)
1767; Delano & Aldrich, 1904; J. Frederick Kelly, 1929; Robert T. Coolidge, 1951; Gregg & Weis Architects, 2002
143 Elm Street, Governor Ralph Ingersoll House
Town & Davis, 1829; Delano & Aldrich, 1918

155 Elm Street

Yale's anticipation of the demise of its small-scale domestic neighbors went awry when the Colonial and its revival became popular among society clubmen and the university's own administrators. Against all odds—the three houses of Elm Street's "Quality Row," more splendid than any of these four, went down in 1908 to make way for the library and courthouse—these houses survive to give a sense of the scale around the Green in the early nineteenth century. That is their virtue on the front, though at the rear all but the Ingersoll House acquired a hodgepodge of additions in the course of a variety of renovations. This architectural patchwork, with the expanse of parking occupying the center of the block, creates a pronounced aesthetic letdown, front to back. The best uses for these structures today would certainly dictate giving them rear gardens and terraces that measure up to the promise of their fronts.

The four Elm Street houses come equipped with interesting social and architectural pasts. The Ingersoll House, a Greek Revival brick block that lost its original stucco or paint finish, was designed very shortly after the formation of A. J. Davis and Ithiel Town's partnership, and so was a near contemporary of Highwood or Sachem's Wood, the vanished mansion that once headed Hillhouse Avenue. The Pierpont House, now appropriately occupied by the Yale Mead Visitor Center, was built for the grandson of Rev. James Pierpont, the First Church (Center Church) minister who was perhaps chiefly responsible for founding the College. Besides being a nice example of the center-hall, center-chimney type, it has associations with distinguished Yale administrators, faculty, and benefactors, including Anson Phelps Stokes, who owned and lived in it during his long term as Secretary of the University in the Hadley administration. Since 1901 the Graduate Club has occupied 155 Elm Street, sometimes said to be an early work by David Hoadley (1774–1839), the designer-builder of the United (North) Church on the Green (1813–15). The house was the home of Eli Whitney Blake, a pioneer door and window hardware manufacturer and inventor of stone-crushing machinery, which revolutionized American road building after the 1850s. Elihu Society, a senior society founded in 1903, now occupies 175 Elm Street, a structure originally dating from the late eighteenth century. It was once home to Tory Tavern, literally counter-Revolutionary, which promoted politics opposite those of the tavern on the opposite corner of the Green, where the Taft now stands. In 1911 Everett V. Meeks, longtime head of Yale's first formal program in architecture, remodeled the house for Elihu.

39. College Street Houses

459 College Street, Elizabethan Club (Leverett Griswold House)
1815
451 College Street (Franklin Hall)
Chapman and Frazier, 1910
Abbey and Mitch Leigh Hall (435 College Street)
Cross and Cross, 1929; renovation, Butler Rogers Baskett Architects, 2005

The remarkable diversity of design styles and uses represented by these three buildings tells something about Yale's history. The "Lizzie" at 459 College Street, dedicated to teas and the appreciation of English literature of Shakespearean times, is enthroned in a crisp little white house that shows off an early example of a gable fronting the street, rather than being turned parallel to it. In so behaving, the Griswold House predicted the temple-front individuality of the Greek Revival, yet did not pull back from the street as many of the houses of that persuasion did. It has a fine little garden at the rear, of just the sort one wishes the old white houses of Elm Street possessed. The latest renovations to house and garden, admirable for their subtlety, were completed by Kenneth Boroson in 1995–96. For a few years, until the 1920s, the Griswold house with its delicate little porch and another wooden house with a Greek Doric porch together made a pair of bookends for Franklin Hall, a chunky Sheffield Scientific frat built in 1910–11 at 451 College by Horace Frazier, an 1883 Sheff graduate. It long had a kitchen and service wing at the back, on the north side, protecting the Lizzie's garden. Yale acquired the building in 1935 and used it first for alumni relations before turning it into the Treasurer's office. It now houses the Comparative Literature, Religious Studies, and Judaic Studies departments. The ailing bulldog gargoyles on 435 College speak of the building's original use as the university's student health center, while the placement of its entrance to the side shows that the architect, John W. Cross, was betting in 1929 that some sort of extension of the Cross Campus across College Street would eventually occur. This explains the choice of Gothic, too, even though Cross was thinking about connecting visually with Richard Morris Hunt's old Divinity School of 1869–70, rather than its successor structure, Calhoun College, finished in 1932. He was very well connected around Yale, having designed the base for the Nathan Hale statue on the Old Campus and just completed the Walter Camp Gateway out by the Yale Bowl. But by now it seems likely his bet is permanently lost; today the building is still another of the variety of neighborhood structures used by the School of Music.

In 2005 Butler Rogers Baskett Architects adaptively renovated 435

451 College Street

Cross Campus

College Street, which had begun life in 1929 as the Department of University Health, as one more in the School of Music's stylistically diverse collection of buildings. It became Abby and Mitch Leigh Hall, with classrooms, faculty studios, and administrative offices filling the rooms once occupied by those ailing bulldogs. The Gothic detailing, surprisingly abundant for health care architecture, inside and out, has been nicely brought back to good health. 435 College over the decades had declined to become a structure of doleful countenance, beyond its original associations with illness. It is good to see the not-quite-impossible dream of its return to appreciation and dignity now realized, and the building named to honor the author of the score for "Man of La Mancha."

40. William L. Harkness Hall
William Adams Delano, Delano & Aldrich, 1927

William L. Harkness Hall, familiarly known as WLH, is perhaps Yale's preeminent "good soldier," a building that accommodates many jobs well and quietly. Since it has no attention-grabbing ornament or notably tasty materials, and now has no distinctive masses except perhaps the squat southwest tower with its seemingly perpetually inoperative clock, William L. Harkness carries a deceptive air of just getting on with business. It comes across as a simple background structure, when in fact it harbors a wide range of academic functions and plays an important role in forming the University's symbolic central space, the Cross Campus.

William L. Harkness Hall

The genesis of WLH really occurred a block and a half away, at the corner of College and Chapel. By the First World War the large classroom building at that location, Osborn Hall of 1888–90, was too beset by traffic noise to be workable, besides itself being too loud aesthetically. Yale College needed to replace the classrooms in a quieter location and in a quieter way. The newly thought-up Cross Campus, formally announced in early 1924, was the logical location. Since the Berkeley Oval and old Divinity School were standing where Berkeley and Calhoun colleges now are, and the University had not yet committed itself to a policy of demolition, there was really only one possible site. That was an L-shaped parcel next to Sprague Hall, the new, elegant but incongruously neo-Federal home of the School of Music. The Cross Campus also needed a commodious classroom building that would provide a good character-setting precedent for new buildings near Sterling Library.

Yale called in William Adams Delano to design a much-needed facility for a tight, aesthetically crucial site. WLH firmly pegs down its corner of the cross axis with the square-topped tower, then sends a shorter leg north toward Commons and a longer one east toward College Street. The structure's superb, banked lecture hall, 201 WLH, with its giant double-layered window, also an escape stair, pushes up against College Street. While different in style from Sprague Hall—that is its purpose—the College Street facade of WLH is almost the same height and width, and picks up the level of its major horizontal subdivisions. (Delano, as a true gentleman, is a gentleman to everyone.) The rest of the building efficiently packs in a variety of classrooms, faculty offices, and a lounge, all managing to be spartan, hard-wearing, yet dignified. WLH underwent well-thought-out renovations by Noyes & Vogt in the mid-1990s, and is back in trim and ready to perform. The renovation inflicted one indignity on the good soldier; the tall, lead-covered tower, or flèche, topping the College Street end was amputated, leaving only the stub of what was once a flourish across space to the lead-covered fantasy castle concealing mechanical equipment atop Sterling Library.

41. Anne T. and Robert M. Bass Library
Edward Larrabee Barnes, 1971;
Hammond Beeby Rupert Ainge Architects, 2006

The Cross Campus Library was a two-level subterranean extension of Sterling Library, covertly occupying the whole width of the grassy Cross Campus space between the two halves of Berkeley College. It was Yale's contribution to the rash of underground libraries that swept across American universities in the 1960s and 1970s. Faced with the onset of the Baby Boomer generation, librarians felt the need to expand undergraduate facilities even when, as was the case with Yale, there was actually not much growth in the number of students. Many times there was either no place else to go with the expansion or, less often, there was a sense that no new structure should compete with prewar libraries that remained the architectural pride of the campus. At Yale, both factors operated. Still, the planning for Yale's undergraduate underground was a tough tussle between Edward L. Barnes (1915–2004), consulting architect to the university after 1966 and technically James Gamble Rogers's successor, and those students and faculty who felt Barnes was undermining Rogers's architectural legacy. An early version of the extension rendered the Cross Campus unusable, not to speak of unmowable, with a dense grid of skylights poking up through the turf; a later version took the skylights out of the middle of the grass and replaced them with linear ones along the length of the side walls, effectively taking away the best places for a little outdoor lolling. Finally, four light and egress courts at the corners of the underground volume were accepted.

Hindsight might make the whole process look like a displacement of Vietnam War draft anxieties, but that sort of dismissal would be to underestimate the significance of the protests not only for this particular building's shape but for Yale's general way of going about planning for its architectural needs. Along with the 1972 scrapping of the proposed Mitchell-Giurgola design for Whitney-Grove colleges, because of the city's insistence on their having new tax-paying commercial space, and Yale's reluctant acceptance of the necessity of commercial

Anne T. and Robert M. Bass Library

space in the Center for British Art, the Cross Campus Library protests shook the administration into realizing that passive acceptance of the benign goodness of any University planning and architectural initiative was a vanished behavior by New Haven citizens and the Yale "family" alike.

The dive down the rabbit hole into the library revealed an efficient, soulless facility that was surprisingly light on the upper level. The people-watching opportunities in the lounge-seating study areas, adjacent to the front light courts, were considerable. A time tunnel passage under High Street-Rose Walk connected two different pieces of architecture—the walk from the library's space-odyssey plastic laminate to Sterling's stone-paved nave was frankly surreal—and two different senses of what it meant to learn. On one end, knowledge was seemingly understood as information, on the other end as religion.

The transformation of the former Cross Campus Library into the Anne T. and Robert M. Bass Library, completed in 2007, is perhaps the most remarkable makeover in the history of Yale architecture. The architects were Hammond Beeby Rupert Ainge of Chicago, led by former Yale School of Architecture dean Thomas Beeby. The building has been updated in its various systems, of course, as would be expected in a comprehensive renovation of almost any building its age, and the Cross Campus grass was removed and put back after replacement of the library's subsurface roofing membrane—not your standard routine roofing job. The main entrance to the library was flipped from west to east, back to front. Moreover, the building has now been given some Architecture in the form of gothicizing ornament inside and out, which reinforces the connection to James Gamble Rogers's Sterling Memorial Library.

Instead of slipping down steps in an open-air light court close to High Street, one enters through an ornamented stone pavilion off Grub Street (the sidewalk over to Commons between Berkeley College and William L. Harkness Hall), discovering inside it an elevator, and beyond it a stair down, connecting to the cafe and circulation desk that formerly monitored the Time Tunnel under High Street from Sterling Library. At first the elaborate Gothic styling of the chunky entry box seems strange, too much on too little. The structure is too small to be a chapel, but it is clearly also not a wandering mausoleum lost from the nearby Grove Street Cemetery. It is a folly, a sort of hybrid of Sterling Library's lead-roofed elevator penthouse, visible atop the stack tower, with a triumphal arch, and as such just good, elaborate fun. The mood swing is enormous from Ed Barnes's abstraction to this jolly appreciation of Yale's Gothic past, and James Gamble Rogers would have appreciated it.

Ornamental treatments inside and out are another collaboration of Tom Beeby and his firm with Kent Bloomer, a sculptor and theorist of ornament who for decades has taught at the School of Architecture. Beeby has a career-long penchant for low, broad-beamed buildings, perhaps most famously demonstrated in the Harold Washington Library Center in Chicago. There, as with Bass Library and elsewhere, Bloomer's work lightens the block of the basic structure. Inside, some of the ornament in the shallow-vaulted spaces pays homage to the hypnotic, repetitive, vegetal/geometric work of another Chicagoan, Louis Sullivan.

The undergraduates using Bass Library, unlike those visiting the Cross Campus Library in 1971, are used to a wireless world in which any information seemingly can be juxtaposed instantly with any other information, anywhere. Jorge Luis Borges's Library of Babel has come true, though without the architecture he imagined. In such a world it is interesting to see Yale assert that distinct architectural character still matters in the places to which its students summon infinite information.

**WALK FIVE: LAW SCHOOL, GRADUATE SCHOOL,
AND THE SAARINEN COLLEGES**

When, in a four-day session in November 1701, the trustees of the new Collegiate School—all ministers—first met formally in Saybrook, Connecticut Colony, they saw fit to call out their intentions. So they recorded at the start of the minutes of the meeting—as their first official act—that their forebears had come to America to plant and propagate "the blessed Reformed, Protestant Religion," and that to perpetuate this design a "Liberal and Relligious Education of Suitable youth" was "a chief, and most probable expedient." The Colony needed two varieties of educated men to lead the communities: laymen and ministers. The Collegiate School was intended to supply both. But it would be wrong to interpret this as a division of labor between "Liberal" and "Relligious" men; all graduates were to be infused with the purpose of vigilantly maintaining the Puritan vision of community based in moral purpose, and guided by their ability to read the Bible in an educated fashion. The distinction drawn was instead between means ("Liberal and Relligious Education") and ends (propagation of "blessed…Religion").

Though they broadened a bit and softened around the edges, Yale College maintained something very like those as its method and purpose for a very long time. Yale College existed to produce an educated elite, the goal of whose leadership was continuous re-creation of a moral society. To keep that broad social purpose in view, it was held, a man's Yale education must not be so arcane as to render him irrelevant nor so specialized as to make him useful to society for only one purpose.

Yale thus paradoxically resisted altering its moral and classical curriculum, even as a growing America increasingly depended upon and valued specialized expertise. Yale College resisted change and specialization precisely because it wished to be relevant. The once-famous *Faculty Report* of 1828, issued under Jeremiah Day a century and a quarter after the Saybrook meeting, declined to alter the curriculum in the direction of what today would be called practical, specialized, or preprofessional subjects. Noah Porter's presidency, which lasted from 1871 until 1886, has usually been interpreted as the last stand of the resistance to diversification, specialization, and secularization.

Porter contended that only colleges maintaining a required curriculum, study of classical literature, and required chapel and church could produce truly liberal men. To become cultured, and therefore liberal, students had to read extensively rather than specifically in an elected discipline, and learn how to think historically rather than scientifically. Extensive reading and historical thinking formed the basis of what Porter called "Christian culture."

At Yale, graduate study, the study of scientific, legal, and technical subjects, and even of specialized religious topics, were all established very early by comparison with many other institutions of higher education. But the University established each in a separate School; whether always consciously calculated to do so or not, the practical result was to remove pressure for change in the College. By the last half of the nineteenth century, cultural tides were flowing heavily against Porter and those who thought like him. The required curriculum gave way under Porter's successor, Timothy Dwight. Porter's interpretation of "liberal" as meaning "broad, but highly scripted, and to the purpose of leadership toward a moral society," still surprisingly close to that of the founders in Saybrook 185 years earlier, was replaced by one that construed it as "specialized, but freely chosen, and secularized."

It is possible to wonder whether this was another instance of Yale undertaking change to get back to original means and ends. Because the world now regards specialized or professional accomplishment as the prerequisite to leadership in a specialty or a profession, as well as to general social, cultural, and political influence, it can be argued that Yale adopted specialization and professionalization in order to keep producing an elite of leaders. If the goal is certainly not promulgation of the "blessed, Reformed Protestant Religion," as it was in 1701, it may at least be considered to be the broader, secular equivalent, the knowing and just society continually recreated.

Among other themes possible to pick out from the location and use of the buildings on this walk, then, is Yale's resistance to, but then adoption of, specialization and professionalization. This includes not only legal professionalism but also the vocation of professional scholarship evidenced in the Graduate School. This is visible today in the campus structure. Very quickly, with the Old Brick Row on what is now the Old Campus, the habit was established of considering the east side, toward the Green, the front of the College. Functions not thought very presentable, like privies, coal yards, and laboratories, were put on the other side, to the west. With the change from College to University, Yale's center shifted from the Old Brick Row to Sterling Library. But the attitude toward what is front (east; the Library faces the Cross Campus) and back (west) remains unaltered, even if the campus has expanded. Thus the power plant, though larger than the Old Campus coal yard, has the same backside relation to the Library that the coal yard had to the Row. Payne Whitney Gymnasium, similarly, holds a rear echelon position equivalent to that of the first Yale Gym, and like it, is regarded as useful because it positively rechannels energies that otherwise might destabilize the community. (It might be noted, too, that amateur, non-preprofessional athletics are defended now with the ardor once stirred by the

Required Curriculum.) The Graduate School is drawn closer than the Gym to the presentable side, but does not quite reach it, and gets a visible tower by way of compensation. The Law School over time has orbited ever closer to front-side status; if Sterling Library's face is Yale's presiding visage, the Law School today sits immediately to its left hand, not quite out of sight.

42. Sterling Law Building
James Gamble Rogers, 1931

Legal education only gradually assumed the central place it now holds at Yale—physically, psychologically, and financially. An early attempt to institute law lectures in the College fizzled when his practice and the enticements of politics distracted the appointed professor. The entity that became the law school started out around 1800, quite separate from Yale, housed in commercial space in New Haven. As the men teaching and studying there were mostly Yale College graduates, the administration was persuaded in 1824 to list the law students in the Yale catalog; it was further persuaded in 1843 to grant a Bachelor of Laws degree to the school's students. After some rocky financial times, the school took heart when, in 1871, New Haven County offered it the use of a floor in the new courthouse on the east side of the Green, apparently in trade for general judicial and professional access to the Law Library. After a quarter century in that situation, the school moved into its first unshared

Sterling Law Buildings

structure, Hendrie Hall, on the north side of the Green and thus that much closer to the rest of Yale. That location still reinforced the idea of a law school poised between town and academy. The Law School's last move, in 1931, brought it into the present set of buildings, next door to Sterling Library and Woodbridge Hall and thus at the strategic heart of the university; ironically, a location resisted at the time both by Dean of the Law School, Robert M. Hutchins, and President of the University, James Rowland Angell. They had wanted the law school to join up with the medical school and other sociobiological entities of the university to form a Human Welfare Group located in the medical complex. Not even two such powerful figures could resist the combined wills of a Corporation majority, the trustees of the Sterling Bequest, and, critically, Yale's consulting architect, James Gamble Rogers. It was one of the times in the history of Yale when architectural vision led university policy, rather than the other way around.

Rogers believed that the Law and Graduate Schools absolutely should not be allowed to escape the vicinity of Sterling Library, because of the atmospheric support they would give. Once that campus-planning goal was secured, Rogers—surprise!—in 1926 received the commission to design a building. The block acquired for the Law School site had an interesting history, having held the Hopkins Grammar School, a New Haven institution older than Yale, and, as noted on a 1748 map, the house of "Jethro a black man." (The corner of Grove and York was long known as "Jethro's corner.") Rogers dallied briefly with a scheme that put a big entrance and a classical block on High Street facing the Bicentennial Buildings. By 1928 he had come up with the strategy the completed building reflects; a complex mass on the east side of the block, occupied by library and classrooms, picks up and continues Sterling's Wall Street tactics and at the same time anchors a set of dormitory ranges defining three interior courtyards. The Law School with its variety of uses—dormitories, dining hall, kitchen, library, classrooms, and offices—proved to be good practice toward the complexities of the colleges, once it was determined over the course of 1929 that Yale would adopt that small-community system for the undergraduates. Rogers indicated some of the complexity inside by choosing a model of exceptional clarity, the Chapel of King's College, Cambridge, for the Law Library's reading room, and then packing around it a dense assembly of variegated lower masses, something King's is completely without.

The Law School's west and south walls showcase some of Yale's most amusing stone carvings, based on a theme of crime and punishment. (The east and north sides are content with great brickwork but little figural ornament.) From the set-piece entry porch inward, the satirical spotlight turns to the legal profession; the architects, painters, and masons seem to have had a particularly good time with this responsibility. The main staircase and the law library's main reading room, renovated in 1998, are fine spaces, while the auditorium has been a pilgrimage spot over the decades for the university's largest classes from any and all departments, such as Vincent Scully's famously popular lectures on the history of art and architecture.

43. Hall of Graduate Studies
James Gamble Rogers, 1932

The Hall of Graduate Studies (HGS) is one of James Gamble Rogers's most inventive ensembles at Yale, as well as having what is certainly the most cocked-hat ground plan. The latter was not at all arbitrary, however, and understanding it offers clues about the stylistic freedom Rogers allowed himself. When Yale was planning HGS

in the late 1920s, it did not own the property immediately to the west, where Stiles and Morse colleges now stand. York Square was there, opened in 1836, a graceful, green, fenced private park of considerable size (roughly the same as the open space of the Old Campus today), defined entirely by two- and three-story houses and row dwellings. The city of New Haven sealed the fate of this ensemble at the edge of the Nine Squares when it moved its high schools here when the center of town, their former location, became too dense, noisy, and expensive. Between 1894 and 1919, the schools chewed up major chunks of the York Square perimeter; in 1927 the city ran Tower Parkway diagonally through the middle, slaloming left and right to dodge the power plant and then one of the schools; and Yale finished it off in 1932 by leapfrogging the school complex and putting Payne Whitney Gymnasium on its west. (The Gym's width matches exactly the long side of the Square.)

Rogers thus faced another impossible urban situation, in which he had to back HGS up against a set of public school buildings while not leaving the new gymnasium feeling isolated from the rest of Yale. He took the odd space available to him, got one small square courtyard in easily, next to Mory's on the south, then used the Beaux-Arts "reflex angle" method, drawn from Parisian hotel planning, to make a larger courtyard symmetrically irregular around an axis through the center of the dining hall. This kind of planning is impossible to describe in narrative, but it is eminently understandable on the ground. The same can be said of HGS's tower; not only is it today a nice conclusion to Wall Street, but when it was built it also signaled the direction of Yale to the front door of the gymnasium, over the roofs of the high schools. The tower said "Yale," but not too loudly, since it was built of brick with contrasting stone trim, like the earlier polychrome city schools.

HGS is a hybrid place, a combination of bold massing and contrasty materials with subtle circulation arrangements and flattened, Deco-style ornament. The walk on axis through the front gates (Samuel Yellin ironwork again), along a covered arcade space between the two green courtyards, then into a cloister corridor that passes the tower elevators and the dining hall before arriving at the common room (newly restored, with an elaborate allegorical ceiling, as of 1998) turns one unawares almost completely around the compass. Then again there are moments when Rogers seems to have delighted in abruptness, as in the unabated plunge of the tower into the smaller, southern courtyard. The ornamental program here has a tone of self-mockery, with stern mustachioed guardian figures, representing architect and donor, flanking the front gates, and caricature heads of graduate school dignitaries in the arched openings. Scattered around the walls are bricks with two peculiar sorts of molded surface impressions, a W+ and a Pac-Man-ish head with little wings. They refer to Wilbur Cross, dean of the Graduate School, and James Rowland Angell, president of the University, and it is up to the viewer to decide whether this is simply honorific, like a Roman brick stamp marking an imperial reign, or an invitation to recall the description of someone being "thick as a brick."

Hall of Graduate Studies

44. The Mory's Association (306 York Street)

pre–1817

Quite by accident, two of the best-known spots for live music in New Haven, Toad's Place, an eclectic stop on a variety of different contemporary tour circuits, and Mory's, are located next to one another. Mory's, a private club of long Yale associations, is the venue of choice to hear the groups, now female as well as male, that continue the centuries-old undergraduate tradition of a cappella close-harmony singing. Monday nights belong to the Whiffenpoofs, most famous of the groups. While all of them perform old standards enough to warm the heart of any Old Blue, they also do inventive arrangements of just about any sequence of sounds, new and old, remotely capable of being called music. It is hardly an embalmed tradition. Mory's interior features hardy, initial-scarred old wooden tables and an assortment of memorabilia and photos accumulated over the course of an association with Yale since 1863. The house that this institution now occupies was built sometime before 1817, with various additions accumulated in the rear as need dictated; it became Mory's in 1912, when the similar old wooden house which had been its home since 1876 fell victim to New Haven real estate pressures. That old location, at the southwest corner of Chapel and Temple streets (hence the "Temple Bar" of the "Whiffenpoof Song") thus was witness to some of the warmer moments—glasses raised on high—in Yale-New Haven relations, as well as one of the all-time low points, the 1854 street murder of a rioting townsman, allegedly by a Yale student. Mory's and Toad's, fortunately, coexist and, together, often generate the sort of spirited weekend life sadly missing from the old centers of American cities.

45. Ezra Stiles and Samuel F. B. Morse Colleges

Eero Saarinen & Associates, 1962; renovation: KieranTimberlake, 2011 and 2010, respectively

Eero Saarinen (1910–1961) created designs that accommodated and celebrated various kinds of movement, whether of whole populations (the St. Louis Arch, officially the "Jefferson Westward Expansion Memorial"), airplanes (the TWA and Dulles Airport terminals), cars (the General Motors Technical Center), or hockey players (Ingalls Rink at Yale). Faced with the commission for the first new Yale residential colleges since before World War II, though, he produced a set of buildings very much concerned with the opposite of movement. Both in their overall configuration and in their stylistic expression, Morse and Stiles work hard to develop a strong sense of stability and rootedness in place. They catch up intact the typology of the prewar colleges, and accept that its elements are the proper ones for doing the job of community creation that was Yale's purpose in adopting the college system in the first place, in the early 1930s. Saarinen, himself a Yale undergraduate in exactly

Ezra Stiles College

those years (he graduated with a BFA in 1934; the first seven colleges officially opened on September 25, 1933), seems to have wholly bought into it.

In building Payne Whitney Gymnasium in 1932, the University had jumped beyond a set of New Haven school buildings and Tower Parkway, which Yale had allowed the city to run across some of its territory in return for the right to close Library Street. During New Haven's urban renewal fever, the University acquired the schools (with a gift from John Hay Whitney, whose family gave the gym) and in 1959 knocked them down. The city deemed the Parkway indispensable. Saarinen therefore could only partly tie the gym back to the main body of the campus. (Morse and Stiles were, however, configured so that a third college, its ranges completing their sweeping arc around the gym, could be plugged in if the Parkway were closed.)

Saarinen and César Pelli, who was in charge of the project for Saarinen's office, designed the two colleges as balanced but not exactly symmetrical entities either side of a walkway to the gym. The intention to use the colleges as a place-specific link is quite clear; the gym tower appears picturesquely framed along the walkway looking one way, and Harkness Tower is framed in similar fashion looking the other way. The walkway rises up several feet, then steps down again, allowing space beneath it for a kitchen shared by the two college dining halls. This creation of artificial topography on a flat site is a design trick of considerable effectiveness, one that Saarinen may well have learned as an architecture student in Weir Hall, on the man-made plateau behind Skull and Bones. Whatever the source of inspiration, it produces a subtle but distinct impression of passing through a special place.

Both budget and a Modernist sensibility made impossible a return to the Gothic of the prewar colleges, so Saarinen looked for a wall-making method that would produce an architectural character sympathetic with but different enough from the older buildings that it would not look like a cheap latter-day version. He adopted a refined version of the "desert concrete" construction Frank Lloyd Wright used at Taliesin West, in which stone rubble was placed loose between formwork panels, then a slurry of concrete injected to fill the spaces between stones. The rubble walls are set out like thick, folded planes with vertical banks of window glass inserted between them. The result is simultaneously archaic and innovative.

Concrete trusses span the dining halls of the two colleges and prove to be acceptable updates of the hammer-beam fantasies in the prewar halls. Stiles's hall has always been judged superior to Morse's because it gets more sun, and besides has the advantage of the Giamatti Moose, a dubious present, dubiously accepted, from the Stiles students to A. Bartlett Giamatti on his retirement from the college mastership. The master's houses are of interest as two of a very small number of residences designed by Saarinen. Built simultaneously with the two colleges was a commercial building on Broadway, originally housing the Yale Co-op. Renovations in 1997 for another tenant completely removed the Saarinen interiors and added the exterior galleria to Broadway.

46. York Square and Tower Parkway

York Square
1836; demolished after 1894
Tower Parkway
1926

The run of high-stooped rowhouses at numbers 90 to 108 York Square Place, beside Payne Whitney Gymnasium, is what remains of York Square. This was a private place built in Greek Revival style in the late 1830s, once one of New Haven's best addresses. Hard as it is to imagine now with Tower Parkway traffic zooming past, some of the luminaries of the Yale faculty in the last third of the nineteenth century lived here, strolling across the green and leafy square to Broadway for the short walk down to the College.

The Square was a 500-foot-long rectangle of space, edged by a fence similar to

York Square

but more delicate than that around the Green. Its perimeter street was fed turbine-fashion by two off-center access streets leading from Broadway (starting where the loading dock beside the Stiles tower now sits) and from Ashmun Street (it remains). The earliest houses around the square were portico-fronted freestanding mansions dating from 1840, while the post–Civil War period saw the construction of rowhouses, some of which are what here survive.

The Square offers an object lesson in the tenet that too great a concentration of single uses, especially when combined with car traffic, kills civility. New Haven moved its three high schools to flank two sides of the Square between 1894 and 1919, cut a deal with Yale in 1926 that allowed Tower Parkway to extend Grove Street past York, right through the middle of the Square, then permitted the enormous mass of Payne Whitney to be built in 1932. In recent years the combination of the traffic-taming measures, the maturation of Stiles's and Morse's crescent of green, and the replacement of a sea of parking by the Swing Dorm has tipped the balance of the area somewhat back in favor of pedestrian life. Turning the Parkway back into a two-way street would help further. Still, no matter what alterations are accomplished, one wonders what the image—and, more important, the livable reality—of downtown New Haven might be today if York Square had survived intact.

Tower Parkway is named for J. B. Tower, who was president of the Geometric Garage Company and New Haven mayor (1925–28). As mayor, he brokered the deal that got New Haven this trafficway.

47. Payne Whitney Gymnasium and Ray Tompkins House
John Russell Pope, 1932; Ellerbe Beckett with César Pelli, 1999

With a footprint measuring 510 feet wide (not including the adjacent 200 feet of Tompkins House) by 206 feet deep, centered on a 200-foot-high tower looking as though it took muscle-building supplements, the gym is one of Yale's largest and bulkiest buildings. Its architect, John Russell Pope, from whose 1919 Plan (see Cross Campus) James Gamble Rogers had adopted critical features into official campus planning, received the gym commission in 1925. Pope's 1919 Plan had featured a gymnasium with tower at the head of his early version of an east-west Cross Campus axis. He seems to have returned to the idea with a vengeance even though Payne Whitney had no sweep of green grass or an axis to dominate, and in fact when built was separated from the campus. It is as though by sheer force of architectural muscle Pope hoped to connect the gym back to the center. It would take another three decades for the university to build out to it, with Stiles and Morse colleges. The gym's great size, but distant placement, reflected the ambivalence felt by the Yale administration and faculty during the great surge of organized intercollegiate athletics into near dominance of college life after the Civil War. Yale had been embarrassed into building its first gym in 1859, on what is now the site of Branford College's Calliope Court, after official town ordinance forced student games off the Green because of sporadic but intense conflicts with local citizens. The second gym, built in 1890–92, stretched deep back into the block from street frontage now occupied by the Trumbull College dining hall, and was knocked down

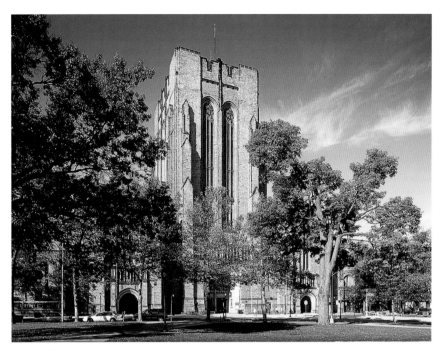

Payne Whitney Gymnasium

(although perfectly serviceable) to make way for Sterling Library. Hence the need for the Pope gymnasium.

Payne Whitney's architecture seemingly makes team sports and personal fitness into divine missions to be accomplished by factory-like specialization, efficiency, and mechanization. The tower's Gothic traceried windows, articulated as though to light a single tall space inside, as does, say, the crossing tower of York Minster, actually open into a stack of high-ceiling rooms devoted to various team sports and specialty exercises. Each wing centers on a major volume, the south one on an exhibition swimming pool with steeply banked seats, the north on an arena. Other, smaller sorts of uses pack around, between, and above the big ones, some even sliding into the spaces between the deep trusses necessary to make the big spans below. Recent renovations have preserved special features from the days of gentlemanly athletics: the leather pony and sloping floors of the polo practice room, for example. In the nave-like transverse entry hall, gargoyle bulldogs with energetic expressions carry appropriate equipment and hats. The trophy room, an inner sanctum, looks out on the nave space from the second floor.

Since Payne Whitney was conceived as a Great Wall backing up to the neighborhoods beyond it, there was no large central corridor opening back from the entry; the tower, instead, took the architectural emphasis vertically. With the opening of the Lanman addition in 1999, a reason for such a hall now exists, and it provides a welcome glimpse of daylight straight ahead. A glance down when passing along it will provide a look at the crew tank with its hydraulically pumped simulation of a river. Next door, Ray Tompkins House, built by Pope at the same time as athletic administration offices and for the Y Club, is like a Tudor country house or a lost piece of Fraternity Row. It has, in addition, the virtue of stepping Payne Whitney's mass down to the scale of the neighborhood.

48. Lanman Addition and Lake Place
Ellerbe Beckett, 1999

When Payne Whitney Gym was built in the early 1930s, fitting its stone bulk into the existing three-story neighborhood of wooden houses and brick apartment buildings would not have been an issue for Yale, even if it had been remotely possible. Starting with a 1941 City Master Plan, on into the 1950s, serious consideration was given to building a major ring-road which would have blown away Lake Place, the block-long street of houses against which the Gym backs, and then connected around behind the Grove Street Cemetery either to an extended, widened Sachem or an extended, widened Trumbull Street. Either way, Tower Parkway could be closed and the Gym tied more securely back into the Yale campus. The disastrous demonstrations provided by other New Haven road and clearance projects effectively short-circuited the idea. Meanwhile, against the odds, Lake Place kept up a changing life on its own, partly in symbiotic relationship not with official Yale but with students, faculty, and employees. In reaction against life in the undergraduate colleges, some boarding houses in the 1960s and 1970s were turned into group houses or communes, and in the 1980s, with different motivations, unofficial fraternity chapters sprang up there.

These developments, coupled with a less peremptory general attitude on the University's part, meant that when the time came around for bringing Yale's close-to-campus athletic facilities up to contemporary needs, it was clear that the Lake Place context needed to be accorded serious consideration. The Pelli addition manages both to provide an enormous volume of new space for the Gym—sufficient for four full-size basketball courts and an indoor track—and to be vastly friendlier to Lake Place than its parent building. It does so by keeping the scale down; by lowering the main level more than a full floor below the adjacent sidewalk; by putting a rhythmically articulated wall of varied materials next to the sidewalk; and by using translucent glazing that shows figures in motion. With horizontal lines across rhythmically regular structural bays, the Lanman addition is reminiscent of some good early twentieth-century modern buildings. Gropius and Meyer's 1913–14 administration building for the Fagus Factory comes to mind, perhaps because of the similar clear-glazed corner stair towers and tightly rectangular volumes. Lanman demonstrates that buildings of that lineage, in sure hands, can make good neighbors and streets.

100 Tower Parkway

49. 100 Tower Parkway
Herbert S. Newman & Partners, 1998

Generations of Yale architecture students pursued studio projects for dormitories
to be built on the large (but never large enough) parking lot that for four decades
occupied the ground between Payne Whitney Gym and the Central Power Plant.
Most of the land had served as the site of New Haven's Commercial High School,
a 1919 building taken down in 1959. Meanwhile, in an all too real situation on the
other side of the same block, the people responsible for the planning, daily care,
and maintenance of Yale's buildings and grounds worked in a dispiriting miscellany
of buildings on Ashmun Street. The impetus to build a new dormitory and to raze the
old undergraduate college facilities buildings came when the University realized it
could not compress its typical renovation project into one summer. Yale came to the
conclusion that it had an urgent need for buffer space to house groups, usually for
one year, as their buildings underwent reconstruction. The often lumbering University
moved with astonishing quickness; it decided in 1996 to gain space for the Swing
Space dormitory by (at long last) moving Facilities Management out of Ashmun
Street and clearing the block of all old buildings except the power plant. Suddenly
the hypothetical dormitory project became territorially plausible and a high priority.

Herb Newman and his partners, involved with Yale's renovations since the 1970s,
delivered the new building in less than two years. The design opted for a U-shaped
range of dormitory rooms open toward the south to form a sun-trapping courtyard.
In the Swing dorm, this basic organization also blocked the winter winds sweeping
in from the north over the Grove Street Cemetery, and provided protection from the
swirling gusts created along Tower Parkway in the lee of the gym's huge mass.

Grove Street Cemetery

The newer building is larger and the site geometries more complicated, yet parallels to Berkeley and other old colleges are apparent. Yale's typological reflex shows up again. There is also an eerie resemblance in detail and proportion—three stories and a 45-degree roof, evenly spaced plain windows—to the first Yale College building of 1717–18. Like Payne Whitney Gym, it recognizes the vanished old outline of York Square.

50. Grove Street Cemetery

1796 and 1814; stone walls and iron fence, 1849; gate, Henry Austin, 1845

Like many features of New Haven and Yale, the "New Haven Burying Ground," as it was officially named upon its organization in 1796 (and act of incorporation in October of the next year), owes its genesis to James Hillhouse (1754–1832). Hillhouse, Class of 1773, was a canny, cryptic real estate developer, politician, and treasurer of Yale for a half century. Each of his activities fed the others; his public improvement projects often benefited private real estate deals. The Grove Street Cemetery was, if not the first, certainly one of the earliest American burial grounds to be laid out with plots of ground permanently owned by individual families and used exclusively for family members' interment. In such a system, the burial place demonstrates family solidarity and stability across generations, rather than just providing the generalized *memento mori* of random burials in the typical colonial churchyard. Hillhouse would have been sensitive to the idea of family plots, for he had been adopted by his childless uncle and aunt, James Abraham and Mary Lucas Hillhouse. It must have been a complicated situation, since William Hillhouse, his father and James's older brother, was still alive at the time. Whatever the reasons, James Hillhouse came to New Haven at age seven to live in the Hillhouse family mansion at the northeast corner of Church and Grove streets. (Grove Street commemorates the Hillhouse's house, Grove Hall.) The elder Hillhouse died two years after his adoptive son's graduation from Yale; four years later, Sarah Lloyd Hillhouse, James's wife, died after less than a year of marriage. By 1796 Hillhouse had remarried and had a seven-year-old son, James Abraham (1789–1841), who survived epidemics of scarlet and yellow fever that swept through New Haven in 1794 and 1795. Others were not so fortunate.

Thirty-two prominent New Haven families endorsed Hillhouse's proposal for this new sort of burial place. Each subscribed money to pay for the original six acres of land and to build a wooden fence around the perimeter. Four more acres were soon added, and another increment of just under eight in 1814 when it became clear that the project was succeeding. The new Yale Medical School, 1813–14, established itself in a failed hotel opposite the Cemetery entrance, on the site now occupied by the Sterling-Sheffield-Strathcona tower. Hillhouse had sold the hotel to Yale, of which he was then treasurer. Some thought the adjacency of medical school and burial ground suspicious, and, sure enough, discovery of a corpse in the medical school basement, resurrected for dissection (even if not from Grove Street Cemetery), lead to several days of attack on the building in 1824. This was not a happy circumstance for mourners' peace of mind or for Hillhouse's real estate values. During the 1830s and 1840s changes in the vicinity of the cemetery, notably a canal and a railway line, added to the pressure for a more secure enclosure. An eight-foot-high stone wall was put up on three sides in 1848–49, while along Grove Street, perceived to be the face, an iron fence maintained some openness.

The most memorable feature of Grove Street Cemetery is the 1845 brownstone Egyptian Revival gate designed by Henry Austin, built to face recently opened High Street. It defined High as a sort of Austinian Yale avenue, since he was just then finishing the College Library (1842–46), now Dwight Hall, built of the same stone a few blocks down. With steam engines whistling by on the other side the cemetery, the stylistic choice reflects the sense that the Egyptians were able to build in ways that resisted change and perpetuated the names of dynasties. Its inscription, "THE DEAD SHALL BE RAISED," will be recognized as an admonition to spiritual, social, and grammatical good order.

51. Rose Center
William Rawn Associates, 2006

In a long-ago world chronologically not far past, what passed for security at Yale consisted of older men in fedoras and trench coats ambling around campus from their quarters in Phelps Gate on the Old Campus. Evenings, one of them was stationed for a while at a little office at the front gate of each of the colleges,

Rose Center

genially waving at more or less anyone who came or went. To say that has changed is to make a major understatement. The university now has both a police department and a security department, and there is a network of several hundred blue-lit emergency telephones dotting the campus night.

The Rose Center is a campus police station for today's world. To the credit of the university and architects William Rawn Associates, it is more than that. What could have been a defensive bunker is, instead, glassy and open to the three streets it fronts. In fact, the northwest corner of the station has meeting rooms used by the Dixwell-Yale Community Learning Center, and a corner lobby shared by Yale police, Dixwell residents, and students participating in community service programs. Rawn used the need for the openness in a real and perceived sense as the basis for design; the large areas of window facing south and west—the worst directions for solar heat gain and glare—have been equipped with heat-rejecting translucent glass and enough horizontal shading fins that, quite opposite to a bunker effect, make the building look ready for takeoff.

The Rose Center must be understood not just as sleek, accomplished architecture, which it certainly is, but also as a key strategic element in the city and Yale's design to support the neighborhood to the north and west of the Grove Street Cemetery as laid out in the University's Framework Plan. The Rose Center marks what will be the halfway point in a walk almost no student ever used to take, from Payne Whitney Gymnasium around to Prospect Street, Ingalls Rink, and Science Hill. Before demolition a generation ago of the 1940s Elm Haven public

Yale Health Center

housing project just to the north, and construction of its more recent replacement with mixed-income HOPE VI houses, the walk would be not only boring and inconvenient but potentially dangerous. If Yale's Framework Plan is to succeed, the Rose Center and the Dixwell-Yale Community Learning Center must also succeed. A police station of garrison-like character has been well avoided by Rawn and the University, and that bodes well for the Dixwell neighborhood, too.

52. Yale Health Center and Lock Street Garage
Mack Scogin Merrill Elam Architects, 2010 (LEED Gold)

At the very least, in the strict technical sense of the term, this building is grotesque. The etymology of the adjective is "of a cave," and the dark ceramic cladding, variable wall thickness, and unconventional, irregularly triangular lobby of the Yale Health Center invokes subterranean associations even as light pours in from overhead skylights. Depending upon the tastes, mood, and health of the beholder, that may or may not be a good thing. Certainly it can be said that spelunking for medical care is an original idea.

The Health Services building (Westerman & Miller, 1971) on lower Hillhouse Avenue was long regarded as obsolescent and occupying a key site better used for an academic building. Its replacement was planned as one link in the Yale strategy to stabilize the area around and especially "behind" the Grove Street Cemetery. The architects selected for the work, Mack Scogin and Merrill Elam, heading an Atlanta firm, appear to have approached the task of designing for a long-disused site, with no Yale associations, with earnestness and energy. In addition to pictures of the structure in construction and upon completion, analytic diagrams of site forces and possible internal configurations abound in their website presentation of the process leading up to the scheme. Yale would have known in hiring them to expect something unconventional, and they delivered.

Four stories and a basement are intricately organized and interconnected, even in comparison with the complexity normal to health care buildings. The Yale Health Center uses an unusual organizational tool, corridors running perpendicular to outside walls, allowing functions to be packed closer together on the tight site and natural light to reach the interiors.

The building opened in 2010, so it is premature to pronounce judgment on its success either as architecture or as a component within university planning. It can be noted that Yale Health Center and its parking deck, the Lock Street Garage, with the Rose Center on the same block, form a pleasant enough green open space facing the brownstone back wall of the cemetery. Rose and Yale Health represent the considerable, eclectic range of architectural character produced by architects in the first decade of a new century.

When the two new undergraduate colleges just east, across the old canal/ rail line now rehabbed as the Farmington Canal Heritage Greenway, are built and populated, it will soon be apparent whether Yale Health Center helps its occupants not to feel consigned to the wrong side of the tracks. A contemporary campus health care facility needs to be open and available around the clock, all year long. On the face of it, though, sick students arriving at the doorstep late at night would not seem the likeliest source of liveliness to perk up the feeling of life behind the cemetery. Restaurants and new model, small-footprint urban groceries more conventionally provide that sense of activity and positive energy, and the well-received small cafe in the Yale Health Center supports that. A grocery would certainly have been welcomed both by the graduate student population on Mansfield Street and by residents of the Dixwell neighborhood. In any event, Yale is betting that this building, its activity, and its site—much more critical than usual to the success of other sites and uses around it—will succeed at doing much more than acquiring mordant nicknames from the student body.

WALK SIX: BEINECKE LIBRARY TO TIMOTHY DWIGHT COLLEGE

If this is the best of possible worlds, what then are the others?
—Voltaire, *Candide* (1759)

This is an area of New Haven, thought of now principally as a part of
the Yale campus, which, from the late eighteenth century on, was an
in-between place, off-center from a couple of different points of view.
It was not certainly a part of either the Green or of the Hillhouse quarter;
it was neither particularly affluent nor poor; nor, until very late in the
nineteenth century, did it develop a strong allegiance to either Yale College
or to the Sheffield Scientific School, the two developing Yale centers
bracketing it. Consequently it is either (depending on your point of view)
one of the messiest or one of the most interesting components of the
campus, with a diversity of building types, styles, and uses, and no one
particularly dominant. If your planning proclivities are toward overarching
patterns, it will look like an opportunity for a cleanup. If otherwise, it is an
argument for the virtues of smallness, localism, and peripherality; for the
complexities of a heterotopia over the clean order of a utopia.

John Russell Pope's 1919 plan (see Walk Four) made this area the link
that would unify the whole Yale campus. Hewitt University Quadrangle,
fronting Beinecke Library, was to be a courtyard receiving the thrust of an
axis from the Old Campus, sleepy little Wall Street was to become a major
east-west mall terminating where the Silliman master's house and Slifka
Center now stand, and Hillhouse Avenue was to have rolled a block further
than it does, across what is now the lower half of the Silliman courtyard,
to terminate at the aggrandized Wall Street. Had that utopian vision come
to pass, most of the older buildings on this walk would have been destroyed
and, even leaving aside Pope's interest in a lockstep Gothic stylistic unity,
there would have been no room left for new ones. Pope's was a totalizing
vision. When something did not fit in, it would remain only when he was
convinced that it was sponsored by powerful interests or mightily expensive
to remove. Even Woodbridge Hall did not meet Pope's visionary criteria
(one guesses University Secretary Anson Phelps Stokes, whose family had
given the building, was not a great fan of his plan), so there was certainly
no hope for such odd leftovers as the Wall Street rowhouses and their
hole-in-the-wall storefronts.

Pope's sweeping plan did not carry the day, of course. It was just too
brilliant and too ruthless. Aspects of it were adapted by James Gamble
Rogers in the 1920s for the Cross Campus, but Rogers's work differed
in one fundamental way from Pope's: it was incremental, opportunist,

and flexible in its boundaries. The difference, grossly stated, is that Pope proposed to fortify the whole of the campus and provide it with a distinct set of monumental entrance squares and focal towers, while Rogers proceeded to fortify the Yale campus in block-by-block fashion, craftily working with many small linkages and only a few major visual pivots. While Rogers in the end was no less ambitious than Pope in controlling the aesthetic experience of the campus, he was content to do it a piece at a time. And, because he valued the appearance of incremental growth (even where he was in complete control), the juxtaposition of conforming and nonconforming elements is less jarring.

For all that it is good, effective Modernism, Gordon Bunshaft's design for Beinecke Library and Plaza displayed the attitudes of a miniature version of the Pope plan. It took the territory allocated to it and set up walls at the perimeter of the Plaza in the way Pope set out boundaries with New Haven—tightly limiting entry and providing an awe-inspiring, hermetically sealed vision at the center. Messy complexities stayed outside or underground. The Pope approach, in other words, was not and is not limited to architects and planners working within historicist premises. At least in theory, it remains available to form a Yale of the future.

This raises a difficult question: what is the real difference between Bunshaft's and Pope's sort of vision, in which the entire University, or one of its pieces, is regarded as an isolable, perfectible island, and Rogers's brand, which certainly gave Yale its share of totally designed courtyard retreats from the streets of the too-messy city? Perhaps, if anywhere, a difference can be located in Rogers's seeming toleration of, even appetite for, interim real complexity on the road to an ultimate pretend complexity. So long as an overall order is maintained, the local stuff can be quite provisional until time comes to spruce it up. In the end, the vision may be no less totalizing, but along the way there is the reassuring operative sense of a genially eclectic taste. The choices presented to contemporary planners, therefore, might be seen as among three, rather than between two, approaches to urban design: the totalization of Pope and Bunshaft, the incrementalism of Rogers, or neither. Some places need planning and others have evolved into pretty good places with comparatively little of it, or even despite it. The area comprising Walk Six, a kind of Bermuda Triangle of lost utopian plans, would seem one such heterotopia.

53. Beinecke Library and Hewitt University Quadrangle
Gordon Bunshaft of Skidmore, Owings & Merrill, 1963

Beinecke Rare Book and Manuscript Library is a beautiful, self-involved structure, an oversized desk accessory, a gorgeous paperweight holding down the mass of documents and scholarly activity below the gray plane of its granite plaza. To change metaphors, the Library is an iceberg, most of it invisible below the surface; perhaps to overextend the metaphor, this iceberg succeeded in sinking the Titanic of the Bicentennial Buildings' prewar traditional urbanism. Gordon Bunshaft's (1909–1990) 1963 design, emphatic in its prismatic modernist singularity, turned away from Carrère & Hastings's idea, initiated with the Bicentennial Buildings, of making the public area at the University's center a defined, greenery-filled, colonnaded square. As architectural confrontations go, the one of Beinecke with its surroundings is one of Yale's more surreal.

And yet what better place for it? Considered in light of Yale's previous architectural history, the Bicentennial Buildings of 1901–02 were themselves an aberration. For all of Beinecke's lack of concern for the styles and spatial language of its immediate context, it can be argued to stand in a Yale tradition of inward-turning strongbox buildings. This one, with the best of its traditionalist predecessors, was certainly studied to a high degree of refinement in its proportions and visual effects. The above-ground part of the Library is all for show, but what a show! The six stories of book stacks, separately air-conditioned, glow with dark bronze and the bindings of 160,000 rare books, while the translucent Vermont marble panels

transmit light whose color varies according to the intensity of sun outside. The panels' granite frames cover steel trusses, which span corner pier to corner pier and make an elaborate light- and weather-screen around the self-supporting, 35-foot-by-60-foot, six-story book tower. East and west faces measure fifteen panel modules wide by five panels high, a perfect three-square proportion, while north and south are ten panels wide by five high, a double square; the walls remain uniform despite the variation in span, since the structure's real context is the timeless realm of weightless geometry. The sunken court on the Woodbridge Hall side provides

Beinecke Library sunken sculpture court

Beinecke Library

marble-whitened light through dark glass to the working part of the Library below ground. Its sculptural pieces and mysteriously scribed floor, *The Garden (Pyramid, Sun, and Cube),* are the work of the Japanese-American sculptor Isamu Noguchi (1904–1988).

Over the decades, the plaza (officially University Court until 1917, Hewitt Quadrangle thereafter) has seen rallies, "happenings," and protests concerned with every aspect of University policy. Among the best-remembered are a replicant Soweto shanty, a protest that itself was burned in protest, and the well-loved Claes Oldenburg *Lipstick,* now in the Morse College courtyard, a dubiously received gift to the Yale Corporation from the Colossal Keepsake Corporation.

Beinecke Library celebrated its fortieth birthday in 2003 with a renovation, which included removal of the Hewitt Quadrangle paving so that the roof membrane on the underground part of the library could be replaced. Along the way, landscape architect Laurie Olin remedied some of the collateral consequences of Bunshaft's 1960s conversion of Hewitt to a nearly dead-level granite plain. The Ledyard Flagstaff was moved closer to the memorial cenotaph and its stepped base, formerly sunk below plaza level so that it seemed a tall, precariously balanced toothpick, was re-exposed. At the northeast corner of the plaza, Olin's design for new steps and a stone bench echoes Woolsey Hall's expansive curves. It also now provides a focused setting for Alexander Calder's primary-colored *Gallows and Lollipops* mobile of 1960, which used to look as though it had freewheeled in by accident. The whole war memorial complex was rededicated on Veterans Day in 2006.

54. Bicentennial Buildings and Woodbridge Hall

University Commons, Woolsey Hall, and Memorial Rotunda
John M. Carrère & Thomas Hastings, 1902
Woodbridge Hall
Isaac Newton Phelps Stokes and John Mead Howells, 1901

The white limestone classicism of these Beaux-Arts buildings was intended to provide a coherent, unifying center for an otherwise chaotic collection of University structures and activities. This group—University Commons, Woolsey Hall, Memorial Rotunda, and Woodbridge Hall—for the first time provided Yale University with

Bicentennial Buildings

its own buildings, distinct from those of its various entities—Yale College, Sheff, or
the other schools. The Bicentennial Group gave physical form to an administrative
policy of centralization and management reform pushed by President Timothy
Dwight throughout his time in office (1886–1899) and continued by his successor,
Arthur Twining Hadley (1899–1921). By building in the new Beaux-Arts style and
limestone, and locating the buildings as a link between the College buildings on
the Old Campus and the Sheffield Scientific buildings on Hillhouse Avenue, the
administration attempted to signal visually that it was beholden to no one piece of
the University more than another. Here was to be the central place that organized,
managed, and served the whole.

Yet considered from a purely stylistic standpoint, the buildings only added
another flavor to the fifty-seven architectural varieties already offered around the
campus. At the very least, critics said, the kind of Gothic Charles Coolidge Haight
had introduced to the College (see Vanderbilt and Phelps Halls) ought to have
been carried through here too. Haight was in fact among the five entrants in the
1899 limited competition for the Bicentennial Group but did not carry the day, no
doubt precisely because his work to that time was for the College. But the choice
of Renaissance over Gothic was also a matter of the University desiring what was
called "largeness of effect," a visual corollary of policy; the competition's architectural
advisor, George B. Post of New York, favored the Carrère and Hastings entry,
observing that "the several designs are a good illustration of the fact that very
much the same relation exists in art between grandeur and picturesqueness as in
mechanics between speed and power—what you gain in one you almost necessarily
lose in the other." Yale chose power.

Woodbridge Hall

Disliked by many architects at the time—even the classicist John Russell Pope took pains to hide the buildings in his 1919 Plan for the University—there is no denying that Commons, Woolsey, and the Memorial Rotunda have power, even if it shades toward the fulsome. Yale had had only a refectory commons since 1842; after 1902 it had a timber-trussed banqueting hall worthy of Valhalla, supported by kitchen facilities to match those of any New York hotel. Woolsey Hall was Yale's first large assembly space to be definitively secular, its 2,691 seats far surpassing Battell Chapel's 1,000. The Rotunda, its tablets commemorating Yale's dead in many conflicts, takes the traditional domed and colonnaded shape of the martyrium type. It is an elaborate, double-scaled version of Bramante's Tempietto, built in 1502 on the site of St. Peter's martyrdom in Rome.

Carrère and Hastings—John M. Carrère (1858–1911) and Thomas Hastings (1860–1929)—met in the offices of McKim, Mead & White and formed their partnership in 1885. They were socially, critically, and commercially successful; the Bicentennial Buildings were a major stepping-stone toward the New York Public Library commission of 1911, the high point of the firm's production.

Woodbridge Hall, the only building of the group not designed by Carrère and Hastings, was by another socially well-connected New York firm, Howells & Stokes—John Mead Howells (1868–1959) and Isaac Newton Phelps Stokes (1867–1944). Since Anson Phelps Stokes, his brother, was Secretary of the University (1899–1921), and the donors were the philanthropist aunts Olivia Egleston Phelps Stokes (1847–1927) and Caroline Phelps Stokes (1854–1909), the reason for the choice of a different architect is not far to seek. For all that the building's trappings are those of a small French Renaissance–styled mansion of America's Gilded Age, Howells & Stokes were pioneers in the study of American architectural history, including Yale's. It is difficult not to see Woodbridge, therefore, as a slightly larger, more ornamental reincarnation of the 1832 Trumbull Gallery which, converted into the Treasury in 1868 with the addition of windows, served as Yale's central administration building until knocked down in 1901.

In 2004 Charney Architects of New Haven tucked an elevator and emergency exit stair in the garden behind Woodbridge Hall. It is a Swiss-watch miniature in copper, imitating a glass garden conservatory, and is an unexpected treat in an odd campus corner.

55. Silliman College
comprehensive renovations: KieranTimberlake, 2007

Byers Hall
Hiss & Weekes, 1903
Vanderbilt-Sheffield Dormitories and Towers
Charles Coolidge Haight, 1906
Dining Hall, Master's House, and East and North Ranges
Eggers & Higgins, 1940

Silliman, finished in 1940, was not only the last-completed of the ten original colleges, it also marked the end of a half century in which Yale tried to unify itself physically and institutionally by means of architecture. Postwar design would proceed from a different philosophy, with visual unity not foremost among its objectives. Otto R. Eggers, who put Silliman's pieces together, gained a reputation as John Russell Pope's principal assistant after 1924 (until Pope's death in 1937). Eggers was known as a master of watercolor wash rendering, a critical factor in Pope's success in compiling his astonishing record of obtaining important public commissions. Eggers oversaw completion of Pope's National Gallery of Art and Jefferson Memorial, and Silliman was a product of the same twilight-of-classicism period.

Silliman is Yale's largest college in student numbers and land area, occupying a whole city block, as well as being the most diverse in its constituent buildings. While other colleges make-believe at being historical assemblages, Silliman genuinely is one; Eggers cobbled a set of early-twentieth-century Sheffield Scientific School buildings together with others of his own firm's design. Somehow the 1903 Petit Trianon of Byers Hall (now holding the college library, seminar rooms, and a gallery) was made to stand together with the C. C. Haight techno-Gothic of the two 1903–06 Vanderbilt-Sheffield dormitory ranges, while the new brick buildings looked toward the Federal-style Timothy Dwight College

Silliman College

of 1935. It is no wonder the job is not entirely successful, but it is professionally interesting to watch the attempt at unity. Eggers's procedure was not to attempt a collage of elements, the 1980s Postmodern method, but to balance like and unlike elements against each other at a larger scale. Thus, the east range of his red-brick additions becomes lower at the center gate, and turns to limestone; this allows Timothy Dwight's tall Federal tower to loom into the Silliman courtyard, balancing the limestone Gothic tower at the center of the west range. It is also instructive to see what Eggers omits; window shutters, for instance, are present only on the master's house, so that Silliman's brick ranges feel stern and less domestic than TD, making a transition of mood rather than of style to the techno-Gothic west side of the college.

Silliman's site has seen a lot of history. Robert Newman's barn, in which occurred the 1639 deliberations that founded the church and civil government of New Haven, stood just north of where the Grove Street gate tower opens toward, and nicely terminates, Hillhouse Avenue. Between about 1670 and his death in 1688, one of the judges who had condemned Charles I to death, John Dixwell, lived quietly in pseudonymous exile as "James Davids" in a house on the Newman property. The barn long gone, its site was appropriately occupied by a clever 1893 building designed by Bruce Price for the New Haven Colony Historical Society. There were limits even to Eggers's willingness to synthesize, however, and down it went, rather than becoming part of Silliman. Another historic structure on the site was only sent into exile; Noah Webster's white wooden house, chunky and square as an unabridged dictionary, stood facing Timothy Dwight from the corner of Grove and Temple until it was sold to Henry Ford and moved out to Greenfield Village, Michigan. It is hard not to think about it as a might-have-been Silliman master's house. Newman's barn and the Webster house are commemorated with stone tablets at their former sites.

Rosenfeld Hall

56. 370 Temple Street (Center for Language Study), Rosenfeld Hall, and Helen Hadley Hall

370 Temple Street (Center for Language Study)
Satterlee & Boyd, 1906
Rosenfeld Hall (St. Elmo Hall)
Kenneth M. Murchison, 1912
Helen Hadley Hall
Douglas Orr, 1958

Two former Sheffield Scientific fraternity buildings, of similar height and rooflines, dark brick, raked joints, and limestone trim, form a sort of gatehouse urban space across Temple Street. They exhibit an appetite for urban coherence, in contrast with the six-story slab dormitory of Helen Hadley Hall, just down Temple, which sits gingerly back from the street rather than trying in some fashion to engage it. Helen Hadley does, to be fair, register its function with a grid of wide-spaced small window openings in a pattern similar to that of the nineteenth-century rowhouses diagonally opposite. The building's blandness was no doubt calculated; as Yale's first women's dormitory built explicitly for that use, its presence on campus was not uniformly welcomed. Also interesting, and more calculated, was the use of a corridor-based room arrangement, instead of the less monitorable entryway system in the all-male colleges.

Helen Hadley, wife of Arthur Twining Hadley, Yale's president from 1899 until 1921, lived nearby in a much more exuberant building. The family house, built in

Timothy Dwight College

1880 at 93 Whitney Avenue (northeast corner of Trumbull and Whitney) and now occupied by a commercial use, was originally a festival of different materials topped by a red-orange tile roof.

57. Timothy Dwight College
James Gamble Rogers, 1935; renovation: Peter Gisolfi Associates, 2002

Timothy Dwight College, known simply as TD, was finished in 1935 in the middle of the Depression, after a leisurely design process that began in 1928. It was James Gamble Rogers's last Yale college and in fact his last building for the University. It shows him adopting a few of the same tactics used in Pierson College, which also is located on the outer periphery of the central campus; both have tall towers to signal their existence and locations, for example. There is a similar range of large- to small-scale masses, but in TD the juxtapositions of scale are more abrupt; immediately on coming under the tall gate tower, through a chunky brownstone tunnel, the white wooden portico of the college library lies dead ahead, unmissably in contrast. Other such contrasts occur inside; common room windows are set low and made to seem even lower by the floor's being below the level of the courtyard outside, while the adjacent dining hall's windows are high above the floor, over a thick, brown wooden liner. It would be going too far to suggest that Rogers was a closet surrealist, but certainly in TD he manipulated scale, weight, and light for dramatic effect.

But, effective as such things were and are, it was not Rogers's goal just to put together a stimulating collection of abstracted architectural qualities. It was all in aid of the ongoing job of creating a sense of community in a population one-third of which turns over every year. In the case of Timothy Dwight, the sense is strong that that job is best accomplished by sorting out the responsibility for different aspects of community-making into clearly differentiated building types, each with an historical resonance. The dorm ranges are in the type of the Old Brick Row, with a little softening touch of southern ironwork. The TD library is like a New England town hall, in which the wisdom and decisions of earlier generations are studied and debated. The lower, larger courtyard, surrounded by a reincarnated Yale Fence, is the town common or green, while the smaller, slightly raised one is like the garden parterre of a governor's house. The dining hall is the most remarkable of all the College's spaces because it is substantially without an exterior; buried behind the common room, backed up against an alley to the east, the library the focus of exterior attention, its architectural energies are turned inward, concentrated on the innately inward-focused act of eating together around tables. Timothy Dwight's is the starkest but most powerful of the undergraduate dining halls, its thick brick walls simply painted white.

Through the course of planning nine residential colleges and the Hall of Graduate Studies, Rogers used the same short list of programmatic requirements—ranges of dormitories, a dining hall, kitchen and service access, common room, library, a small number of classrooms and offices, and usually a master's house—in such a way as never to repeat an overall pattern, and always to respond to light and air requirements and tight urban sites in workable and appealing fashion. Timothy Dwight capped off this remarkable sustained performance.

58. Theodore Dwight Woolsey House

Builder unknown, circa 1820s

At 250 Church Street is an overlooked building that recollects a symbolic turning point, not in the expected direction, in Yale-New Haven relations. This was once the home of Theodore Dwight Woolsey (1801–1889), nephew of Timothy Dwight, professor of Greek in Yale College from 1831 to 1846 (during which period he built or bought the house), then Yale's president from 1846 until 1871. The Yale Corporation, on electing Woolsey, permitted him to remain in his own New Haven residence rather than moving into a Yale-owned house on or near campus. It was the first time in the history of the institution that such permission had been granted, though not the first time it had been desired. Ironic, then, that Woolsey presided over the intensifying town-gown problems of the 1840s and 1850s, including the 1854 siege of the College by a mob equipped with cannon, and went on to play a central role in the decision to tear down the Brick Row and turn Yale's face away from the streets of the city. As far as can be made out through the neglected and altered state of the building, the original house was an interesting attempt to have

Theodore Dwight Woolsey House

a life in the city but a green retreat too; the pilastered side was pulled close to the street and even given a frontal pediment in good urban fashion, while entry was through a porch whose principal orientation was to a wide garden stretching to the Grove Street corner on the north. (The building at 258 Church Street, now known for the Willoughby's coffee shop on its ground floor, was built on Woolsey's garden shortly after his death in 1889. It was the residence of Mr. and Mrs. Oliver Bennett, she a Winchester, before they moved up to their stylish McKim Mead & White house on Prospect Street in 1903. That house was demolished for the Divinity School, perhaps as ghostly Dwight-Woolsey what-goes-around-comes-around retribution.)

59. Slifka Center and Wall Street Rowhouses

Joseph Slifka Center for Jewish Life (Yale affiliated)
Roth and Moore Architects, 1996

Wall Street between Temple and College is an unexpectedly narrow, shaded, busy but intimate block. It is a low-scale architectural heterotopia par excellence, making a case for the virtues of what can result when many planning, esthetic, and economic forces overlap but none ever acquires the power to dominate. The street features some of New Haven's few remaining nineteenth-century rowhouses, whose ground floors house some of the longest-running businesses in downtown New Haven; it is unexpected but wonderful to find these small businesses here, long blocks away from any other services or restaurants. The block probably sprang up to serve the Sheff students' needs for beer and laundry—Rosey, of Rosey's Tailors, might well

Slifka Center

have been here then himself—then were grandfathered in when New Haven adopted zoning codes. Many grand plans have been offered up for the deep block to the south of Wall Street, but so far surface parking is the use that has trumped them all. The concern is that one day one of these grand plans might be realized and, by accident, kill the street's life and diversity.

The Slifka Center shares the low proportions and some of the details of Roth and Moore's Mudd Library; on the interior it reveals an admiration for the tonalities and oak of Kahn's British Art Center. Its Wall Street facade melds together some of the larger scale and rhythms of C. C. Haight's 1903–06 dormitories and gateway opposite with the brick-and-stone rowhouses next to it. On the south terrace, protected from the messy expanse of midblock parking by a brick screen wall, an even unlikelier hybrid is pulled off; industrial mushroom columns and heavy timber make a sukkah, at once a contemporary and primitive exemplification of the type.

60. Stoeckel Hall, Sprague Hall, and St. Anthony Hall

Stoeckel Hall (Chi Phi Fraternity)
Grosvenor Atterbury, 1897; renovation: Charney Architects, 2009
St. Anthony Hall
Charles C. Haight, 1913
Sprague Hall
Coolidge and Shattuck, 1917; renovation: KBMP Architects, 2003

Until after the Civil War, College Street north of Elm was lined with prosperous middle-class houses dating back to the eighteenth century, a number of them owned or occupied by Yale faculty. Yale itself stepped across Elm in 1869-70 with the construction of Richard Morris Hunt's East Divinity on the site now occupied by Calhoun College. At almost the same moment, two blocks to the north, the Scientific School also began to build on property previously private and domestic. Sheff, and to a lesser extent Divinity, began to generate a drift in the character of College

Street and adjacent areas, not so much by the size of their own buildings as by the fact that, unlike Yale College, neither provided housing for all their students. Sheff, in fact, provided none at all. Consequently, the Sheff students organized their own fraternities and societies, which rented houses or found property and built on the blocks around lower Prospect Street and Hillhouse Avenue where the School's activities were concentrated. Gradually these blocks of College Street became given over to the two branches of Yale and their students.

The intersection of College and Wall streets shows off the heterogeneous results of the fifty-year transformation from a New Haven to a Yale identity. Of the four corners, Scroll and Key went earliest, in 1870. In 1894 St. Anthony Hall, a Sheff society, went up at the northeast corner, but not the building seen today. The earlier building was a Richardsonian brownstone design by Heins and La Farge (son of the painter and stained-glass artist); its ornamental iron gate was recycled for the corner entrance on the present octagonal tower. The ubiquitous Charles C. Haight designed the second St. A's in 1913, built to provide more space and to fit better with the two limestone Vanderbilt-donated halls (1903–06) flanking it. The seemingly perpetually sun-washed Venetian terra-cotta and brick structure at the southeast corner, now Stoeckel Hall, one of the Music School's buildings, was designed by Grosvenor Atterbury (a Scroll and Key man) for the Chi Phi fraternity in 1897. The remaining corner was one of the more significant in the area from 1886 until 1899, holding the tall mansarded house of Timothy Dwight, president of the University. Dwight, who was principally responsible for the new Divinity College buildings, bought it when a professor. On his retirement from the presidency, he sold the house to the University, which gave it over to the recently formalized (1894) School of Music. In 1916 the old house, one of the last vestiges of the residential street of a half century earlier,

Sprague Hall

was knocked down. In its place in 1917 Coolidge and Shattuck of Boston built Sprague Hall, a reserved but not at all unfriendly brick Georgian facility for the School of Music. It was the last piece in what is now one of the more pleasantly surreal intersections at Yale, with stylistic representations of North Africa, Boston, Venice, and northern France coexisting there, and with music always in the background.

In 2009 Charney Architects completed a full exterior restoration, interior renovation, and substantial side addition to Stoeckel Hall. It is a tour de force work: the terra-cotta of the original building alone is worth a sidewalk full stop to admire, and the building earned a LEED Gold rating besides. The School of Music and the Department of Music continue to add to their own quirky campus-within-a-campus. Earlier, Sprague Hall was completely renovated in 2005 by Toronto's Kuwabara Payne McKenna Blumberg Architects. That project restored, respectfully jazzed up, and improved the acoustics of the School of Music's main performance space. It also added a nearly invisible rear connection of the building to William L. Harkness Hall, which wraps it on two sides.

61. Scroll and Key
Richard Morris Hunt, designed 1864; built 1870

Scroll and Key may not be so well known to the world outside Yale as is Skull and Bones, but "Keys" (legally, Kingsley Trust Association) is almost as old and arguably at least as influential in its impact on Yale planning and architecture. It was founded in 1842, ten years after Bones, apparently after some sort of altercation within the older society involving selection order, Southerners, Junior societies, and other matters not now much worth decoding. Like all the various societies, fraternities, and eating clubs that then dominated undergraduate life, it happily rented out rooms on the upper floors of downtown New Haven commercial buildings for a few years.

Skull and Bones raised the standard of society life with the construction of its High Street tomb in 1856. Keys members began agitating for a hall of their own. Progress toward the goal was fitful. Expectations were set high, not merely out of a sense of competition with Skull and Bones but because Keys had, from the outset, artistic ambitions; the founding members had dedicated themselves to "the study of literature and taste" and vowed to make their meeting place "the home of friendship, the hall of literature, and the studio of fine arts." They were assisted toward achieving such ends in a permanent hall by a number of circumstances, not least of which was the marriage in 1855 of one of their founders, John Addison Porter (1822–1866), by then a faculty member of the newly founded Yale Scientific School, to the daughter of Joseph Sheffield, the railroad entrepreneur. (Sheffield lived on lower Hillhouse Avenue in the old Ithiel Town house.) By 1863 Keys owned property on Prospect Street, backing up to Sheffield's garden, and New York architect Richard Morris Hunt was engaged to make plans for a hall. A design close to the one eventually

Scroll and Key

built was accepted in January 1864, but there ensued still another chase for a site, a real estate chess game, one suspects, with Yale acting as a cat's paw for Skull and Bones to frustrate its rival. Finally, in 1869, Keys bought the present site at College and Wall streets from Berzelius, the secret society of the renamed Sheffield (what a coincidence) Scientific School, and built Hunt's design in 1869–70. Funds were tight however, in part because Hunt had gone over budget; many items inside and out—the stone and cast iron fence, for instance—were added later over the years.

Richard Morris Hunt (1828–1895) was the first American architect to train at the École des Beaux-Arts in Paris. His Tenth Street Studio Building in New York City was the site of Hunt's own atelier and of the studios of any number of well-known American artists. Even if the architect nearly sunk the men of Keys with cost overruns, they could not have found anyone in North America better suited to giving them the exotic but tasteful art-studio ambiance they sought. The hall's alternating bands of light and dark stone, pattern-pierced stone window screens, and exotic column capitals at the entrance are all extracted from Islamic architecture. Nineteenth-century artists' studios commonly had exotic orientalia lying about to suggest that the painter was sophisticated, well traveled, and in touch with mysterious powers; Hunt's Scroll and Key is one instance in which the trope got turned into a building.

Scroll and Key has provided many patrons and designers of Yale buildings. Patrons include Sage, McClellan, Bingham, Mellon, and Whitney. Architects include Walter B. Chambers (McClellan and Bingham Halls), Grosvenor Atterbury (Connecticut Hall and Medical School buildings), William A. Delano (Divinity School, Sterling Chemistry, W. L. Harkness Hall, and others) and, most notable, James Gamble Rogers, the one person most responsible for the shape of the campus today. Scroll and Key was extensively renovated in 2010.

WALK SEVEN: HILLHOUSE AVENUE AND LOWER PROSPECT STREETS

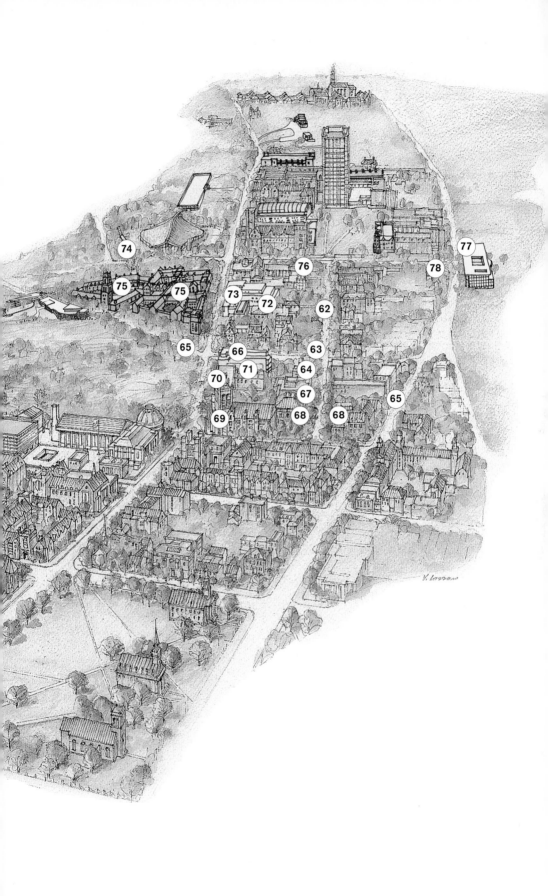

Roy Lichtenstein's 31-foot-high stainless steel *Modern Head* (1974, 1989; placed here in 1993) turns its Greek profile wide-eyed and with parted lips, away from the top of Hillhouse Avenue. If, in its flat, deliberately blatant echoes of Picasso and Art Deco, there is a kind of insouciant play with viewers' recall of slides memorized for art history classes, the *Head* is also a subtle prompt to reflect on the imagery of classicism, which for all their modernity, underlay much of that artist's and that style's work. Lichtenstein (1923–1997) loved that sort of double play; the weird scientist in one of his 1960s pop-art paintings demands, "What? Why did you ask that? What do you know about my image duplicator?" Here, at the foot of the Hill, science and technology meet aspirations to timeless art; this is the Hillhouse Avenue of architect Ithiel Town, inventor and painter Samuel F. B. Morse, and scientist Ben Silliman, who also was plotter of the Trumbull Gallery. At its peak, few streets in the country could exemplify the ideal of America as an Arcadia or Eden redeemed by human ingenuity, the place of the Machine in the Garden, better than this one.

Morse, Silliman, Town, and many other men and women of note came to this avenue because of one name, Hillhouse, which for over a century and a half was central to New Haven's and Yale's development. To local ears the name has an archetypal ring, for the Hill-houses lived in the House (Highwood, later Sachem's Wood) on the Hill (Prospect, now usually Science). Family and house are gone now—the house was willed to Yale in 1942 by the last Hillhouse, but with the stipulation that it be torn down and the site never built upon—but they left behind an imposing emptiness at the head of Hillhouse Avenue, like a vacant throne.

Two Hillhouses deserve mention, James (1754–1832) and his son James Abraham (1789–1841). Both were innovators and developers who thought in terms of remaking whole environments, suffusing them with spiritual and didactic content while at the same time making money. The elder Hillhouse masterminded many projects in which real estate, social reform, and aesthetics converged, notably the Trumbull Plan for Yale College (1792) and the Grove Street Cemetery (1797). The great New Haven elm planting for which he pushed hard was not far behind in significance. It began in 1784, the post-Revolutionary year in which New Haven formally named its streets. In 1787 a new street, Temple Street, was laid out through the center of the Green and continued out to Grove Street. Temple Avenue, later renamed Hillhouse, was staked out, 150 feet wide, and its elms planted in 1792. (A young Hillhouse employee, Jeremiah Day, drove the guiding stakes; he would be Yale's president from 1817 until 1846.) In one direction the line of the Avenue aimed directly at the point where Temple Street left the Green, and it is strongly to be supposed that Hillhouse in making the alignment hoped to carry through the connection to the city's center. Uphill the other direction, the aisle of elms converged on a site where, as the trees prophesied for thirty-six years before it happened, James Abraham eventually built a family mansion, designed by A. J. Davis in 1828–1830. While the trees grew, Hillhouse senior and then his son found buyers and tenants intrigued by the Virgilian situation. An enterprising young Yale chemist, Benjamin Silliman, who in 1807 had bottled and sold the first soda water in the United States, was the first. In the fall of 1809 he brought his bride Harriet Trumbull to an innovative house—timber-framed, with traprock infill that was then stuccoed—which Hillhouse had built for himself but not occupied, at what is now the northwest corner of Trumbull and Hillhouse. Slowly at first, but at a pace accelerating from the 1820s on, the Avenue attracted a growing collection of accomplished people and interesting buildings.

Meanwhile Hillhouse engaged in other projects, many of them to do with developing transportation and trade networks in the new nation. In 1798 he organized the building of a turnpike tollroad, now Whitney Avenue, almost arrow-straight up to Hartford, literally from his doorstep at Whitney and Grove. At the corner of Grove and Prospect he built a hotel, which failed when Jefferson's 1807 Embargo killed New Haven's foreign trade. Hillhouse nimbly sold the building to Yale for its new Medical School, organized under Silliman's leadership between 1807 and its opening in 1813. Thus the first two buildings of the Hillhouse area, Silliman's private residence and the mixed blessing of the science-based educational institution (see Grove Street Cemetery), set its subsequent hybrid character.

When Hillhouse built the hotel and what would have been his own house, the one Silliman later occupied, they were separated by the upper reaches of East Creek, a stream that wandered southeast before taking a turn to set the east face of the Nine Squares and reaching New Haven harbor. That changed dramatically with the chartering of the Farmington Canal in 1822, a scheme intended to suck western New England's trade away from the Connecticut River and Hartford in favor of the Canal and New Haven. Under Hillhouse's direction East Creek was turned into the first leg of the Canal, with a large turning basin dug out between Whitney and Temple streets. Barges, tow-horses, and gangs of laborers now slid or trudged across the Avenue vista framed by the growing elms, and to no one's consternation; all was in fulfillment of the biblical admonition to subdue the earth and enjoy its fruits. Housebuilding on and near the

Avenue accelerated at the same time, in good part because James Abraham Hillhouse returned to New Haven in 1823 after sojourns in Boston, London, and New York, equipped with poetic and builderly ambitions and the financial backing of his wife's, Cornelia Lawrence's, wealthy New York merchant family.

Hillhouse the younger cut Trumbull Street across from State Street to Prospect by 1828, providing additional frontage for development in anticipation of the Canal's success. Within the Hillhouse property between Whitney and Prospect, Trumbull made a *decumanus* to cross Hillhouse Avenue's *cardo*; it was the year in which the Yale faculty under President Day issued a once-famous report affirming the primacy of Greek, Latin, and classical studies in a college education. In the same year, James Abraham commissioned Highwood, and its two-story Greek Ionic portico culminated the Avenue after 1830. A. J. Davis (1803–1892) designed the house in the fervor incited by his encounter with Stuart and Revett's *Antiquities of Athens*, loaned to him by the New Haven architect-builder-truss inventor Ithiel Town (1784–1844). It was renamed Sachem's Wood after the death of the elder Hillhouse in 1832, and James Abraham published *Sachem's Wood: A Short Poem, with Notes*, describing the view down the Avenue:

> Now, from this bench, the gazer sees
> Towers and white steeples o'er the trees
> Mansions that peep from leafy bowers,
> And Villas blooming close by ours…

One of the notable "blooming" villas was Town's for himself, on the site now occupied by the 1958 addition to Dunham Laboratory. Built around 1832 during the period of the partnership he had formed with Davis after Highwood, it housed Town, his family, and, until its dispersal after Town's death in 1844, the largest collection of architectural and engineering books in America. Town was generous in allowing access to the library, and it was consulted by, among many others, the members of the Society for Architectural and Rural Improvement, formed in 1833 by James Abraham and some Yale and New Haven worthies.

The name reveals an attitude that was less disturbed than one would imagine when the Canal enterprise failed and, beginning in 1847, barges were supplanted by the cars and engines of a railroad line, the city's third. This new variety of machine in the garden was more intrusive, but then science and technology were everywhere becoming more important and visible in the country. Fundamentally the conviction held that one could have the virtues of the rural and the comforts of the city, precisely because science's feeding of the human ingenuity exemplified in the railroad would see to it that virtues and comforts would advance together. Under the influence of Ben Silliman (still very much alive and now trainwatching on Hillhouse Avenue), Ben Silliman Jr., and others, Yale founded Schools of Applied Chemistry (1847) and Engineering (1852) which were combined in 1854 as the Yale Scientific School. In 1855 a professor in the school married the daughter of the man who had run the railroad through the Canal cut, and Joseph Earl Sheffield bought 38 Hillhouse, an 1833–34 Town and Davis design, as a wedding gift for Professor and Mrs. John A. Porter. In 1858 Sheffield, following with more of the in-law support which, arguably, made the Avenue happen, bought the old Medical School building from Yale (now SSS's site), expanded and refurbished it as classrooms and laboratories, then gave it back for the use of the (gratefully rechristianed) Sheffield Scientific School. He also bought the Ithiel Town house, added to it, and moved in to watch over his railroad, the school, and his daughter and son-in-law's household.

Sheffield's gifts and rebuildings effectively reinforced the division of upper and lower Hillhouse Avenue—the upper sedately residential, and the lower section dominated by larger buildings housing occasionally noxious activities. The upper-lower pattern, in which buildings of divergent uses and scale on the lower part were operated by the residents of the upper, both pulled together by the broad sweep of the elms from Grove up to the Hillhouse mansion, persisted well into the twentieth century. More large buildings came along on the lower end, a few houses vanished or were replaced by larger ones on the upper; the architectural pattern continued, but then the stuff that held the buildings together began gradually to disappear. Dutch Elm disease destroyed the grand old trees planted by James Hillhouse in 1792, the supervising gaze of Sachem's Wood vanished in 1942, the faculty gradually fled from living in the vicinity of campus, and the terrible postwar mistake was made which turned Trumbull Street into a car sewer serving Interstate 91. All combined by late in the century to erode not only the physical appeal of Hillhouse Avenue but, more importantly, comprehension of its *rus in urbs* reason for existence. Hillhouse Avenue once dreamed of the city of man as an immanent garden, profitable to both the spirit and the bank account, with Nature's and Man's beauty, usefulness, and ingenuity everywhere visible. Yale now owns all the properties on Hillhouse. It is to be hoped that the University's intention to make the foot of Science Hill the "Ecological Campus" will also reclaim the older, related vision of the Hillhouse family and the Avenue.

62. Hillhouse Avenue Houses

A walk down the Avenue, though still good by any standard, is only distantly like one when the famous elms still lined it. Some of the best houses survive, and though the old trees are gone one can still puzzle out James Hillhouse's vision of unified man-made and green grandeur, and appreciate its broader urban design implications. Hillhouse's 1792 approach to the Avenue's elm planting was interestingly different from the one he had used in 1787 for the trees of Temple Street, then newly cut through the Green. The two streets grew to become the city's most beautiful, indeed they largely made New Haven's reputation as a beautiful city. They had very different characters, not only because one was religious and civic (its three churches and the Green) and the other residential, but because, thanks to Hillhouse, their trees created distinct moods. Temple Street, its elms placed symmetrically just outside both sides of the roadbed (perhaps 45 feet separating their lines across the street) became a green cathedral, dark and vertical, because the tree crowns met overhead; Hillhouse Avenue, its trees outside the street and sidewalk lines (hence their lines perhaps 90 feet apart, too far for treetops to meet) grew into a horizontally proportioned grand corridor lit by a central channel of sky. Temple's elms helped produce an environment of civic-minded spirituality, the Avenue's trees pulled individual houses into civic unity. Both places resulted from the underlying notion that trees and buildings, together, define the city's essential nature.

It helps today, then, to imagine the Avenue's houses set in long washes of dappled shadow on both sides of a brightly sunlit street. People ought always to be imagined here, figures moving out of each house doorway and into every other doorway up and down the Avenue, for its history is a complex tangle of patrons, architects, families, intermarriages, moves of families, moves of houses. Only a brief sketch of Hillhouse Avenue houses, and how they played into Yale, New Haven, and the country, can be given here.

Three architects of national significance designed houses on the upper Avenue: Ithiel Town (1774–1844) and A. J. Davis (1803–1892) in the early part of the nineteenth century, Bruce Price (1845–1903) toward the end of it. Town's and Davis's work, individually or as partners, is to be found at 56 and 46 Hillhouse,

31 Hillhouse, and around the corner to the east at 85 Trumbull. One should always remember, too, the vanished Sachem's Wood at the top of the hill. At number 38, Price's design in 1892 replaced an 1833 Town and Davis house.

It is probably fair to class New York architects Russell Sturgis

43 Hillhouse Avenue, the President's House

Hillhouse Avenue

(1836–1909) and Josiah Cleaveland Cady (1837–1919) a notch below the first three, and Henry Austin (1804–1891) and Sidney Mason Stone (1803–1882) as regional builders-designers of considerable accomplishment. Sturgis in 1871 designed 43 Hillhouse, much remodeled and since 1937 the Yale President's house. Cady contributed number 28 in 1884, on the site of the Avenue's first house, whose pieces had already been moved away in various directions in 1871. Austin worked almost everywhere on the Avenue, remodeling many houses designed by others, but also designed numbers 24 (see Dana House) and 52 from scratch, both in the same year, 1849. Stone designed number 55, a fine and well-preserved example of his work.

Moving down Hillhouse Avenue, even numbered houses are on the right, to the west, and odd numbers are to the left, on the east. Town and Davis built 56 Hillhouse about 1836 for Mrs. Elizabeth Apthorp and her four daughters. She conducted Mrs. Apthorp's Young Ladies Seminary in this masonry cube, and the house later served as a school or dormitory for women. It was the home of the second Timothy Dwight after his retirement from the Yale presidency in 1899.

Sidney Mason Stone built 55 Hillhouse, the Pelatiah Perit House, sometime between 1859 and 1861. Painted brown, in contrast with the white or yellow of earlier Town and Davis houses, it retained the idea of a simple cubic block loaded up with fine detailing around openings. Since 1960 senior University administrators have lived here.

52 Hillhouse is one of the Avenue's stars, and the site of one of its sadder stories. Henry Austin designed and built it in 1849 for the young professor John Pitkin Norton and his family. Norton worked himself to exhaustion in the Scientific

School and died at age thirty in 1852. Major additions in the late nineteenth century bulked it up, disturbing the original character in which house and landscape design reinforced each other.

51 Hillhouse was built in 1862, designer unknown, for John Graves, treasurer of the New Haven Gas Company. The company had proven an enormous success since the first demonstration of gaslight at 34 Hillhouse only fourteen years before. The house was long the residence of president Dwight's older brother James.

47 Hillhouse, built in 1862 for James M. Hoppin, was razed in 1941. Hoppin was first a professor in the Divinity (Theological) School, then taught the history of art and architecture in the School of Fine Arts, 1879–99. The house served as President James Rowland Angell's residence between 1924 and 1937. Its demolition demonstrated the insignificance Yale too often attributes to the buildings in which its own history has occurred.

46 Hillhouse was first the home of Aaron Skinner, who ran a boys' boarding school in the house; Town and Davis probably designed it in 1831–32. The two-story Greek Revival portico, with its four expensive Ionic columns, complemented the same feature on Sachem's Wood. Before Henry Austin filled the front corners out with a second floor in 1859, the likeness of the house to a classical temple would have been more pronounced. A subsequent resident donated Kirtland Hall on lower Hillhouse to the Scientific School, and its architect piously reproduced the porch.

43 Hillhouse, since 1937 the home of Yale's presidents, was built in 1871 for Henry Farnam (1803–1883). Farnam was a surveyor and engineer who came to New Haven to work on the Farmington Canal. He hooked up with Joseph Sheffield on the railway, which succeeded the Canal, and then on subsequent railroad ventures centered on Chicago. He built the first railway bridge over the Mississippi River, fighting off steamboat companies in the course of doing so. Retiring in 1863 at age sixty, he returned to New Haven. Following the lead of his partner, Joseph Sheffield, in donations to Yale, Farnam gave the gift of Farnam Hall, built 1869–70 on the Old Campus. Farnam also employed the dormitory's architect, Russell Sturgis, to design this house for him. As originally built it was a condensation of the same elements—rounded towers, a stone porch, wooden Gothic dormers—found on the dormitory. If the original building represented surplus design energy from the Old Campus, its 1937 reconstruction by Kimball & Husted looks to be Colonial Williamsburg overflow.

The current 38 Hillhouse is the second house on the site. The first, the Nathan Whiting house, was an 1833–34 Greek Revival design by Town and Davis. It became the residence of John Addison and Josephine Sheffield Porter and their sons. In 1895 Bruce Price built the present villa on the site, equipped with the crisply archeological Greek details often associated with Academic Classicism in the 1890s. His client was Henry F. English, son of James E. English, New Haven builder and clock manufacturer, U.S. senator and Connecticut governor.

37 Hillhouse, built in 1866, is more distinguished for its list of residents than its architecture. It was the home of Daniel Coit Gilman, Yale's librarian from 1858 until he left in 1872 to become President of the new University of California, then of Johns Hopkins. He organized the art exhibitions that led to the foundation of the School of Art (see Street Hall). Members of the Farnam family, who also built 43 Hillhouse and 28 Hillhouse, followed Gilman.

35 Hillhouse is another Town and Davis design, constructed in 1837. It is a straightforward house to the front of which a giant Corinthian portico has been attached, and was built for Mrs. Mary B. Prichard and her three daughters. Just the previous year Mrs. Apthorp and her four daughters had moved into 56 Hillhouse, and the Avenue became a street much visited by young men. One Prichard daughter married future Yale president Theodore Dwight Woolsey.

The land that held two successive houses at 34 Hillhouse is now the grassy lawn of the Luce Building. The wooden first house, built elsewhere around 1808–11, moved here around 1826 and moved out twelve years later; it now stands at 58 Trumbull Street, where it was the residence of J. F. Weir, first head of the School of Art. In 1840 Professor and Mrs. Benjamin Silliman Jr. put up a brick house on the lot; his parents occupied 28 Hillhouse next door. The Sillimans were innovators and entrepreneurs, and the younger professor installed New Haven's first gaslighting in the house in 1848. Walter Camp (1859–1925), who helped found American football and instigated naming All-American teams, later owned the house. He thought up the idea of marking a football field in a measured "gridiron," and regulating play by time and a series of downs; Camp worked for the New Haven Clock Company (owned in part by the English family, of 38 Hillhouse), so the idea might well have come naturally to him. Yale razed the house in 1936.

31 Hillhouse, as originally constructed in 1826, formed, with the original 34 Hillhouse, a more or less matched pair of five-bay wooden houses facing each other across the Avenue just above newly laid-out Trumbull Street. Half-sisters, Mrs. Apthorp and Mrs. Abigail Whelpley occupied the two houses. James Abraham Hillhouse, eager to bring residents to the area that shortly would be crossed by the Farmington Canal, set up the whole arrangement. When Mrs. Apthorp moved up the street into 56 Hillhouse in 1837, her former house was spirited away to Trumbull Street, the gatehouse-like symmetry vanishing along with it. Noah Porter had Henry Austin "modernize" 31 Hillhouse in 1866–70, shortly before Porter became Yale's president in 1871.

30 Hillhouse is today the least distinguished house on the Avenue. It was not always so; when built in 1884 for Edwin S. Wheeler, it had something of the red-brick Queen Anne character of 28 Hillhouse, built next door in the same year. All original references were modernized away in a 1908 remodeling and stuccoing by another member of the English family.

Dana House

28 Hillhouse is the address of another Avenue lot with a complex architectural history. On it in 1807 James Hillhouse built a house he intended for his own use. Due to financial difficulties suffered as a result of President Thomas Jefferson's embargo, Hillhouse stayed in the family mansion, Grove Hall, at the corner of Grove and Church streets, and sold the new house to Benjamin Silliman. Silliman lived there with his family and mother-in-law, Mrs. Trumbull (in whose honor the street was named) until his death in 1864. That house's timber frame was moved around the corner, providing the basic structure for 87 Trumbull. Charles H. Farnam, son of Henry (43 Hillhouse), hired architect Josiah Cleaveland Cady in 1884 to put up the present house on the 28 Hillhouse site. (It has also been attributed to Russell Sturgis, back in New Haven at the time to work on Lawrance Hall on the Old Campus.)

27 Hillhouse was built in 1866 for George Park Fisher, another Divinity professor. Mrs. Fisher was the sister of Mrs. Benjamin Silliman Jr., across the Avenue at number 28; to call Hillhouse Avenue relations ingrown is an understatement.

Around the corner at 85 Trumbull Street, at least for the moment, is another James A. Hillhouse–commissioned house "carefully built, in 1837, after an elevation by A. J. Davis, Esq.," according to an 1839 advertisement. In 1998 Yale announced plans for its demolition as part of an agreement in which the University agreed to save and renovate other historic houses in its possession. Some preservationists oppose the decision and contest the Yale assertion that the building has been so denatured over the years as no longer to have historic worth.

63. Dana House and Vicinity

24 Hillhouse (former James Dwight Dana House)
Henry Austin, 1849
87 Trumbull Street
circa 1807; 1872
Wolf's Head Society Tomb
McKim, Mead & White, 1885
17 Hillhouse
Westerman & Miller, 1971

Henry Austin built 24 Hillhouse in 1849 for Professor James Dwight Dana, the same year he did the house for John Pitkin Norton, another Yale scientist, at 52 Hillhouse. The two together show Austin at his most balanced, between the tight, rather dry character of the old Yale Library (now Dwight Chapel) of 1842–46, and the excess of the 1849 New Haven Railroad Station, with its East Indian–inspired tower. Restored in the late 1990s, the Dana House today gives a clear idea of Hillhouse Avenue architecture before the Civil War. Its inventive ornament referring more to plant forms than any specific historical style, Austin's work was here more profusely detailed and exotic than Town's and Davis's, but it proceeded from the same basis in tight, light-colored geometric masses under low-pitched, widespreading roofs.

Mrs. Henrietta Dana was the daughter of Benjamin and Harriet Trumbull Silliman, at number 28 Hillhouse, just across Trumbull, and James Dwight Dana was Silliman's student and protégé. The house stayed in the Dana family until sold to Yale in 1962; the building mass on the north is an addition of 1905, built—amazingly enough considering the date—in the style of the original, no doubt owing to the family continuity.

It is more a matter of historical curiosity than one of architectural interest that the pleasant but nondescript 1871 house at 87 Trumbull Street is built on the bones of the 1807 Benjamin Silliman house, the framing members moved from the 28 Hillhouse Avenue lot next door. And yet perhaps it was living with the sense of being in a Yale reliquary that inspired Reuben Holden, secretary of the University and a resident here in the early 1960s, to put together *Yale: A Pictorial History*, a book of enormous value. (My copy sits beside me now; it was a primary inspiration for this guide.) Another resident of the house, 1969–76, the period of his highest national visibility during the Vietnam War and the Black Panther trial, was University Chaplain William Sloane Coffin Jr.

McKim, Mead & White designed the brownstone building at 77 Prospect, with its crowstep gable facing Trumbull and a beautifully handled corner entry splitting its attentions between the two streets. Built in 1884–85, it is the only surviving building in New Haven designed by the famous New Yorkers. (The houses once at 404 Whitney Avenue and 423 Prospect Street, the latter the site of the Divinity School, are long gone.) Wolf's Head was designed as the "tomb" for the third oldest of the Yale College secret societies, established in 1883 in reaction against the perceived excessive secrecy and snobbery of the first two. The fact that the building has real windows, unlike Skull and Bones or Scroll and Key, was in its day a policy statement. The organization moved out in 1924, leaving for larger quarters on York Street (see Fraternity Row).

Back on Hillhouse Avenue, 17 Hillhouse, the former Health Services Center, is notable for two aspects, neither having to do with the quality of its design. First, its construction necessitated demolishing The Colony (Henry Bacon, 1898) at 17 Hillhouse, the genial, large-porched, almost Southern feeling dormitory of Berzelius, one of the Sheffield Scientific student societies. Second, the Health Center was the first large nonresidential building to step beyond the Farmington Canal, and so broke a pattern that had held since the first construction on Hillhouse Avenue in 1807. Acceptance of Trumbull Street as a major traffic distributor has kept upper Hillhouse alive despite such contradictory signs as the Dana House renovation. In 2010, 17 Hillhouse saw its last patient as Yale Health moved to the Yale Health Center on Lock Street.

64. Leet Oliver Hall and the Mathematics Building Competition

Leet Oliver Memorial Hall
Charles C. Haight, 1908
Yale Mathematics Building Competition
1969; Venturi and Rauch, winner; unbuilt

Leet Oliver was built in 1908 to provide classrooms for the Sheffield Scientific School. It was yet another example of the ample, functional, pleasant but usually somewhat dry limestone Gothic style of Charles Coolidge Haight. Haight here provided a straightforward masonry-bearing wall building, which proved itself adaptable over the decades, and its large staircase and ample central halls served circulation and social purposes well. Their presence necessarily made the building a thick one, a fact Haight artfully disguised with the same massing trick—pulling vertically proportioned bays forward from the blocky body of the building—he had used on Vanderbilt Hall in 1893.

The Mathematics Department moved into the building in the early 1940s and, while appreciative of the structure, proceeded to prove the old academic theorem that communal, shared space, like classrooms, will always over time be colonized and privatized. By the 1960s Leet Oliver was a maze of offices and

Leet Oliver Hall

other backstage spaces made by partitioning former classrooms, and, with the rapid growth of the department, the idea of renovating and adding on to the old building prompted the most famous and controversial design competition in Yale's history.

Charles Moore, then the head of the architecture program at Yale, organized the two-stage competition on behalf of the Mathematics Department in 1969. By the submission deadline of January 5, 1970, the extraordinary number of 468 entries had been submitted. Taken together, the entries' wide range in character, organizational strategy, and stylistic tactics documented serious changes afoot in the architecture world. Venturi and Rauch won the competition in April 1970, four years after the 1966 publication of Robert Venturi's *Complexity and Contradiction in Architecture*, with a design that exemplified the tenets of his "Gentle Manifesto" and also delighted the mathematicians. Neither the design nor the fact of its winning pleased most architects, however, and the howl that went up—that the whole thing was precooked, intended to select Venturi, who was on the Yale faculty, from the outset—certainly did nothing to endear the project to a Yale administration already distracted by the pressures associated with the Vietnam War and, as well, perhaps made leery of architects generally by the June 1969 fire at A&A. The fact that the jury included architectural voices sometimes raised against Venturi and his ideas, and that the runner-up entry by John Fowler and John Paul McGowan was particularly different and interesting, did not register with the many vociferous critics. The upshot was skittishness by Yale administrators and potential donors, which eventually proved fatal to the project.

Venturi and Rauch's Math Building design was one of the earliest casualties in the civil war within the architectural profession over postmodernism. No definitive conclusions came of that war, yet it can certainly be said that with the profession and the public alike, new architecture today must be extra careful when it steps into old neighborhoods having Hillhouse Avenue's historic significance. That sense was not generally shared in 1970, as many of the nonwinning competition entries demonstrated, and Yale itself showed at the time with Becton Lab and the Health Services Building (17 Hillhouse). Forty years later the Venturi and Rauch design retains the power to raise tempers, but it can at least be agreed that its big curve, sweeping away from the Avenue, would have been a definitive announcement that big buildings should go no further up the street. In so doing it summed up and ratified, like no other entry, the history and character of Hillhouse Avenue.

Farmington Canal

65. Farmington Canal

Between Leet Oliver and the Dana House, Hillhouse Avenue rises noticeably and then sinks again. The bump is not the residuum of some vanished hillock but a ghostly topographic memory of the need to get over the tops of vehicles that once passed by below Hillhouse Avenue. A look down from the sidewalk will reveal, under the tangle of locust trees and weeds, the crumbling stonework and bed of what was from 1825 until 1847 the Farmington Canal, and thereafter a railroad line, connecting New Haven harbor up to the Connecticut River at Northampton, Massachusetts, 76 miles away. It is the physical remnant of another episode in the economic and political rivalry between Hartford and New Haven; the basic notion was to divert the flow of trade away from the Connecticut River, on which Hartford lies, to make New Haven the mouth of a trading basin encompassing all of western New England as far north as the St. Lawrence River. Because Hartford blocked public aid from the Connecticut legislature, funding for the canal and then the railroad came from private investment, much of it from New Haven citizens.

Besides the Hillhouses, as always, two other figures important to Yale figured in the tale of the Canal and subsequent rail line. Joseph Earl Sheffield (1792–1882), who had made money in the cotton trade between Mobile, Alabama, and Europe, settled in New Haven in 1835 and quickly became the principal investor in the enterprise. Henry Farnam (1803–1883) was a surveyor and engineer who helped lay out and maintain the Canal, then assisted Sheffield on the railroad endeavor. No one made much money from the Canal or the railroad, but Sheffield and Farnam used the experience as a warm-up exercise for much larger and more profitable railroad projects, principally involving connecting the rapidly growing city of Chicago west to the Mississippi and eastward toward New York. Both settled on Hillhouse Avenue, Sheffield in 1859, Farnam in 1871. The house Farnam built (see Hillhouse Avenue Houses) for himself at 43 Hillhouse now serves as the University's President's House.

Yale announced in the fall of 1998 that the section of the Farmington Canal running through the campus would be made available for a Rails-to-Trails project. The two unusual green pedestrian bridges carrying the Hillhouse Avenue sidewalks over the old canal were installed in 2010. Their structural engineer was Guy Nordenson and Associates, working with Pelli Clarke Pelli, architects of the nearby Malone Engineering Center. The design in its diagonal latticework not only does its job but is also a historical homage to New Haven architect-engineer Ithiel Town, whose early-nineteenth-century invention of a simple, strong, relatively inexpensive wooden truss for bridges enabled a better national road network. It also allowed him to build his own house on the site now wasted on the Dunham Laboratory Annex.

66. Daniel L. Malone Engineering Center
Pelli Clarke Pelli Architects, 2005 (LEED Gold)

The glassy north facade, slightly but visibly curved and precise as a Japanese sword, gets the lion's share of attention in photography of this building. It is very hard to resist the play of leafy greenery, or better still of colored fall foliage, in the Farmington Canal Heritage Greenway against the lenticular grid, or not to be fascinated by the ant-farm-like movement of people inside along the cantilevered corridors visible through the reflections.

But that face of Malone is no more to be admired than the massing and detail of the limestone-clad Prospect Street facade. It manages, via a small terrace setback of the top floor, to acknowledge not only the mass of J. C. Cady's staunch old red-brick Watson Hall immediately next door, but also the height and light coloration of Marcel Breuer's Becton Center down the block. Pelli's punched-in variety of windows echoes those stacked on Watson, while the limestone panels at

the same time recall Breuer's precast pieces on Becton. Given the historic antipathy of Becton and Watson— two other red-brick Cady structures, also originally built for the Sheffield Scientific School, were torn down to make room for Becton—there is a sort of magisterial equanimity in evidence here.

Daniel L. Malone Engineering Center

In its quality and contextuality, Malone capably fends off a ghost still haunting the site just east on the Farmington Canal, where Robert Venturi never got to build his winning Yale Mathematics Building competition entry of 1970, with its similarly convex north facade. Venturi's design implicitly promised that Yale would build no new large buildings on Hillhouse Avenue north of the canal, while Pelli's building, a quarter-century later, in effect promised that it *would* do so, at least on Prospect Street, but that they would be done with urbanity and savoir faire. That is the standard set for two other deans of the School of Architecture: Fred Koetter for Rosenkranz Hall and Robert A. M. Stern for his two new undergraduate colleges.

Internally Malone uses the triangular site, wider at Prospect Street and narrowing eastward, to sort out a spectrum of laboratory suite sizes. The long corridor connecting them, glass and views on one side, labs on the other, acts like a large version of the narrow corridor through old Yale Station, working as a social condenser to ensure meeting and mixing of those using the building.

Just over the Farmington Canal from Malone, at the northeast corner of Prospect and Trumbull streets, Charney Architects in 2008 completed still another of their modestly sized but intricate puzzle-palace renovations, this one for the Institution for Social and Policy Studies. It knits together nineteenth-century houses at 87 and 89 Trumbull and McKim, Mead & White's crowstep-gabled 1884 building, the original home of the Wolf's Head senior society. The Charney brothers' house-sized addition also makes a south-facing suntrap courtyard out of what was previously a throwaway side yard.

67. Dunham Laboratory and Annex, Town-Sheffield House, Collection of Musical Instruments, Mason Laboratory, and St. Mary's Church

Dunham Laboratory and Annex
Henry G. Morse, 1912; Douglas Orr, 1958
Mason Laboratory
Charles Coolidge Haight, 1911
Ithiel Town-Joseph E. Sheffield House
Town & Davis, circa 1832; Henry A. Austin, circa 1859
Collection of Musical Instruments (Alpha Delta Phi Fraternity)
W. H. Allen, 1894
St. Mary's Roman Catholic Church
James Murphy, 1876

The block of Hillhouse Avenue below the Farmington Canal is a quiet riot, a century and a half of dramatic social and technological change represented today by a group of mostly solid and fairly ordinary buildings. The vanished structures and

Dunham Laboratory Annex

names, taken together with those currently occupying the sites, make for a study in transformation of the block's expectations and associations. The most notable absence, of course, is that of the house once on the site occupied by the 1958 Dunham Lab Annex. As built around 1832 by and for architect Ithiel Town, the house had a crisp, upright, central two-story block of three Greek-detailed bays, and short,

St. Mary's Roman Catholic Church

story-and-a-half wings with colonnades of square piers. It would have been at home in Karl Friedrich Schinkel's Potsdam. Henry Austin's 1859 renovation and expansion of the house for Joseph Sheffield's use was one of the more restrained productions of an interesting career often marked by heavy-handed exuberance and a kind of exotic pieciness. Austin parked a single-story Renaissance-style porch in front of the main block, gave it a more assertive tympanum, flanked it with asymmetrical Italianate towers, and attached two little houselets to the ends of Town's side wings. Town had his Romantic tendencies but they were restrained within an ideal of classical reticence; Austin and Sheffield seem to have delighted in the display of references transported across distances and overcoming time. Still, it was an amazing house and a period piece. In 1958, an utterly banal structure, one of Yale's earliest modern buildings, replaced it.

If there is little to be said for the Dunham Annex, the building to which it is appended deserves a bit more attention. While the 1912 Dunham Laboratory (originally for electrical engineering) is nothing particularly special, it is still interesting to see how the typical Yale techno-Gothic of this century's first decade and a half comes out when handled by someone other than C. C. Haight; compare this building with Mason Lab across the street and Leet Oliver next door. Henry G. Morse's design has an asymmetrical facade and a shallower, more fanciful, and delicate touch. The building, in a certain way, is a spiritual successor to the Benjamin Silliman Jr. house, once just up the Avenue on the site occupied by the Luce Center's cryptic lawn, which in 1848 showed off the first gas lighting in New Haven. Austin C. Dunham, donor of the building, was a pioneer in electric lighting; his company, the Hartford Electric Light Company, began providing electricity to that city in 1883.

Across the street on the east side is a tightly packed range of three disparate buildings. The earliest of the three is St. Mary's Church, built in 1870–76 by an Irish Catholic congregation, which many considered a greater intrusion on august Hillhouse Avenue than Joseph Sheffield's smoke-spewing locomotives. Though there had for a long time been private schools on the Avenue, they were conducted in houses. St Mary's, the first distinctively nonresidential building on the Avenue, was designed by James Murphy (1834–1907), a Providence architect who had just split off from an association in New York with the older and better-known Patrick C. Keely; together and apart, the two designed literally hundreds of Catholic churches around New England, serving successive waves of Irish, Italian, Polish, and other immigrants who came to work in the America that the likes of Sheffield were industrializing. In the basement of St. Mary's in 1881 Father Michael J. McGivney (1852–1890) organized the Knights of Columbus. Founded to provide burial benefits to members' families, it has grown into an international fraternal order with a large, self-run life insurance company, as well as architectural ambitions. In addition to the Knights of Columbus Building, the Knights have been responsible for, among other little projects, renovation of the facade of St. Peter's Basilica in Rome. St. Mary's exterior has the discrete confidence of one who knows exactly what are considered to be good manners, and deliberately steps slightly over the line; the tower, with its very large second-story windows, is assertive without being aggressive. The church must have made a nice pairing with the Sheffield mansion opposite.

As if having Catholics around wasn't challenge enough, lower Hillhouse in the late 1880s and 1890s began to be graced with fraternities for the jolly lads of the Scientific School. While not much different in size than the houses further up the street, they adopted a different architectural demeanor, studiedly grave or antic.

In 1894–95 W. H. Allen built a dark, handsome, Richardsonian mini-palazzo for the members of Alpha Delta Phi, a Sheff organization. It provided the students some dining and socializing facilities, but no dormitory space. Around its central entrance the block carries the carved ornamental equivalent of secret handshakes to decode. Occupied since 1960 by the Yale Collection of Musical Instruments, still another of the University's assortment of wonderful oddments, the interiors have given up most of their original character in favor of a softened, pleasing abstraction.

Caught between St. Mary's upwardly mobile Gothic and the fraternity's well-grounded block was the house built in 1856 by Dr. William Hillhouse, son of James Abraham. Yale bought and demolished it in 1910, and presented the job of filling the gap to its veteran peacemaker, Haight. Given his successful insertion of Vanderbilt, Phelps, and Linsly Halls into similar tight and stylistically disparate sites, it would have been surprising had anyone else been tapped for the design of Mason Lab. The major piece of its large bulk is wedged up against the church, but out of sight. The facade fronting Hillhouse Avenue, however, is a study in architectural reconciliation with an admirable economy of means. It has an emphatic stringcourse set just at the level of ADPi's cornice line, the story above it giving just the visual weight necessary to hold down the thrust of the buttresses mimicking those on the St. Mary's tower; nothing could look more unassuming.

68. Warner House and Kirtland Hall

Warner House (formerly Cloister Hall)
H. Edwards Ficken (or Clarence H. Stilson), 1888; Metcalfe and Ballantyne, 1915
Kirtland Hall
Kirtland Kelsey Cutter, 1902

Late in the nineteenth century, as Hillhouse Avenue closed in on a century of development since 1792, it had attained genuine beauty and (to use a term of the day) refinement. The elm trees, which accounted for its parklike character, had grown into magnificence; the dignified procession up to Sachem's Wood was lined with elms, paved sidewalks, wide swaths of grassy street border, stone curbs, and underground drainage for the finely crushed gravel street. At the foot of the Avenue, where it met Grove Street, bollards across the sidewalks and a pair of stone and iron fence sections subtly announced that one was entering something, which, if not quite a private drive, was also not a common New Haven street.

In 1888 a group from the Scientific School built Cloister Hall, now the Warner House, a fraternity building that excused its presence by pretending to be merely a picturesque gatehouse for the Avenue. It was in the spirit of A. J. Davis's 1857 Gate Lodge for Llewellyn Park, New Jersey, or more recently, Bruce Price's for the

Warner House

posh Tuxedo Park preserve in 1885. Warner House, with its imaginative chimney, jerkinhead tile roof, and stone strapwork above the original entry porch on Grove Street, also has the sort of Hanseatic League overlay (see also the crowstep gables of 77 Prospect, Wolf's Head Society, 1884), which had come to signify student solidarity and *Brüderschaft* by architectural reference to medieval German university life. (Not too long afterward the same group decided on a different model, building the Greek Ionic white marble Book and Snake Tomb in 1901.)

Price himself (1843–1903) was working at Yale at the same time, his eyebrow-raising Osborn Hall (see Bingham Hall) of 1886 having gone up, its donor's gift secured by the efforts of John W. Sterling, at the corner of College and Chapel. But the winds of cultural change were blowing a different way, which in architecture meant a shift in the direction of a French-based Academic Classicism. Price had had a year of training in Paris, so he followed the trend, with effects felt on Hillhouse Avenue. Up the Avenue, the other side of the Canal, he designed 38 Hillhouse (see Hillhouse Avenue Houses) in 1892

Kirtland Hall

for Henry F. English, and in 1893 with funding from English, a building for the New Haven Colony Historical Society. Appropriately enough it occupied the site of Newman's Barn, where in 1639 the Colony had formally organized its governance. Since it was built as a more urban, party-wall version of the English House, with very similar materials and Beaux-Arts architectural detailing, the Historical Society once again reaffirmed upper Hillhouse's private patronage of public institutions on lower Hillhouse. At the same time, conveniently, it asserted the continuity of New Haven's deepest roots with its refined, sophisticated present. The Historical Society building was torn down in the late 1930s to make way for the Silliman College dining hall.

By the turn of the twentieth century, the entry to Hillhouse Avenue was watched over by Warner House and the Historical Society, two buildings symbolizing continuity—the former with European ideas of university life and the latter with New Haven's prefigured destiny. The two were joined in 1904 by Kirtland Hall, placed in the side yard of the Town-Sheffield House. It was an homage to Hillhouse Avenue, offered with typological faithfulness. Mrs. Lucy Boardman, who lived for almost a half century in 46 Hillhouse (see Hillhouse Avenue Houses), gave the funds for Kirtland; it was a gift in memory of her uncle, one of the earliest graduates, in 1815, of the Medical School, housed then at Prospect and Grove streets in the former Hillhouse hotel. The building was for the use of the Geology Department of the Sheffield Scientific School, thereby placing the study of geology at the entrance to the street on which had lived Dana and the Sillimans, father and son. The architect, Kirtland Kelsey Cutter (1860–1939), was a relative, of course, called back from a burgeoning practice in Spokane, Washington. Cutter tellingly chose local East Haven brownstone as his material rather than following the example of the brand-new Bicentennial Buildings and importing limestone. He also gave the building a four-columned Ionic portico, which duplicates the size, spacing, and detailing of the 1839 Ithiel Town portico on 46 Hillhouse, the donor's house. The forms and themes, the money and bloodlines, of Hillhouse Avenue eerily restated themselves in Kirtland.

69. Sterling Tower, Sheffield Hall, and Strathcona Hall (SSS)
Zantzinger, Borie & Medary, 1932

The enormous University reorganization that began at the end of World War I and continued through the 1920s left the Sheffield Scientific School alive in name but little else, its undergraduates absorbed into the College, its various faculties hived off into separate departments. In 1930 Sheffield Hall, its first building put up around 1807, was Yale's second oldest after Connecticut Hall (1750–53). Unlike Connecticut it held no place in the hearts of old graduates, and thus received no reverential offerings of funds for renovation. Having knocked down Osborn Hall in 1926, the University needed another large auditorium. Since Woodbridge Hall

*Sterling Tower, with Sheffield Hall on the left
and Strathcona Hall on the right*

Sterling Tower

could not be expanded, physically or symbolically, administrative office space for dozens of new workers tending the larger flow of paper accompanying reorganization were also needed. These demands converged at old Sheff, and in 1932 the three-component new building called SSS supplanted it.

Two familiar names show up in the portmanteau commemoration. The Prospect Street wing of SSS is the Sheffield part, remembering the old building and its donor, while the John W. Sterling bequest accounts for the central limestone tower. The third name, Strathcona, is less familiar around Yale and indeed generally this side of the border with Canada. Lord Strathcona, Donald Alexander Smith (1820–1914), was one of the two principal builders of the Canadian Pacific Railroad (completed 1885), as well as a banker, politician, and philanthropist. After 1888 he retired to England, leaving the conduct of his business affairs in the hands of—surprise—John W. Sterling. The Strathcona wing, along Grove Street, has a large, well-lit ground floor auditorium and an extensive supply of ornament concerned with railroads, buffalo, guns and other Winning-of-the-Northwest themes.

Zantzinger, Borie & Medary was a versatile, well-connected Philadelphia firm, producing styles selected at the pleasure of the client. It designed Gothic dorms for Princeton and, evenhandedly, the Philadelphia Museum of Art. Clarence C. Zantzinger, PhB from Sheff in 1892, fulfilled the near-absolute requirement of the day that every design commission Yale gave out had to be handled by a Yale graduate. The choice of a cool whitish limestone for SSS, instead of the more romantic seam-faced granite in which many of Yale's buildings of the era were constructed, was owing to the limestone Bicentennial Group just across the Grove-Prospect-College intersection. Ironically, the design of the SSS tower owes considerably to the one John Russell Pope showed at the end of the axis from the Old Campus in his 1919 Plan (see Walk Four), deliberately blocking the view of the Bicentennial Group, which he detested. Zantzinger's tower provides an appropriate terminus for the long view north on College Street, but up close it is a perennial cause of confusion. It looks as though the tower is courteously signaling the location of a diagonal through-passage into the block beyond, especially so to those who have just traversed the Memorial

Rotunda from Beinecke Plaza. "How very nice (if slightly humorous)," generations of visitors have thought, "the tall tower complements the short rotunda," and then blundered their way down into the Registrar's Office looking for the way through.

70. Becton Laboratory and Applied Science Center
Marcel Breuer & Associates, 1970

The precast concrete panels and sculptural concrete base piers of Becton Lab are characteristic of the late buildings of the Hungarian-born Marcel Breuer (1902–1981). It has siblings as near as New Haven's Interstate 95 frontage (the Pirelli Building, built as the Armstrong Rubber Co., 1968) and as far as—well, around the world. Breuer is deservedly well-remembered for his furniture, especially the "Wassily" chair of 1925 and the ubiquitously knocked-off cantilever "Breuer" chair of 1928, most of it designed early in his career while teaching at the Bauhaus. He was also one of the first real postwar international power architects. Breuer designed museums, factories, office buildings, and campus buildings in North and South America, Asia, and Europe. These buildings share an attention to the system of their component pieces that no doubt had been made instinctual by his furniture-making and, even more, by his teaching of furniture making. This is perhaps the virtue of his individual buildings and certainly the problem with Breuer's ensembles, even ensembles made up exclusively of the man's own work. His buildings seldom relate at all to their surroundings, even when their surroundings are each other; they are hermetically self-contained, essentially large pieces of furniture that function, more or less, as buildings. This is true of the 1966 Whitney Museum in New York, of the 1976 Hubert Humphrey Building just off the Mall in Washington, DC, and of Becton Lab.

Becton Laboratory

Becton Laboratory

Vincent Scully has long derided it, famously, as "the world's largest table radio."

Beinecke Library, a building slightly earlier than Becton and with some of the same instincts, is redeemed by luxe materials, a spectacular interior space, and a center-block plaza animated by a campus circulation pattern that brings through large numbers of people. Becton has none of these three, though ironically, given the antipathies of the parties involved, Robert Venturi's unbuilt Yale Math Building would have done very good things for Breuer's rear plaza by drawing movement through the block to its prominent back entrance. Other than Davies Auditorium, buried beneath the rear plaza, the only interior space of note in Becton is the ground-floor library. One would like to report that the upper, working floors have operated well and flexibly over the decades; one cannot.

Becton stands on the site of Winchester (1892–1967) and North Sheffield (1872–73; 1967) halls, both designed by Josiah Cleaveland Cady, the much underesteemed architect of the old Metropolitan Opera House and the earliest wing of the American Museum of Natural History, in New York. Both were squarish, highly crafted brick boxes with round-arched exterior walls and interior columns, and some care given to the design of ventilation flues. They were essentially heavily constructed loft buildings of the sort which, like the surviving Cady building next door, Sheffield Chemical (now Watson Hall), have proven over the decades to be eminently malleable.

71. Arthur K. Watson Hall
Cady, Berg & See, 1895; Roth & Moore, 1986

Now past its centenary, Watson Hall is the only survivor of the row of three magnificent utilitarian cubes—North Sheffield Hall, Winchester Hall, and Sheffield Chemical (1894–95), as Watson was originally named—which architect Josiah Cleaveland Cady placed along Prospect Street for the Sheffield Scientific School. In the decades after the Civil War, Sheff, exercising its growing financial muscle, expanded out of its original home at the corner of Grove and Prospect and added the three structures on what had been the gardens of the Town-Sheffield mansion. Photographs of the grouping make it look distinctly like a train chugging down Prospect; old Sheff, its front tower and cylindrical observatory dome like an engine stack, confidently pulls the three Cady buildings along behind.

Arthur K. Watson Hall

Cady (1837–1919) clearly loved working in brick. His library survives intact at his alma mater, Trinity College in Hartford, and it contains many books on brick and terra-cotta construction, most of them in German. When he is remembered at all, Cady is often mislabeled as a follower of Henry Hobson Richardson when in fact his training and designs were in the line of the contemporary round-arched German architecture of Berlin and Munich, the *Rundbogenstil*. It is important to an understanding of nineteenth-century Yale to recollect the high prestige then enjoyed by German education and methods; clear evidence of this is the fact that all three Yale presidents under whom Cady executed commissions, Porter, Dwight, and Hadley, did graduate work at German universities. Watson's round arches and corbel tables are in the line of descent from such buildings as Karl Friedrich Schinkel's 1832–35 Bauakademie, which held a key location at the center of Berlin until after World War II. (And thus Prospect Street played industrial Berlin to Hillhouse Avenue's pastoral Potsdam; the two environments were mutually supporting opposites.)

By the late 1960s all three Cady buildings had become technically outmoded and were often considered stylistically embarrassing. They had in addition, during the time of the Vietnam conflict, the terrible bad luck to house both the program in Southeast Asia Studies and the headquarters of the various Reserve Officers Training Corps. In 1967 two of the three went down despite protests; the University was already case-hardened against demonstrations more intense than those of pioneer preservationists. Becton Lab was built in their place. In the mid 1980s Roth and Moore performed a meticulous adaptive reuse to transform Sheff Chemical into Arthur K. Watson Hall (named for the donor, one of the IBM Watsons) for the burgeoning Computer Science Department. Among other self-effacing things done by the architects was the addition of the northernmost part (left, as seen from Prospect) of the building's front mass just as originally designed; it had never been constructed because of an intransigent holdout row of townhouses. The building now contains computing labs and department offices. Sadly, this has not meant an escape from headlines, since it was the site of one of the antitechnology Unabomber explosions of the 1990s.

72. Henry R. Luce Hall

Edward L. Barnes, 1994

Every so often at Yale a building comes along that makes you wonder if anyone involved with its planning and design was actually conscious of what was being created. Luce is one of them. It offers Prospect Street a gate, a fence, and a parking lot, so clearly that must be the back, or so one imagines; yet it is set far back from Hillhouse, has a mousehole-in-the-baseboard of an entry on that side, and sends only a tentative arc of sidewalk in that direction. Perhaps judgment should be withheld pending construction of a feature that might make visible, let alone useful or meaningful, the Luce Center's imaginary "axis" from its north face up the middle of the block toward the former School of Management. In its current state the building's siting is, in the euphemism of architecture school reviews, "unconvincing." Bending over backward to defend the architect, it looks as though the University had not formulated a clear policy about the scale of new buildings north of Trumbull Street, nor the one governing such buildings' relationships to the historic houses on Hillhouse and Trumbull.

But then there is the problem of the architecture itself. The vacillation that shows in the building's siting occurs again with its massing, materials, scale, and proportions. Seen from Hillhouse, the building tries to lessen its apparent size by jiggle-joggling into three subsidiary masses, but then gives the central one an elevation derived, in an absentminded way, from Louis Sullivan's monumental small-town banks with their large arches on small boxes. From that model the round-topped second-story openings get five, count 'em, five layers of brick voussoirs to form

Henry R. Luce Hall

arches, as though handicraft still ruled the building trades. But then the windows filling the openings are made of two very large sheets of dark glass with dark mullions, a standard late-modern try for the old abstract "void." The arches and the glass combine to give the building something of the look of a 1980s renovation. To be sure, Edward Larabee Barnes's (1915–2004) hesitancy surely grew out of the sense that the mid-block siting put Luce in potential competition with the Hillhouse Avenue houses, and therefore needed to be made more bland. If so, that is an excuse that only recalls attention to the prior problem of its location here in the first place.

By way of a comparison, old photographs show the Town-Sheffield House on lower Hillhouse with the vibrating polychrome block of North Sheffield, its front door right up on Prospect Street, behind. They were just fine in that nonrelationship, each building being itself, because the architects of both (Ithiel Town and Henry Austin for the former, J. C. Cady the latter) gave them an assertive relationship to the street in front of them, and a strong sense of front, sides, and back. On a campus that promises in the new century only to get more densely packed, there could be some new usefulness to this old urban lesson.

73. Rosenkranz Hall
Koetter Kim & Associates, 2009 (LEED Silver)

The architectural theory battles of the 1970s over what it means to design "contextually," and how to do it, still echo around Yale, lo, all these decades later. It was certainly a consensus that whatever it means or however one does it, Edward Larrabee Barnes's Luce Center failed on that count in the early 1990s, both on its Hillhouse Avenue and Prospect Street sides. Among other, more positive,

Rosenkranz Hall

Rosenkranz Hall detail

reasons for creation of Rosenkranz Hall, there was the remedial one of screening Luce from Prospect.

Such architectural sequestration is not unprecedented on the Yale campus. William A. Delano himself, for example, used the long, thin L-shaped massing of William L. Harkess Hall to screen Sprague Hall's classicism from the unified Gothic of the Cross Campus. The open question with Rosenkranz is, sequestration from what? There is no current unified character to this area of campus, and not likely to be any easy one in the future, what with the two neo-Gothic colleges intended for the other side of Prospect from Rosenkranz. Not only that, but in general Yale seems to have backed into a version of Eero Saarinen's famous "style for the job," each new building on its own recognizance to behave well urbanistically no matter how, exactly, its architects determine it will look. Witness the neo-modern School of Management in construction only a long Sachem Street block east of the new colleges' site.

Performing its screening function means, for starters, that Rosenkranz has lengthy corridors in its own L-shaped plan, and as well a high ratio of exterior wall surface to interior constructed space. (It is a bit surprising that the building achieves the respectable energy efficiency rating it does.) The glassy main entry to the corridor system is, logically enough, at its center at the bend in the L, but it is around the corner from Prospect and faces north, presumably to avoid high heat gain from afternoon sun on the west as well as to be available to a new east-west pedestrian path between Hillhouse Avenue and Prospect Street that leads to the new colleges. As logical as the decisions might be, they combine into a "where's the front door?" problem that compounds the basic identity issue of a building shape essentially conceived on the defensive.

Rosenkranz's Prospect Street elevation is dominated by a set of slightly angled, shallow, vertical glass bay windows, which succeed in balancing out the long elevation and, no doubt, preparing to sympathize with Stern's oncoming Gothic across the street. There is a lot going on in not much depth, with irregular layers of limestone, windows jogging slightly in and out, and a metal-clad top floor barely back of the limestone parapet. Veterans of the aforementioned architectural theory wars will be reminded of the classic essay "Transparency: Literal and Phenomenal" by Colin Rowe, Fred Koetter's English-born mentor, and understand that Rosenkranz is influenced by the now century-old heritage of the shallow, fluctuating, pictorial space of Cubism. Indeed, the whole strategy and demeanor of the building make it a late illustration of the antiheroic urbanistic ideas in Rowe and Koetter's *Collage City* (1978).

The building plays well with Luce, not only bridging to it respectfully but forming with it a pleasant outdoor courtyard centered on a rear bay on 38 Hillhouse Avenue. Inside, classrooms and offices, no two alike in size or shape, are assigned with almost mandarin discernment of hierarchy among members of the Social Science faculty. It makes for humorous comparison with Kroon Hall, just a bit further up Prospect Street, in which either by dint of the building's highly regular structure or because of some strong egalitarian streak in the Forestry and Environmental Studies faculty, there is almost no such hierarchy visible.

74. Hammond Hall and Seeley G. Mudd Library

Hammond Hall
W. Gedney Beatty, 1904; demolition, 2009
Seeley G. Mudd Library
Roth & Moore, 1982

This entry is retained from the first edition, not to sow confusion but to remind readers that the Yale campus is still a work in progress, a place of ongoing difficult architectural decisions.

On lower Mansfield Street, tucked out of sight, are two buildings that do not deserve to be as out of mind as they now seem to be. Because of their contents—

Hammond Hall

Hammond Hall, afar from other Arts buildings, housed studios for the sculpture department, and Mudd contains books and publications infrequently requested at Sterling, or for which other campus libraries no longer have space—there is seldom reason for most students and faculty to make a trip there. The long north face of Mudd's quietly elegant brick and concrete block turns Winchester Avenue's traffic (now much less heavy than in the glory days of the eponymous Arms Company) into Sachem Street, the cross street over to Prospect, Hillhouse, and Whitney. In so doing it forms an urban eddy where once the roistering Hammond could be discovered; Mudd now backs up to the quiet, overgrown banks of the old canal cut.

Mudd clearly owes something to its architects' memories of the old brick laboratory buildings for the Sheffield Scientific School, by J. C. Cady, and to their admiration of Louis Kahn. The quiet, urbane massing, careful, flush articulation of frame and cladding, and the corner entry, assert that, besides fulfilling its programmatic purpose, the building is an homage to the Center for British Art.

Seeley G. Mudd Library

The bumped-up massing of three stories to four in front, and the abstract reminiscences of *cheneaux* (small ornamental cornice elements) on its parapet, show Mudd's consciousness of Hammond, its old neighbor. Inside, the building's north-facing reading room is one of Yale's most pleasant contemporary spaces.

Hammond was built in 1904 as the Metallurgical Laboratory for the Sheffield Scientific arm of the University. In good Beaux-Arts typological reportage, the massing revealed classrooms and offices in the palazzo block on the street, and a big train-shed-like high space with smelters, forges, and other heavy

equipment at the back, adjacent to what, when the building was constructed, was an active railroad line. The architect, W. Gedney Beatty, at a guess, was picking up on the lead of the Bicentennial Buildings, but heated things up with some demonstrative contrasts of brick and stone, and, again, an announcement of function in the hammer motif in the splendid copper cornice. The donor, John Hays Hammond, a Sheff Scientific graduate, was an associate of Cecil Rhodes in South African mining enterprises. Even if the Sculpture Department knew of that origin in 1970, when, fortuitously, the building became available to the refugees from the burned-out A&A Building (Becton Lab had just taken over for Hammond), not even the most politically conscious student chose to say anything, given the prospect of getting this sort of space. Although chopped up for individual studios, the grandeur of the volume under the shed could still be sensed.

Hammond Hall was demolished in 2009 and Mudd Library is scheduled for demolition to make way for new residential colleges. Their fate was sealed when their sites became considered central to the campus.

75. New Residential Colleges
Robert A. M. Stern Architects, 2015, projected (LEED Gold targeted)

The University's decision to expand the undergraduate student body for the first time since Yale College became coeducational in 1970 is momentous. It dominoes out into a wide variety of consequences for the campus and its character, not to speak of the need to enlarge the faculty and perhaps revisit the curriculum. The two new colleges to accommodate the enlarged number of undergrads will arguably be the most important new buildings Yale has constructed since A. Whitney Griswold, Yale's president fifty years ago, oversaw the University's wave of notable new modernist buildings, including Stiles and Morse of 1962, the last pair of new colleges. (An attempt to build the thirteenth and fourteenth colleges at the northwest corner of Whitney Avenue and Grove Street, to a design by Romaldo Giurgola, was repelled by the City in 1973.) The buildings Robert A. M. Stern, dean of the School of Architecture since 1999, and his firm are designing will be significant for Yale principally because they will culminate the attempt to better knit the campus together by creating a linked set of new buildings along the north side of the Farmington Canal, an area long thought of as behind Grove Street Cemetery. (In real estate analysis terms, the area has been "shaded" by the cemetery from the activity of the central campus and downtown New Haven.) The fact that Stern's large new colleges are shaped and styled in homage to James Gamble Rogers's Gothic of the 1920s and 1930s is interesting and mildly controversial, but less important than the potential shift in the University's psychological center of gravity and sense of its own balance and integration.

New Residential Colleges, rendering

The most immediately striking consequence of the new colleges is demolition (or disassembly) of around a dozen buildings to clear room for them. These include structures dating from several eras in New Haven architectural history, from historic houses to a recent, well-regarded, prefabricated modular temporary structure designed by Centerbrook Architects. The most significant buildings to go down are Hammond Hall and Seeley G. Mudd Library, both of which were well designed and constructed, hard working, and of proven flexibility. The demolitions, needless to say, do not sit well with preservationists. There is some loud sentiment voiced that Yale is arrogantly and needlessly adopting the mindset that, in the 1950s, excused so much destruction of history in New Haven in the name of renewal.

Besides the big gamble of building behind the cemetery in the first place, Yale is betting on Stern's buildings being good enough to make people forget the losses, assuming they knew and cared about them in the first place. Stern, as knowledgeable about Yale's history as any architect working on the campus since Rogers, can argue with good evidence that this is just Yale once more destroying part of its fabric in order to remake itself in some way more like it was originally. Yale's aboriginal Typological impulse (see introduction) is again served.

Beyond whether the new location is judged acceptable for student living, the test of whether that idea of Type repetition works in reality will likely come in the issue of whether the new colleges are simply too large and functionally specialized to be coherent, architecturally and socially. Each is more or less the size of Silliman, currently the biggest college, but arranged around multiple smaller courtyards rather than Silliman's large, subtly subdivided one. The larger footprints Stern was asked to plan for are the result of escalation over the decades, not only in what size rooms students expect to live in, but in the sheer number and variety of educational and recreational amenities now regarded as essential. If the idea behind the college system was to make going to a growing Yale once again an experience of living and studying in a small, close-knit community, everyone knowing everyone, then it is to be hoped that the ambitious program Yale has handed Stern does not prove too large and elaborate to provide that unifying experience.

The University and its architects are certainly doing everything they can think of to make sure the new colleges are coherent and feel connected to other colleges and the Old Campus. The architectural renderings capably emulate the style of Otto Eggers's drawings for John Russell Pope's famous 1919 Plan for the campus. There is a central pedestrian passage between the colleges almost embarrassingly riffing on Library Walk, between Branford and Jonathan Edwards, with features quoting Berkeley thrown in. Stern and his colleagues have strategically placed two towers, one for each college (at the time of writing), to wigwag back to Harkness Tower, signaling the fact of the colleges' existence back along Prospect Street and, an ominous portent to some, down the central axis of the cemetery.

76. Former School of Organization and Management

52 Hillhouse Avenue (Steinbach Hall)
Henry Austin, 1849
56 Hillhouse Avenue (Thomas M. Evans Hall)
A. J. Davis, 1837
60 Sachem Street (Watson Center)
Gordon Bunshaft of Skidmore, Owings & Merrill, 1961
135 Prospect Street (Founders Hall)
pre-1882; Andrew F. Euston, 1956
Additions and alterations
Edward L. Barnes, 1978

Coming around the corner of Prospect and Sachem streets, going back up the slight rise to *Modern Head*, one encounters Yale's premier architectural palimpsest. Appropriately enough it houses the School of Management; none of the School's courses could ever offer a better case study in melding disparate tendencies toward a single purpose than its own buildings. Edward Larrabee Barnes's early (1978) demonstration of adaptive use knitted together structures of high and low historical interest as well as high and low degrees of stylistic standoffishness.

The Apthorp and Norton Houses (see Hillhouse Avenue Houses) are distinguished pieces of Yale's and New Haven's architectural heritage. Of different but real worth is 135 Prospect Street, which deserves mention and respect for the odd but important duties it has helped perform. The "unpretentious little brick structure just north of North Sheffield Hall, on Prospect Street," as it was described

Former School of Management

in 1882, was a little observatory from which, under a contract with the State, "the College daily transmit(ted) the exact time to every railroad station in Connecticut." Similarly, it housed a "thermometric bureau," to which temperature-measuring devices could be sent for certification that they conformed to a single standard.

Less glamorous than the College Clock on the Athenaeum tower in the Old Brick Row, the building nonetheless is equally part of the story of the standardization of the country's means and methods of measurements—a story central to the history of American science and technology, certainly, but also of medicine and, appropriately enough, business. The central part of the SOM frontage on Sachem Street is occupied by a glass and dark gray aluminum structure of Miesian mien, designed by Gordon Bunshaft of Skidmore, Owings & Merrill in 1961, two years before he produced Beinecke Library. As originally built it was even more aloof from its surroundings than Beinecke, floating on a recessed white base in a shallow moat of white marble chips. The building was named in honor of the Watson family, of IBM, and was the University's first purpose-built computer center. And also perhaps its last; the machines quickly became first larger and more demanding, then smaller and more pervasive. The University's major computer center in 1968 moved into a rehabbed 1924 building at 175 Whitney Avenue, the new Management School was given the Bunshaft building in 1977, and the Watson name has now moved down Prospect to dignify the adaptively reused former Sheffield Chem. It took less than a decade for 60 Sachem Street to become outmoded; a building created in the image of new technology could not keep up with the complex reality of it.

77. School of Management / Edward P. Evans Hall
Foster + Partners with Gruzen Samton Architects, 2013, projected
(LEED Gold targeted)

From existing in the most cobbled-together architectural setting of any major program on campus, in old houses along Hillhouse Avenue and Prospect and Sachem streets, the School of Management with its new Edward P. Evans Hall has gone to the other extreme, in keeping with the schools at peer institutions. Its elements are here condensed into a blocky structure whose only massing rivals in the university system are Sterling Memorial Library and Payne Whitney Gymnasium, or perhaps the former Richard C. Lee High School now serving the School of Nursing. With its long face to Whitney Avenue, and a central open-air courtyard on the axis of Sachem Street, the building reaches deep into the unusually large block between Bradley and Humphrey streets; the block was once one property, the Wayland estate, for which the appealing mid-1850s cottage at 135 Prospect served as a gatehouse.

Prior to discussion of the architectural character and merits of Lord Norman Foster's design, two questions must be asked. First, is the sheer size (242,000 square feet) of this structure testimony to the hold the banking and finance industry

Edward P. Evans Hall, rendering

has—or at least had prior to the post-2007 Great Recession—on the American and world economy? Edward P. Evans, Class of 1964 donor for whom the building is named, was a horseman and breeder, not a financier, but the question is almost obligatory given the current state of national finances. This book, though, is not really the place to consider whether this is *de facto* Wall Street's embassy at Yale. (It is, however, for the second question: why here?) The building represents a giant step across Whitney Avenue into a neighborhood made up mostly of small older houses and genial minor office buildings. Why here and not, for one possibility, on medical campus land near the train station, a literal direct line to Wall Street? Surely a building as impressive as Foster's would have made, if nothing else, a great advertisement for the University in the old heart of New Haven, with convenient access via train to the business centers of Boston and New York.

One can surmise that the answer is simply inertia and a large Yale-owned site. The School of Management faculty and students are used to being on this end of campus, have worked out their parking privileges and commuting routines, and like the environment. If that is the case, good for them. But that operational model for a school of management seems better suited to the 1970s, when corporations built large suburban headquarters office campuses, than to the early twenty-first century, with corporations like Aetna, Union Carbide, and Schlumberger—just to name three

Connecticut examples—now abandoning and even tearing down such formerly prized trophies.

Leaving the two questions aside, the School of Management's new home does a variety of things to soften its bulk and create architectural interest. It is light colored and massed as a collection of sub-buildings beneath a unifying roof, the latter supported by a vertically proportioned high colonnade. One will be able to sense from outside the lightening provided by the aforementioned central courtyard, which is of a size and wall height close to those of the much-loved fountain courtyard on the north side of the Sterling Library nave.

Lord Norman Foster, whose practice is based in London, has designed distinguished structures around the globe, perhaps first among equals the renovation and new dome for Berlin's Reichstag. Evans Hall is a homecoming to New Haven for Foster, who earned his MArch degree at Yale in 1962, under Paul Rudolph, at the very beginning of his career. Le Corbusier was of course the preeminent architect of that day, but in America, Edward Durell Stone was getting a lot of attention with thin-columned, elegant boxes like the 1959 American Embassy in New Delhi. The new building will certainly be of a quality commensurate with the rest of Foster's Pritzker Prize–winning œuvre, the latter now extensive enough that its arc can be thought about with some justice. There is an old observation that as architects age they unconsciously emulate, but then correct, the heroes of their youth. Evans Hall has more than a few features in common with some of Stone's prominent commissions, both the Indian embassy and the 1971 Kennedy Center in Washington for instance. But if something of Stone is lurking just at the edge of Foster's design consciousness here, the influence is stiffened and heroicized by a memory of the north facade of Le Corbusier's High Court building in Chandigarh, also in India. That building, too, features a single high roof sheltering a regular march of structure and asymmetrical secondary masses. Courts, embassies, cultural centers; Evans Hall's affinities, if this is an accurate reading, are cause for reflection on the blurring line between public and private institutions in the twenty-first century.

78. John North House (158 Whitney Avenue)
Sidney Mason Stone, 1836; addition, 1909

10 Sachem Street renovation and addition
Tai Soo Kim Partners, 2007

Back across Whitney Avenue, Tai Soo Kim, another Yale-educated architect and near contemporary of Foster with a distinguished international record, has done yeoman work in renovating and adding onto the 1836 John North House for the Department of Anthropology. The North House should really be thought of as part of the Hillhouse Avenue collection of historic houses, though there is no surviving

Sachem Renovation and Addition

record that Ithiel Town, from his residence down the street, had any hand in the design. More than any other house of the era in the neighborhood, though, the

North House looks like a lost piece of Karl Friedrich Schinkel's early-nineteenth-century work in Potsdam, outside Berlin. There is something of the same measured balance and lightness beneath a bold, abstract cornice plane. Kim's work has often shared those qualities, so it is interesting and good to see a determinedly contemporary designer well matched to historic structure. This was a project in which much of the work, such as a new basement inserted below the house and a large rear addition, became simple backdrop upon completion, leaving the old house as a renewed intensification of itself.

Roy Lichtenstein's Modern Head *(1974, 1989)*

WALK EIGHT: SCIENCE HILL AND THE DIVINITY SCHOOL

In 1802 Yale President Timothy Dwight surprised young Ben Silliman (1779–1864), a recent graduate about to embark on a law career, with news that he had been appointed to the newly founded professorship of Chemistry and Mineralogy. Dwight announced it with certainty and rightness, even inevitability, as though he had been given special knowledge of what a Calvinist God had foreordained for Silliman. Whatever the source of his insight, Dwight, the great preacher and descendent of Jonathan Edwards, had his man. Silliman spent a long, distinguished career pursuing research and teaching in the basements, attics, and backyard buildings of the Old Brick Row. The space allocated to the sciences reflected the Yale hierarchies; Silliman's work was background for that of the traditional "Discipline and Piety" curriculum, strongly grounded in Greek, Latin, and Hebrew, and taught in the premium spaces of the Row buildings. Even Silliman added his own essay on the role of religion in the sciences, called "Coincidence of Geology with Sacred History," to his edition of a geology textbook. Silliman read nature as Dwight did the Bible, and the buildings of what might as well have been called Silliman Row floated like tugs behind and beside the larger vessels of the Row itself.

During the same years, another Dwight student and protégé, Nathaniel W. Taylor, was teaching the "New Haven Theology" in the Divinity department, formally founded in 1822. In 1835, Divinity was accorded the left-handed compliment of its own new building at the north end of the Brick Row. Taylor's teachings apparently disturbed more traditional alumni enough to affect their donations, so housing his department in a separate structure both gave it distinction and separated it. Yale behaved spatially and architecturally, then, not only to delineate hierarchies, as with Silliman, but also to define the relation of explicit doctrinal teaching to its core curriculum. These two instances foreshadow later patterns of university planning generated by two paired, but opposite, movements within the College's curriculum and the University's balance of power. Generalization though it may be, it is accurate to say that the push to bring science and technology into Yale, and the struggle to push religion out, strongly affected the shape of the campus as it is today. The walk around Science Hill, and from there up to the Divinity School, carries that as its continuous subtext.

The buildings on this walk are sited where they are because of a linked sequence of curricular and spatial events. In 1847 a Department of Philosophy and the Arts, forerunner of both the Graduate School and of the Scientific School, is founded, taking up quarters in the superannuated President's House on the Campus; then, upon obtaining the strong support of Joseph

Earl Sheffield, for whom in 1861 it was renamed, the Scientific School begins to develop its own faculty and curriculum, student body, and set of buildings on lower Hillhouse Avenue and Prospect Street. Meantime, the Divinity program has become moribund, and Divinity College is knocked down for the sake of making room for Durfee; the program is saved almost single-handedly by Timothy Dwight, a Divinity professor and grandson of the first Dwight, and new buildings are put up to house Divinity across Elm from the College on the site of Calhoun College. Rivalries develop between Sheff and the College, and programs and classes are duplicated between them. Buildings for both programs take up resources and increasingly scarce land. In the first and second decades of this century, the property now called Science Hill is acquired from the Hillhouse estate, with the idea of using it for science buildings and housing to be shared by the two programs. In the course of major University-wide reforms in the early 1920s, Sheff and the College are folded together, resulting in a larger student body, which in turn greatly helps precipitate the transformation of the central campus almost exclusively into a collection of undergraduate colleges and classroom buildings for teaching the liberal arts. Yale College's science buildings are knocked down for a college; Divinity, its center-campus land also coveted for the college system, is persuaded to move up Prospect Street by the promise of a beautiful new setting. The overall result is a University split between a central area with student housing and the liberal arts, and a northern quarter of science buildings with a dormitory, ironically, only for the Divinity School.

79. David S. Ingalls Rink

Eero Saarinen, 1958

The "Yale Whale" is a spectacular modern building beached in an unlikely tidepool, neither truly on the Yale campus nor part of the neighborhood of working-class, triple-decker houses it adjoins. (It was to have been connected by an unbuilt ring-road to Payne Whitney Gymnasium.) Even though Louis Kahn's Art Gallery attracted a good deal of attention when it opened in 1953, it was really Eero Saarinen's design for the hockey rink that awakened the world to the fact that staid, traditionalist Yale, under the presidency of A. Whitney Griswold (1951–1962), had embarked on a major modern building program. Kahn's building presented a subtle, near-blank wall to puzzle the uninitiated, while by contrast Saarinen's broadcast a message of exhilarating innovation as loud as a Chuck-Yeager-piloted experimental jet breaking the sound barrier.

David S. Ingalls Rink

Forty years later Ingalls still catches the attention. It has proven over time that Saarinen's sculptural styling of a deceptively simple structural premise is more than the architectural equivalent of late 1950s automobile tail fins. As the largest hall on campus (3,000 spectators for athletic events, more than 5,000 when the arena floor is also used), the Whale has been the backdrop to sports dramas and real-life ones. Perhaps most notable among the latter was the series of tense, public meetings during the Black Panther trial of spring 1970, after one of which a bomb exploded in the north end of the Rink. Miraculously, there were no deaths, and the highly strung structure rang and held.

The Yale hockey team of the early 1950s had rented out the now long vanished New Haven Arena for practice and games—no formula for beating Harvard. Juan Trippe, chairman of Pan American Airways and a member of the Yale Corporation, suggested Eero Saarinen was the designer to produce a sufficiently sensational structure. Yale-educated (BA 1934), newly emerging as a favorite architect of the Eisenhower-era military-industrial complex (General Motors Technical Center, 1949; American Embassy in London, 1956), previously vetted

David S. Ingalls Rink addition

on-campus work (Drake, Vassar, MIT), Saarinen was also a veteran of World War II in the Office of Strategic Services, forerunner of the Central Intelligence Agency, a fact perhaps not lost on Corporation members Dean Acheson and McGeorge Bundy.

The strategy Saarinen found for the Rink had both good Yale precedent and radical ancestry. On the ground, earth was simply excavated and piled up around the edge of the hole to form a crater of seating, in exact miniature repetition of the technique used in the 1914 Yale Bowl. In the sky, to cover this little neo-bowl, Saarinen conceived a central arch-spine from which roof-support cables could be hung laterally. Lower in proportion, the arch was close kin to the architect's 1948 design for the St. Louis Arch, and both were based in the architect's knowledge of similar heroically scaled arches of the 1920s and 1930s by pioneering Russian and Italian modern architects. While the idea of the design came fairly quickly, its exact sculptural treatment and the painstaking technical evolution took considerable time, worry, and money. The single most critical decision, which gave the building its graceful liftoff, was to jut structurally useless neck and tail pieces from the basic concrete arch span; these turn the exterior gesture of the overall profile back up toward the sky, while the invisible concrete inside, which is really doing the work, nose-dives into the ground.

Ingalls Rink was extensively renovated in 2009, with a mostly underground addition to the west, by Kevin Roche John Dinkeloo and Associates. The Varsity Team Center accommodates much improved facilities for both men's and women's hockey teams, masking them with a curving glass block, pitched glass, and a sculpted concrete screen in gentle emulation of the Whale's side wall. It is only just that Kevin Roche and his firm, as successors to Eero Saarinen, would be architects of the extension.

80. Osborn Laboratories, Pierson-Sage Plant, and Sage-Bowers Hall

Osborn Memorial Laboratories
Charles C. Haight, 1914
Pierson-Sage Boiler and Refrigeration Plant
Charles C. Haight, 1913
Sage-Bowers Hall
William A. Delano, Delano & Aldrich, 1924

The first two of these three structures are representative of the hardworking, mostly unglamorous crowd of buildings still in service from Yale's turn-of-the-century version of Gothic (1895–1915). They get little respect either for age, like Dwight Hall (Old Library) of 1842–46, or for picturesque appeal, like Memorial Quadrangle of 1916–1921. It might be called techno-Gothic, since it was favored for the Sheffield Scientific School and for early Yale buildings on Science Hill; yet Linsly Hall of 1907 on the Old Campus is as much a group member as Leet Oliver of 1908 at Sheff. All are quite spare on the exterior, mostly built out of an

Osborn Laboratories

unsexy, monochrome brownstone, with tough, serviceable interior spaces, which over decades have proven fairly adaptable. Osborn was the second Yale structure built on the former Hillhouse estate grounds (Sloane Physics Laboratory preceding it by a year), and it had the job not only of providing laboratory, classroom, and office space, but of accommodating itself to a site still dominated by the 1828 A. J. Davis-designed Hillhouse mansion, Sachem's Wood. Charles Haight, Osborn's architect, by this time was expert at making Yale entrances, having previously designed Vanderbilt, Phelps, Van-Sheff (see Silliman College), and a number of memorial gateways. Here he provided his boldest variant on the same type-theme, altering proportions and topping the paired corner towers flanking the gateway with battlement crenellations in an obvious homage to Davis's recently demolished (1911) Alumni Hall (see Skull and Bones). He also placed Osborn's gate-piece at an angle to the street corner, recognizing that students approaching would see Davis's building on axis up the hill ahead of them. It was a symbolic buttoning-back of the Science campus to the Old Campus.

Seen from Prospect, Sage Hall is usually noticed for the imaginative indignities dreamed up by Forestry students for the stone woodsman attending the front door. It is a blocky structure front and back, opened in early 1924, with Bowers appended without much ceremony in the rear in 1931. This was the first building built explicitly for the School of Forestry, which had become increasingly cramped inside its original quarters in Marsh Hall, the old Othniel Marsh house, just up the street. Sage-Bowers's exterior spareness is even more pronounced than in the C. C. Haight buildings next door, but, as usual with William A. Delano's work, there are surprises inside. The Bowers auditorium, for example, is a reserved but graceful space. Delano (1874–1960) was an architect of considerable versatility and good social connections, producing Yale buildings ranging in character from the uptight Wright Hall to the open, subtle Divinity School, and elsewhere working on buildings as diverse as the first LaGuardia Airport Terminal and the White House.

81. Kroon Hall

Hopkins Architects with Centerbrook Architects, 2009 (LEED Platinum)

Kroon Hall, built for the School of Forestry & Environmental Studies, set out to be Yale's most ecologically responsible building ever. It reached that goal (although KieranTimberlake's Sculpture Building was the first LEED Platinum building in the state of Connecticut), and did so with a structure that is much more than a flat-footed technical and ethical achievement; this is very fine architecture, managing to flout expectations and affirm traditions at the same time. In a time when climate and environmental management are together a very large scientific, political, and economic issue, Kroon Hall guarantees that Yale and its graduates will be central to its discussion.

Kroon is on the site of the old Pierson-Sage Boiler and Refrigeration Plant, which served Science Hill since Yale began building there in the early twentieth century. It was rendered superfluous by new lines brought up from the central campus plant. With only a narrow frontage westward to Prospect Street, and a considerable drop from Sage-Bowers to the north down to Osborn Memorial Laboratories on the south, the site was not an easy one. Hopkins Architects, from England, with Centerbrook Architects, noted that Sage-Bowers and Osborn are set much closer to the street than the other Prospect Street buildings further up the Hill, the larger setback starting with Sloane Physics Laboratory just north of Sage-Bowers. By dropping a simple rectangle of building into the slot behind where the power plant had been, set back from Prospect the same distance as Sloane, three exterior courtyards of different sizes, levels, and purposes could be formed: a small public entry court

Kroon Hall

facing west; a medium-size private court shared with Sage-Bowers, Forestry & Environmental Studies' home base, on the north; and a semipublic large court on the south, shared with Osborn and entered via its diagonal tower. If grace is defined as an economy of means to multiple ends, Kroon Hall quietly exhibits a very graceful strategy indeed.

Within the rectangular perimeter set by that basic idea, the architects designed a long east-west building form that defies two long-standing conventions of solar orientation: do not orient glass walls east or west because of the high heat gain from the lower sun angle in those directions, and make roof pitches asymmetrical to take advantage of the difference between north and south solar exposure. Kroon Hall instead is symmetrical in cross section and glassy toward the setting sun. The latter makes for the round-shouldered, muscular, hooded presence of the building, and the former provides the excuse for an abstract wooden sunscreen that looks like some sort of ritual matchstick mask.

Inside, the building stacks a couple of levels of classrooms and offices on a linear central stair and hallway, saving the warm, wood-vaulted top level for a library and auditorium. Curving laminated wood structural bents, spaced with utter regularity, combined with the exterior stone cladding, lend it the air of an enormous traditional communal building, like an English tithe barn radically updated in its technology for a restive twenty-first century. Intentional or not, that character comports well with the public-mindedness of the Forestry & Environmental Studies program.

More locally and eerily, Kroon Hall also evokes Yale's Old Brick Row. Look at the building from the south and imagine the roundish, draped roof changed to a very similar gambrel. Notice the window pattern alternating between three longer sections of identical vertical windows and two shorter sections centered on front-facing square windows. It takes only a bit of soft squinting to see Connecticut Hall in the center, with two of its long-vanished Brick Row brethren on either side. The common denominators are practicality, respect for repetition, and idealism about a civic educational mission.

82. Silliman Statue, Sloane Physics Laboratory, and Sterling Chemistry Laboratory

Benjamin Silliman Statue
John Ferguson Weir, 1884
Sloane Physics Laboratory
Charles C. Haight, 1912
Sterling Chemistry Laboratory
William A. Delano, Delano & Aldrich, 1923

Benjamin Silliman Statue

When the statue of the great Yale scientist and academic entrepreneur Benjamin Silliman (1779–1864) was unveiled in 1884, there was considerable criticism, much of it to the effect that it made a big, heavy man look even bigger and heavier. It proved in fact to be light on its feet, moving around the campus in a route that marks Yale's centers of sciences. It stood first in front of Farnam Hall on the Old Campus, commemorating the work Silliman did in the laboratories in the old President's House on that site before Farnam came along. Weir, head of the School of Art, modeled Silliman in a pose, in garb, and on a pedestal all very like those of Launt Thompson's nearby Abraham Pierson Statue of 1874. Pierson's Puritan figure holds a book, presumably a Bible, while Silliman, in a long greatcoat, holds a mineral specimen. The message of Weir's work near Thompson would have been clear: both men traveled far to read and teach the word of God, as found in what they held in hand. Pierson worked from Scripture, Silliman from Nature.

The Silliman statue then migrated to a position in front of the Library's (now Dwight Hall's) south wing, actually closer to its Pierson mate, then standing next to the School of Art in Street Hall. Some unknown time later, it took up a different post between the College's first buildings for scientific research and teaching, Kent Lab of 1887–88, and Sloane Lab of 1882–83, on land now occupied by Jonathan Edwards College. In 1922, with the consolidation of a Yale science campus serving both Sheff and the College well underway, Silliman was moved to the side of Sterling Chemistry Lab, then in construction, the vantage point he has held since. The location must have seemed less out of the way then than now, since it commanded the drive up to Sachem's Wood, the old Hillhouse mansion.

Sloane Physics Lab of 1912 is another of Charles Coolidge Haight's reserved pieces of techno-Gothic. It was given by the same good-natured donor who funded an earlier 1882–83 Sloane Lab next to the Old Campus; in 1912 that building was taken over for the popular, softer sciences of psychology, economics, and sociology, and the physical sciences and their students trekked north to Science Hill. Haight's building, like his others at Yale, exhibits the high-quality but deadpan stylistic details that distract the viewer from noticing how he made something interesting out of a serious contextual problem. Sloane shows an ambition eventually to hook up with Osborn, to form a kind of science college with a courtyard, and to do this despite the considerable site elevation differences. This would have been several years prior to the beginning of Memorial Quadrangle, well before Yale was used to the idea of living life entirely closed off from city streets, on courtyards.

Sterling Chemistry Lab, a large, low building on Prospect Street, disguises itself as a bumpy, picturesque series of smaller structures. Despite the size, this is a much more freewheeling building than one might have expected, at least at this date from the old Yale regular, William Adams Delano. The architectural language is slightly peculiar, dry early-twentieth-century Gothic now pushed toward who-knows-quite-what—perhaps Baltic Renaissance; ornamental brick corbel tables appoint the upper facade, and the chimney-pot-topped "exhaust stacks" are the sort of mechanical-services-as-sculpture one normally thinks of as coming only much later in the century. Most of the interior is plain lab space, topped by a sawtooth factory roof, but the high, transverse hall inside the south entrance is a grand, if dark, room.

83. Kline Biology Tower and Kline Chemistry Laboratory

Kline Biology Tower and Library
Philip Johnson, 1965
Kline Chemistry Laboratory
Philip Johnson, 1964

Yale had a clear agenda in its late-1950s and early-1960s building activity on Science Hill. It was, as President Whitney Griswold said, to ensure that Yale science had facilities "second to none in quality." The three Kline buildings addressed that agenda. Architect Philip Johnson (1906–2005), had an extra one or two goals of his own. Even as he was showing himself a so-so student of Louis Kahn's Richards Medical Buildings at Penn with the "ductitecture" of the Yale

Kline Biology Tower

Laboratory for Epidemiology and Public Health, down at the medical end of campus, Johnson on Science Hill was inventing postmodern architectural historicism. Less than a decade after his work with Mies van der Rohe on the Seagram Building, Johnson produced here what is arguably the first referential

Kline Biology Tower

tall building of the post–World War II era. With massing pinched in at the corners in the fashion of early-1930s Rockefeller Center slabs, in order to get more dramatically vertical end elevations, and with a vocabulary of stone spandrels and round brick piers making reference to the fortified late-thirteenth-century cathedral at Albi, France, Kline Biology Tower hinted at a new-old agenda for American architecture. When postmodernism has its history definitively written, Kline Tower ought certainly to figure into it.

The building's status in architectural history has done little for the working lives of the scientists in it. Complaints abound: the floor plate is too small and inflexible in layout; the bracing is insufficient to keep sensitive instruments from registering useless readings when the wind gusts up, and so on. Fitful consideration has even been given to such alternatives as turning Kline Tower into graduate student housing. Difficulties acknowledged, the building undeniably does certain things well. The idea for a hilltop courtyard on Science Hill predated Johnson, but his cantilevered-slab U colonnade, with the Tower inside the court but off-center, provides a sculpturally powerful terminus for Hillhouse Avenue and a modicum of weather protection. The chunky round columns that are the leitmotiv of the three Kline buildings give the Tower's base the grandeur of an Egyptian hypostyle hall. The courtyard-lit underground Library and the top-floor cafe, with its views, deserve visits.

Outside the colonnade but nearby, hooked at both ends onto the north face of Sterling Chemistry, is Kline Chemistry Lab of 1964. It is interesting to compare the brick cylinder and stone spandrel motif as used on this two-story building with its configuration on the Biology Tower's fourteen. In the Chemistry version, the piers are wider apart and even irregular in rhythm. While different structural and environmental considerations apply to the two buildings, it is really their urbanistic prominence that is being gauged. Johnson seems to have decided that the further from public view a building is, the more it can afford to let up a bit on the stiff upper architectural lip.

84. Gibbs Laboratories, Wright Laboratory, Pierson-Sage Garage, and Nancy Lee and Perry R. Bass Center for Molecular and Structural Biology

Josiah Willard Gibbs Laboratories
Paul Schweikher, 1955
Arthur W. Wright Nuclear Structure Laboratory
Douglas Orr, de Cossy, Winder & Associates, 1964
Pierson-Sage Parking Garage
G. B. H. Macomber Company, 1974
Nancy Lee and Perry R. Bass Center for Structural Biology
Kallman McKinnell & Wood, 1995

Gibbs Laboratory is named to honor the great, reclusive Yale professor of mathematical physics, Josiah Willard Gibbs. The building has more of its namesake's quiet traits than his greatness. (Yale, inadvertently to be sure, seems inclined to the left-handed compliment with respect to Gibbs; an inscription on the garden wall of the Berkeley College master's house records the fact that his house was knocked down to make way for the College.) This is not to say that Gibbs is a bad or uninteresting building, simply that it is reticent in the extreme and that, while its virtues are several, they fall into the category of self-control and deferred gratification. Gibbs was one of the earliest of Yale's Modern buildings, opening in 1955 not long after Kahn's better known Art Gallery extension. It was designed by Paul Schweikher (1903–1997), who was chairman of the Yale architecture department from 1953 to 1956.

Gibbs rides the edge of the Science Hill plateau, working with the east faces of Sloane and Sterling Labs to define the sides of the stage that Kline Tower eventually stepped in to occupy; the Bass Center more recently provided the stage backdrop. With its close-set columns, uniform curtain wall, and expressed roof slab, Gibbs is unmistakably an attenuated classical stoa, thin but still quite capable of defining the agora space in front of it. The stoa's repetitive market stalls bespeak the architect's ideas of the Lab interior; quite simply, undifferentiated,

flexible space, ordered by the yard. It is impressive for its sheer disciplined repetition rather than its detail, and in that sense is a legitimate heir to the Old Brick Row.

The northern limit of Science Hill is set by Edwards Street, which edges down from Prospect Street to the flat, busy run of Whitney Avenue,

Gibbs Laboratories

Bass Center

the old 1798 turnpike which headed out to the Eli Whitney factory and on in a straight line to Hartford. The two Yale buildings holding down the Whitney-Edwards corner are almost unrecognizable as buildings, but seem more the slope-and-terrace remains of Mesoamerican temple-mounts, or outcrops of the Hill itself. The 1964 Wright Nuclear Structure Lab and the 1974 Pierson-Sage Parking structure, while perhaps a tad less romantic, are certainly impressive bunkers housing two American obsessions, atoms and autos.

Kallman-McKinnell's Bass Center for Structural Biology of 1995 picks up cues from its context in every direction, yet still manages to assert its own identity. It is long and thin like Gibbs Lab, enfronting the agora before it, but is less reluctant to draw attention, so its ridge line exhaust stacks punctuate the sky in a rhythmic order that exaggerates the chimney-pots of Sterling Chemistry's south facade. Cues from the latter building, too, inform the Tudoroid elements connecting the Bass Center to its neighbors at both ends. Seen from the east paired but opposed sloped roofs slip past each other to reveal the building's section in good orthodox functional fashion, and to announce the presence of a high-design public stair and entrance. The architects have claimed a focal position in whatever future construction occurs on the expanses of surface parking between the Hill and Whitney Avenue.

85. Class of 1954 Chemistry Research Building
Bohlin Cywinski Jackson, 2005 (LEED Silver)

On every campus certain buildings have significance out of proportion with their size. They mark edges and centers, entry and exit points, places of symbolic gathering. In the languages of countries that once fortified their towns, phrases like *hors les murs* came to describe not just a location but a social condition or state of mind.

Bohlin Cywinski Jackson seem to have taken and run with the fact that, north of the building site, the character of the streets subtly shifts, and freestanding "object buildings" predominate over ones that try to define the edges of streets

Chemistry Research Building

and blocks. Even though there are many Yale buildings beyond Edwards Street, they are outside invisible walls, *hors les murs*, outliers.

The Class of 1954 Chemistry Research Building, tongue firmly in picturesque cheek, styles its outside as a remnant of a fortification wall, complete with buttresses, crenellation, a dry moat, and a metal-gated entry arch facing Prospect Street that is deeply recessed in the manner of medieval gates with flanking towers to cover anyone approaching. There is even a projecting tourelle with a hint of the embrasures evolved to protect archers and crossbowmen. It is architectural make-believe in the manner of the Philip Johnson-designed Science Hill buildings which drew on motifs from the fortified cathedral at Albi, France, unexpectedly decorative in the same mode as the fine ornament on William Adams Delano's Sterling Chemistry Laboratory. In the Chemistry Research Building the play is a way of enlivening what is basically another long rectangular building that, like Kroon Hall, forms a fine courtyard with the preexisting building beside it, in this case Kline Chemistry Laboratory, one of the Johnson buildings.

The gate from Prospect Street is notable, another of the creations of the expert ornamental sculptor Kent Bloomer. In this instance the gate's motifs are elaborately allegorical, referring to aspects of synthetic organic chemistry, inorganic chemistry, and chemical biology, the three specializations within the laboratory, each of which has its own floor of the building. (The interior laboratory design, as intricate as the ornamental gate, was by Cannon Design.) Bloomer worked out the symbolism in collaboration with faculty.

86. Prospect Street Houses, Greeley Laboratory, and Mansfield Street Apartments

Betts House (former Davies Mansion)
Henry Austin and David R. Brown, 1868
276 Prospect Street, Old Yale Infirmary
J. C. Cady, 1892
Marsh Hall (360 Prospect Street)
J. C. Cady, 1878
310 Prospect Street, Schwab (President's) House
R. Clipston Sturgis, 1896
William B. Greeley Laboratory
Paul Rudolph, 1959
Mansfield Street Apartments (Married Student Housing)
Paul Rudolph, 1961

After the Civil War, New Haven's upper middle class and wealthy built large houses along Prospect Street, lining what had been a leisurely bridle path on the west shoulder of Prospect Hill's ridge line and the Hillhouse estate. Many of the houses remain, a number of them now owned by Yale and Albertus Magnus College farther out. Among the earliest, in 1868, was a mirror-image pair at 425 and 393 Prospect Street, upright and proud as General Grant steam engines, designed by Henry Austin for Oliver Winchester and his partner in the Winchester Repeating Arms Company, John Davies. The Winchester house was torn down to make way for a 1901–03 McKim, Mead & White house, which the Divinity School replaced in 1932. The Betts house has grand views in all directions, particularly over the sawtooth roofs of the former Winchester munitions factory—now Science Park—and out to West Rock's red mass.

Reliable Josiah Cady, architect of Sheffield Scientific buildings and the first Peabody Museum, in 1878 contributed the Othniel Marsh house at Prospect. He designed it for the Peabody's director, nephew of London-based American banker George Peabody, who willed this appealing stegosaurus to Yale in 1899. (Yale had already acquired a presence with two porch-rich wooden houses in 1882, at 459 and 477 Prospect, for the officers of the (guess the donor) Winchester Observatory; the Observatory survives as the core of the Day-Prospect School.) With the idea that ailing students could recover better in cleaner air away from central New Haven, Cady was called on again in 1892 to do the old Yale Infirmary at 276 Prospect, a taut-volumed, functionally fenestrated brick structure that matched the character and scale of the street's houses. If it is ironic to mention clean air in connection with a building whose front lawn today is completely filled with asphalt and cars, it is no less ironic to see the front of 310 Prospect reduced to the same condition. That house, built in 1896 by the elegant Boston architect R. Clipston Sturgis in the English half-timber mode, clearly gained no permanent respect by serving as Yale's President's House from 1920–23.

Another building that has fallen from grace is Paul Rudolph's Greeley Lab, built for the Forestry School on the grounds of the Marsh house below the mansion. As Rudolph's first Yale building, it opened to considerable and positive press coverage in 1959, four years before A&A. The architect's bent for inventive sculptural play with structural forms shows in the double-branching Y columns (standing for Yale, or representing trees, according to the standard campus oral tradition) and a concrete ceiling slab configured as a graph of its internal forces. Better-maintained than most of Rudolph's New Haven works, it is generally regarded by its occupants as outmoded and unworkable.

Rudolph's Mansfield Street Housing of 1960–61, designed for married students (and their children), has endured even harder wear than that from foresters and architects, yet has fared well over the years. Like Saarinen's Stiles and Morse Colleges, it shows the powerful pull away from the glass-box international version of Modern, which was then being exerted by the masonry hill towns of the Mediterranean.

87. Betts House Renovation and Addition
Vincent Benic Architects (exterior), 2000; Helpern Architects (interiors), 2002

Maurice R. Greenberg Conference Center
Robert A. M. Stern Architects, 2009 (LEED Gold)
Leitner Family Observatory and Planetarium
*David Thompson Architects, 2005 (observatory), 2009 (planetarium);
originally Roth Auditorium of the Culinary Institute of America,
Carlin-Millard Architects, 1959*

The buildings here tell the same story twice, in one larger and one smaller version. The plot is of decline, neglect, and finally respect and reuse in reminder of the good cause of wider vision.

Betts House (named in honor of the family of Roland Betts, an imaginative New York entrepreneur and former Senior Fellow of the Yale Corporation) was built in 1868 to the design of Henry Austin as the John M. Davies House, for a partner in Winchester Arms. It was a private residence until 1947, when it was bought by the Culinary Institute of America as a place to train restaurant chefs; Yale's dining halls were where many of them served apprenticeships. In 1972 the Institute pulled out of gritty New Haven in favor of a more bucolic location in the Hudson Valley, where it has since had good success. The old house fell, though, on still harder times, and was bought and boarded up by Yale. Its high visibility, the reciprocal of its having

Leitner Family Observatory and Planetarium

been built for the great views, made it the poster child for those inside and outside the university voicing concern for Yale's historic preservation record. In 2002 Helpern Architects, a New York firm with a lengthy preservation portfolio, finished renovating the mansion to house the Center for the Study of Globalization, the Office of International Affairs, and the World Fellows Program. Since guns and food are major international problems, Betts House now silently offers a kind of karmic hospitality to their discussion, along with other issues.

The Maurice R. Greenberg Conference Center complements Betts House's office and classroom capabilities with additional large-gathering and dining facilities. As large as the Davies/Betts structure, and with the need to connect to it, Greenberg's program had too many large spaces to treat it as a subsidiary building tailing out from the old house. Robert A. M. Stern and his partners instead set a large geometric block, with one super scaled opening, on a masonry plinth, its simplicity contrasting with the old house's Civil War-era complexity. Small-scale detail, stucco finishes, a curving glass connector like a conservatory, and a sympathetic color scheme then pulled the two buildings into being complementary visually as well as programmatically.

Slightly downhill from the road winding up to Betts and Greenberg, the little Leitner complex, designed by David Thompson Architects, amalgamates twin new observatory domes and a viewing terrace between them with an unpretentious, adaptively reused concrete block building now topped by a lower, larger dome

Betts House and Greenberg Conference Center

Betts House

marking the planetarium. (The original structure was designed by Carlin and Millard as an auditorium for the Culinary Institute.) The Observatory has a pair of historic nineteenth-century refracting telescopes (i.e., lens-, not mirror-based) as well as a larger contemporary reflecting scope. No less than its public statues (see Walk One), the places and travels of Yale telescopes are a wandering epic revealing the school's history in unexpected ways. The college's first major telescope was housed in an unlikely cylindrical canister set atop the tower of the Athenaeum, the Old Brick Row building once immediately south of Connecticut Hall—which is to say, central to Yale physically and intellectually. Winchester Arms profits paid not only for the Davies House but, in 1880, the school's first purpose-built observatory, demolished in the late twentieth century, a block north of the two new domes. It is good to know that the old telescopes are appreciated and in good company at a new home. Similarly, the flat-roofed, formerly neglected, now adaptively reused 1950s building that houses the planetarium has a simple geometric dignity that sets off the detail of the domes and their entry gateway in much the way Greenberg and Betts complement each other.

88. Divinity School (Sterling Divinity Quadrangle)
William A. Delano, Delano & Aldrich, 1932

It is not the purpose of this guide to weigh in on one side or another of the argument over the programmatic fit and preservation fate of the Divinity School's buildings.

Sterling Divinity Quadrangle

Visitors need only be informed that by the late 1990s some parts of the Sterling
Divinity Quadrangle of 1932 have been brought back from the deteriorated condition
in which an earlier, University-wide deferred maintenance policy had left them. Yale
has pledged to Divinity students and faculty, and to preservation groups inside and
outside the University, that it will conserve and "adaptively reuse" most elements
of the complex, leaving the Divinity School's classes and administration in place.
(It remains to be seen what the fate of the non-reused components will be.) The
controversy is intense because it goes much deeper and broader than the relatively
simple questions of whether the operation of the Yale School of Divinity today fits
well with a Depression-era set of structures, and whether the architecture is capable
and worthy of renovation.

The larger issues, too briefly, are these. First, the Divinity School case brings up
once again the broader policy (and real estate) matter of Yale's relations with New
Haven. Given the standard sorts of late-twentieth-century urban deterioration, should
Yale give up on Divinity, its northernmost buildings, pull back to a tighter campus
perimeter, and concentrate its resources? A subsidiary part of that problem is how
or whether Yale should relate to other forces, ranging from community groups to for-
profit developers, seeing their own uses for the buildings. Second, the case causes
people of all degrees of religious conviction to ask why Yale still has a Divinity School
at all, and, since it does, why it operates in such perceived isolation from Yale and the
city: Yale arrived in New Haven as an intensely Calvinist Congregational institution;
since then, religious education has become broader and physically has moved ever

farther from the center of campus. Third, because William Adams Delano's design owes much to earlier eras of architectural history, the case also prompts discussion of what weight is to be accorded to artistic originality as well as the nature of "originality" in the first place. There are other issues as well, but even these three coming together is an unusually bad piece of luck.

Back to the buildings: Delano executed commissions for a number of other Yale buildings and was one of the best-known and well-respected architects of his day. Even a brief look at the Divinity Quadrangle makes one understand why. The School's site planning shows a subtle but powerful relationship among site levels, program, and the image of the facility. The housing for 160 students, with two guest pavilions, was arranged on the gentler western slope, around six small courtyards opening off the common lawn. This maximized the feeling of a single, connected community, while maintaining variety and small scale. The living pavilions focus uphill toward the shared academic and religious facilities, the chapel, classrooms, and library. The court flattens and broadens in front of them, announcing this as the place of the common central work of the School. The remaining components—a common room, dining hall, and originally, a gymnasium, all large spaces—are a full level downhill to the east, taking advantage of the naturally steeper fall on that side to keep down the apparent scale of the whole and to allow the more symbolic elements visual dominance. Stylistically the Divinity School is a lovingly wrought piece of historical fiction, set in 1822, the year of the School's founding. A walk up Prospect and through the Divinity complex is highly recommended, both for enjoyment of the architecture and for reflection on its place, and its program's place, in a changing world.

Following much controversy over possible demolition, the Divinity Quadrangle was eventually comprehensively renovated by R. M. Kliment & Frances Halsband Architects in 2003. The buildings were saved and adaptively reused, though in places by methods at wince-inducing cross purposes to the original design.

89. Peabody Museum of Natural History and Kline Geology Laboratory

Peabody Museum of Natural History
Charles Z. Klauder, Day & Klauder, 1924
Kline Geology Laboratory
Philip Johnson, 1963

When the first Peabody Museum was torn down to make way for the Memorial Quadrangle, Othniel Marsh's dinosaur bones and the museum's massive collection went into storage for several years, until resurrected, again, in 1923–1924 in the present Peabody building. It is now the most visited building at Yale, an important

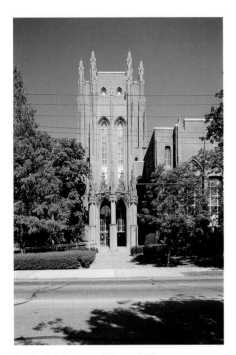

Peabody Museum of Natural History

contributor to area education and tourism, as well as providing significant research facilities with the expanded Class of 1954 Environmental Studies Center.

Perhaps stimulated by the Memorial Quadrangle's example, Yale's early-1920s Gothic in other quarters of the campus began to allow itself some spiky expressiveness. Charles Z. Klauder's design for the Peabody Museum is nearly contemporary with William A. Delano's for Sterling Chemistry Lab, for instance, though the Yale buildings with which it has the greatest affinity are Sterling Power Plant for the Medical School, and the Central Power Plant of 1918, now on Tower Parkway. The two power plants are also Day & Klauder works. The Klauder buildings share a dark brick and light stone trim combination not much found at Yale, and more importantly a great sense of how to dominate a corner site. The Peabody Museum puts up a very vertical tower on the corner of Whitney Avenue and Sachem Street, favoring Whitney because it is the busier street, and gives to it as well the flashy roadside ad of a flamboyant, bifurcated entry porch. But Sachem is hardly ignored, the axis of the sculptural public stair and a side wing carefully angled to recognize the side street. Even architecture buffs who come inside to see some interesting vaulting and experience the staircase should take some time with the collections and, of course, the outdated but still fabulous "Age of the Dinosaurs" mural, painted by Rudolph Zallinger in 1942–47.

The sea-green curtain walls, pressed concrete, and linoleum corridors of Douglas Orr's 1959 Bingham Oceanographic Lab were conceived to link Peabody visually with Gibbs Lab, higher up on the hill, and so to pull the museum into the sciences ensemble, Bingham Lab had neither the strength nor the explicit Peabody ties to pull that off and has since been demolished.

Kline Geology Lab of 1963, the slightly older sibling of the Kline Biology Tower, shows the same rounded-brick piers and stone spandrels applied to a three-story box. Geology is much thicker, with more brick infill wall between the wider-spaced piers. Kline also contains a lot of windowless rooms, as though study of the subject demanded an underground atmosphere. The attempt at compensation, a tall and off-center entry atrium, serves more as an orientation device for the long corridors than as a light source. The Lab's north face aligns with Gibbs Lab to make a route to the hilltop; Johnson, like Douglas Orr with the Oceanographic Lab, wanted to affiliate his building with the complex on top of the hill rather than the early-century buildings, Osborn Lab and its kin, the other side of the Hillhouse axis.

90. Class of 1954 Environmental Science Center
David M. Schwarz Architects, 2001

Until Stern's two new residential colleges are complete, the Environmental Science Center and the Chemistry Research Building, both funded in good part by the Class of 1954, will be the favorite Yale contemporary targets of architects, and even some real people, interested in reenacting the ancient Style Wars battles. In their eyes, traditional form is still an unforgivable offense against proper, "original" expression of the Spirit of the Time. The arguments from both sides are very familiar indeed; one wishes debates about originality could become more original. At the very least they distract from appreciation of the design intelligence in evidence, beyond style, in such buildings as this one—the ESC, as it is known.

If one grants that a walkable environment is a worthwhile goal based on criteria of human health and environmental sustainability, then the intelligence of presenting large, necessarily feature-poor, internally focused building uses (such as laboratories and storage) as smaller, more detailed, and more outgoing ones is a positive trait, not dissimulation. The ESC's motivation seems to have been just that. It is organized and presented to contribute to a more walkable, hence more sustainable, Yale campus.

Adjoining the Peabody Museum, and serving as its backstage support and research facility, the 100,000-square-foot ESC is actually larger than the 90,000-square-foot museum. The plan is organized to wrap an L of offices and classrooms around a blank big box of labs and storage, with a tower-marked corner entrance and adjoining stair at the angle. The seam between the two components is a skylit canyon into which walkways cantilever from the wrapper side. The layout is thus very much like that of the Luce Hall–Rosenkranz ensemble, by Koetter Kim & Asociates, around the corner on Prospect Street. ESC's and Rosenkranz's long facades are in fact very close in length, and they are the same number of stories. It makes an interesting thought experiment to compare the two in their urbanistic, stylistic, and internal functional success.

David Schwarz's octagonal corner tower defers, as it should, to the rather zippy one on the Peabody Museum, the public attraction side of the amalgam. Horizontal stringcourses and window rhythms tie the ESC tower firmly into the outside-facing L, but it still breaks upward in a way reminiscent of any number of corner-chamfered early-twentieth-century setback towers, an ancestral parade

Environmental Science Center

led by the much larger Tribune Tower in Chicago. Windows on the building's longer facade, clustered into groups by skinny buttresses, are graduated larger to smaller as the building rises to dormers and a false-front angled roof. The ESC's dormers and lean-to roof slim down its apparent bulk in a clever way; Vanderbilt Hall on the Old Campus does something similar, hiding the fact that it has a lot of flat roof up out of view. The ESC's brickwork is notably precise, with diagonally patterned, higher-fired headers and lighter stretchers—the term of art is "diapered"—that tie the various elements together like a taut mesh net.

The ESC was set up to assist interdisciplinary research among faculty from different departments. The building also houses the intrinsically interdisciplinary Institute for Biospheric Studies and the Center for Earth Observation. With its basic programmatic motivation being a reach for connection, it is no wonder that the ESC reaches west on Sachem Street toward Osborn Laboratories, its—Gothic, yes, and similarly scaled—neighbor on the other side of the Hillhouse Avenue axis. Together the two make a subtle, low-scale entry setting for Science Hill and the ghost of Sachem's Wood, the old Hillhouse mansion that once stood on the brow of the hill.

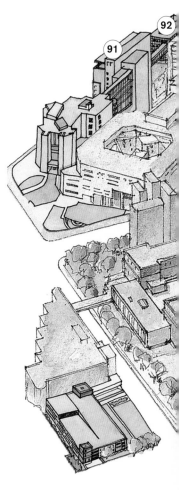

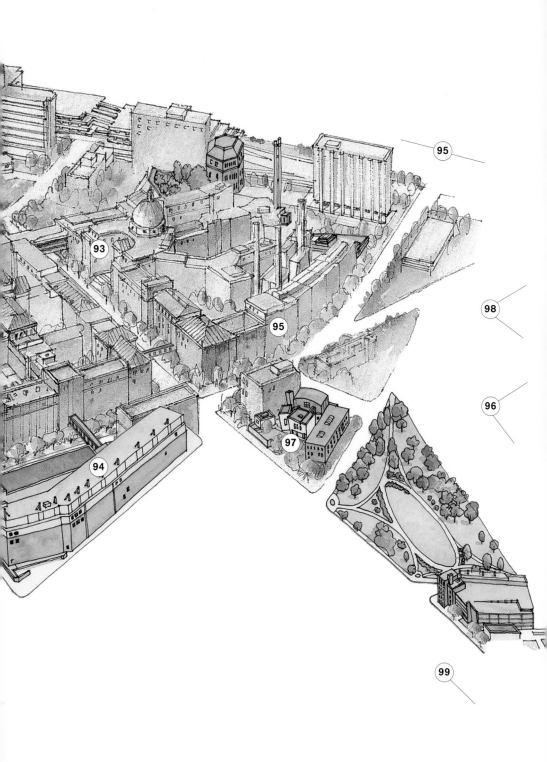

The Hill was the wrong side of the tracks even before tracks were invented. It began life poor in 1638 as the area where those settlers who were not shareholders in the New Haven Colony were given small lots outside the Nine Squares. The neighborhood name is shortened from an old nickname, Sodom Hill, and the area has been not only poor but also too often regarded as dirty and spiritually and physically threatening for the last two centuries. It seems to have been a reputation created in the classic way, by a combination of noxious uses (leather manufacturing, which used West Creek, whose bed is now covered by the Oak Street Connector, as its sewer) and a regular supply of traders and travelers passing through (Davenport Avenue was the road to New York). All this made for cheap land, a population drawn by jobs that others disdained, and cheap housing. Construction jobs on the Farmington Canal in the 1820s and 1830s also attracted laborers, and many of them, Irish with families, settled here. In 1834 they built the first Catholic Church in New Haven on ground now occupied by the South Pavilion of Yale-New Haven Hospital, in the heart of the Medical Campus.

It was hardly accidental that the church was just across the street from the first building of New Haven (originally State) Hospital, completed two years earlier, in 1832, to a design by Ithiel Town. The hospital was a charity institution, established in a poor neighborhood where it was particularly needed and where a whole block of land could be gotten for comparatively little. Town's impressive building, with a three-story Doric portico similar to the Ionic one on the brand-new Hillhouse mansion on the other side of the city, looked back down a street axis to the Nine Squares. Through the nineteenth century the hospital grew by addition of semidetached pavilions, all on the original block bounded by Cedar Street (on which it fronted) and Congress, Howard, and Davenport avenues. It was almost the only block in the area whose outline did not change during the period; as is often the case in the history of cities, when an area is poor it becomes susceptible to having new roads pushed through it, its old roads realigned or simply closed if inconvenient for traffic passing through. Maps of this area from the 1820s on look like snapshots of an urban-scale pick-up-stick game, some of the complexity of which is still visible in the puzzling alignments and orientations of older buildings.

Many people are surprised to learn that the Yale Medical School was not always here, intertwined with the New Haven hospital complex. In fact it fully arrived only in 1923, more than a century after it opened in October 1813 (see SSS). The Medical School was first housed in a converted hotel at Grove and Prospect, from which it moved in 1859–60 to a building built specially for it, on the west side of York Street between Chapel and Crown. (The site was formerly occupied by a house reserved for the holder of the professor of Divinity, since Divinity was then going through one of its periodic near-death experiences.) The School grew to occupy a disjointed set of hand-me-down buildings at that location and elsewhere around the campus. Despite this growth, the School was financially weak and suffered from acrimonious relations with the hospital and the rest of the University during late nineteenth and early twentieth centuries. Under the leadership of a new Dean, Milton Winternitz, it was nevertheless decided to move the entire School across to the Hill, with funds from the Sterling bequest of 1918 used to put up a whole new complex of buildings to accompany the couple of Yale structures already there. (The Jane Ellen Hope building dates from 1901, the Brady Lab and Boardman Building from 1917.)

Since the 1920s, the development of the medical-hospital campus has been enormously complicated. In broadest terms, four patterns describe the growth and change. First, on the block on which the hospital was founded (bounded by Cedar, Congress, Howard, and York), the perimeter has been gradually filled in at the same time as the original nineteenth-century buildings, at the center of the block, have almost all been replaced with newer structures. It is as though, on the Old Campus, the Old Brick Row had been completely surrounded by street-edge structures (which it was), but then replaced with new buildings rather than simply vanishing. Second, opposite the original block, the Sterling-funded complex (Sterling Hall of Medicine and its multiple wings) grew in conformity to various street lines, then saw those streets obliterated, expanded again to front other streets, and in turn saw those wiped out. Sorting out what are and what have been the fronts, sides, backs, and even the interiors of individual buildings is therefore a task of near-Roman complexity. Third, since the 1950s a set of large, modern pavilions for the hospital, of varying degrees of architectural interest, has grown up west of York Street. Finally, since the 1980s, a diverse collection of laboratories, clinics, and offices, some in new and others in renovated structures, has appeared around the edge of the medical-hospital campus, with non-Yale but medically related buildings now showing up even on the other side of the Oak Street Connector.

Overall, the Medical School, the Hospital, and all their client buildings form a formidable labyrinth. To outsiders, especially patients already under stress from illness, it can be enormously intimidating and difficult to navigate. At the same time, for those working, studying, and teaching there, it often becomes a place of workaday interest and intricate vitality.

The oddly formed area at the heart of the whole complex, where Cedar and York meet at what was once the site of the city's first Catholic church, has a lunchtime street liveliness as great as anywhere else in Yale or New Haven.

The Oak Street Connector cut off the Hill and the Medical Campus from the rest of Yale and from downtown New Haven in the 1950s. The Air Rights Garage (Orr, de Cossy, Winder, 1976–80), straddling the end of the highway, definitively reaffirmed the disconnection. During the same period and since, any numbers of plans were announced for dealing with the continuing poverty and problems of the Hill; none has made very much difference. At the moment, when the intense growth of the Medical Campus reflects America's preoccupation with the dream of prolonged life, the hope is held out that jobs generated by that dream will help fulfill another dream—the fitful but persistent resurrection of the Hill.

91. Smilow Cancer Hospital, Yale-New Haven Hospital
Shepley Bulfinch Richardson Abbott Architects, 2009

Hospitals, judged by the standards of good city planning, often seem to embody urbanism's version of the Vietnam era's famously paradoxical utterance: "We had to destroy the village in order to save it." The Smilow Cancer Hospital is a massive structure, a half million square feet of the most advanced treatment facilities, and judged by the standards of health treatment and philanthropy it is nothing but exemplary. Judged by the wheeled traffic its presence generates in the surrounding streets and the Hill community, it falls well short of that.

Strictly considered as a building, Smilow does a variety of things to disguise its bulk and make itself attractive to those viewing and using it. It was an uphill battle, since the building is a massive fourteen-story nearly cubic block, with only one corner cut away a third of the way up on the southeast corner. Portions of the facade pop out and get different surface treatments in order to disguise the basic bulk a bit, darker spandrel panels make visual slits and slots toward the same end, roof features jig and jog, the colors and textures are warm, and the building goes to considerable trouble to make space at its base for grass and plants. Occasionally Shepley Bulfinch, a venerable Boston architectural firm, probably goes too far in the lighten-it-up department. The flying entry canopy on Park Street, for example, is a sculptural pylon holding cables that suspend the canopy proper, which does not use the body of the building for support; this looks to be a nice instance of creating a problem in order to show off by solving it. The interiors are pleasant enough and surprisingly light, with a lot of consideration shown for patients, their families, and staff. That chopped-out corner at the southeast is used to make a rooftop public terrace, with good solar orientation, for the use of all.

The open question at Smilow is whether the whole basic model—not the building but the organizational idea behind such places as Yale-New Haven Hospital—is a good fit with the medical economics and cities of twenty-first-century America. Specialized "centers" concentrated in clusters at hospital "complexes" have become so massive, baroquely elaborate and expensive that that way of providing health care may no longer be tenable. Smilow could prove to be one of the last of its species. Impressive in size, design, technology, and care as both the building and the hospital are, size and complexity sometimes engender fragility rather than protect against it.

92. 55 Park Street Clinical Laboratory at Yale-New Haven Hospital
Behnisch Architekten with Svigals + Partners, 2011

Its principal function to house clinical laboratories supporting the hospital, 55 Park Street is a simple prism of a building wearing a surprising multicolored lab coat. The first striking thing is certainly the curtain wall, but the building is unusual and accomplished in several other ways. It is a demonstration that a simple premise—here, that this would be a building of straightforward, efficient shape—need not result in dumb architecture.

55 Park Street Clinical Laboratory

55 Park is the first building west of the Air Rights Garage, the aircraft-carrier-sized structure intended originally not only to provide hospital parking but to be the gateway through which ran Route 34, the Oak Street Connector. With the Connecticut Department of Transportation's 2004 decision not to extend Route 34, all of the land cleared in the 1960s to hold it became available for redevelopment. It is an astonishing opportunity for New Haven. But it presents every new building in that corridor with the responsibility to reconnect the neighborhoods north and south, even while performing whatever function its owners intend for it.

Earlier buildings along the corridor have only lackadaisically lived up to that urbanistic responsibility. 55 Park, in contrast, lines its ground level with retail space and ties the movement of people coming into the building from the street with that of others entering from the Air Rights Garage at an upper level, offering all a way to bridge over the traffic maelstrom which is South Frontage Road. The four-story volume inside the southwest corner of the building is more than just the staircase it contains. With light from two sides, and a bright palette of yellows and grays setting off natural wood (some of it with actual knots, a horror for more conventional architects), it is a space that tempts people to linger.

The building's curtain wall also contributes to the sense that walking Park Street is once again a reasonable and interesting thing to do. The strictly rectangular harlequin cladding, in three panel sizes, is a high-performance mosaic of nine different glass types and six different metal panel and screen types claimed to tune the skin precisely to different uses inside. It doesn't matter much how accurate that is, since the pattern, or lack of pattern, tempts passersby to try the visual game of figuring it out. At times it seems a light-colored building turning dark or clear, at other times just the reverse. There is a certain Northern European, M. C. Escher–like combination of precision and whimsy at work here, a sense of metamorphoses caught midway between end states. The building, after its single large-scale premise about being a simple mass, jumps down to the arrangements of small-scale panels, with no readily legible middle organizational scale. 55 Park engages the hardwired human instinct to look for order at that scale, benefiting both the architecture and the urbanism.

93. Sterling Hall of Medicine and Medical Library

Sterling Hall of Medicine
Charles Z. Klauder, 1924
Institute of Human Relation
Grosvenor Atterbury, 1929
Harvey Cushing/John Hay Whitney Medical Library
Grosvenor Atterbury, 1941; Alexander Purves and Allan Dehar, 1990

Sterling Hall of Medicine

The Sterling Hall of Medicine formed the nucleus of the Medical School after its transplant in 1923 to the Hill, adjacent to New Haven Hospital. As originally planned by Charles Z. Klauder, but only partly built, this was to have been an ensemble of buildings around a courtyard, overall making a kite-shaped plan whose limits were set by three streets no longer existing. The original front entrance to Sterling, the top of the kite, was through the right-hand part of the current concave Cedar Street facade, while the power plant was in the tail location. Sterling Med's overall character was sparer than now, with much more brick than limestone, and infinitely more astringent than the Sterling-sponsored buildings on the main campus.

Two of the three streets hemming in the Hall of Medicine were eliminated in the late 1920s, which cleared the way for joining the Hall in 1929–30 with the new Institute of Human Relations (now I Wing) to the north. The Institute's architect, Grosvenor G. Atterbury, gave the two structures a new, shared limestone entrance facade and dome; this is what stands today on Cedar Street. Atterbury (1869–1956) was a versatile, quietly inventive architect, known for his experiments in low-cost housing but also as a pioneer in historic restorations, and for museum and country house design. At Yale, he had overseen in 1905 the first major renovation of Connecticut Hall; earlier still he had designed the Venetian mini-palazzo that today is Stoeckel Hall. I Wing's other entrance, on the north, which now opens onto a grassy courtyard in front of Harkness dormitory, originally fronted a busy street; Davenport Avenue continued straight on past it, into the center of the city, rather than curving off into York Street. In other words, this originally was a densely urban area of traffic-filled streets and street-fronting buildings. The change to freestanding buildings with occasional patches of green only came about in the 1950s and 1960s.

A multitude of buildings and structures have been inserted into interstices or attached to the rear of this complex over time. Most notably, Atterbury added the Medical Library onto the rear of the main building in 1941; in turn, Alexander Purves and Allan Dehar extended it in 1990 with an addition that makes much use of natural light in a dense situation.

94. The Anlyan Center for Medical Research and Education

Venturi, Scott Brown and Associates with Payette Associates, 2003

The School of Medicine's 2003 Anlyan Center for Medical Research and Education, designed by Venturi, Scott Brown and Associates, with Payette Associates, is a 457,000-square-foot building at the edge of the convoluted core of the medical campus. It is the large visual anchor for the south end of the medical school and hospital complex, a role the nearly identically sized Smilow Cancer Hospital now plays on the north. Because their sites are quite different—Smilow is closely hemmed in, while the Anlyan Center occupies a block by itself—the two take opposing massing strategies. Smilow is a large, compact chunk of a building, while Anlyan is two long wings connected by a lobby running down the canyon between them. The result for Anlyan is a building almost automatically very different when encountered from different directions.

Anlyan runs down the catalog of design features that over the decades have come to be characteristic of Venturi, Scott Brown's work. Cladding and windows get played with in wallpaper games to break down scale and signal entries and other centers; cartoonish metal trees soften the building on the Howard Avenue side; and there are echoes and insider acknowledgments of other, older buildings and spaces in the area. In this case the curving entry plaza at the corner of Cedar Street and Congress Avenue, part of it defined by a freestanding run of

The Anlyan Center

limestone-clad wall, is a tip of the hat to the little concave entry of Sterling Hall of Medicine, just down Cedar. That might have been expected, since the latter was designed by a fellow Philadelphian, Charles Zeller Klauder. Less predictable is the way Anlyan's entrance plays well with the rear of Frank Gehry and Alan Dehar's 1990 Yale Psychiatric Institute, bringing its small-scaled angled forms into an architectural conversation kitty-corner across the street.

It is a startling contrast to turn the corner down Gilbert Street and encounter Anlyan's long, high, rampart-like south wall, like some sort of urban Carcassonne, laboratory exhaust stacks punctuating the sky. Though vastly larger in scale, Anlyan's angled facade recalls the curving, two-toned, windows-as-wallpaper facade of the Venturi firm's unbuilt winning entry to the 1970 Yale Mathematics Building competition, for a site on lower Hillhouse Avenue. James Hillhouse, Yale's treasurer in the early nineteenth century, built and owned the structure that first housed the

Yale School of Medicine, in 1813. As often happens on the Yale campus, odd, faint, multiple historical echoes bounce around here.

95. Hope Building, Sterling Power Plant, Boyer Center, Laboratory of Epidemiology and Public Health, and Oak Street Connector/Route 34 Redevelopment

Jane Ellen Hope Building
Leoni W. Robinson, 1901
Sterling Power Plant
Charles Z. Klauder, 1924
Boyer Center for Molecular Medicine
César Pelli and Associates, 1991
Laboratory of Epidemiology and Public Health
Philip Johnson, 1963

This disparate quartet of buildings share two things only: they all pertain to the Medical School, and all were shaped to a large extent by the streets around them. The Hope Building, an elegantly detailed brick cube with a beautifully contrasting patinated copper cornice, originally stood in a sort of prow situation, at the tip of an odd protrusion from the block formed by the dogleg of now-vanished Rose Street; this placement made it an "object building" long before most any other buildings in the area were thought of in that way. The Sterling Power Plant, today askew from any of the other buildings in the area, was packed tightly up against two long-gone

Laboratory of Epidemiology and Public Health

streets; its visual power, seen close up from them, must have been even greater than today. Its architect, Charles Klauder, had previously designed the Central Power Plant with his late partner, Frank Miles Day, and both Yale power plants show a consciousness of the dramatic effects to be had from smokestacks and overscaled windows in an urban situation. César Pelli's 1991 Boyer Center picks up the articulated brickwork of the Hope Building, turns it polychrome, and uses the resulting exaggerated horizontality to emphasize the sweep of College Street into Congress Avenue. A driver crossing

Boyer Center

over the Oak Street Connector on College sees the long horizontal lines swerve dramatically out of sight, in contrast with the verticals of the Sterling Power Plant stacks. Philip Johnson's 1963 Epidemiology Lab is a reminder of the "ductitecture" mode of its era, but here, unlike the case of many such laboratories, there is some contextual justification for its sculptural exaggeration and tiny windows provided by the adjacent traffic of the Connector. On the Connector side, Johnson raised the building on a high, defensive podium, which, on the opposite side, opens out at the level of a south-facing, grassy garden.

Interstate 95 opened in 1958, the Oak Street Connector in 1959, and Interstate 91 in 1966. The virtues and problems of all three roadways are well enough known that they need not be repeated here. In late 2011, as this is being written, New Haven is in the midst of a debate over how best to heal the cut made by the Connector more than half a century ago. There is consensus that downtown and the train station area must be tied back together east of the Air Rights Garage. At issue is how to handle traffic still headed to and from the ARG, the still-burgeoning Yale-New Haven Hospital area, and points west. As well, the City has identified four developable parcels over the former channel of the Connector. Buildings on them might help knit things back together, but at the cost of generating their own additional traffic on the frontage roads north and south of the cut. The outcome of the debate is highly uncertain.

What is clear is that, even as opposition to it in both theory and practice gain strength, the old way of building limited access highways, and rebuilding them ever larger, more baroquely elaborate and expensive, still has tremendous technocratic power and a powerful road-building industry behind it. Just east of downtown, I-95 over the Quinnipiac River is receiving the new Pearl Harbor Bridge, and a breathtaking new flyover ramp from the highway into downtown has recently opened. This is occurring as funds for maintenance of existing roads and other infrastructure become increasingly scarce. The spectacle in New Haven in 2011 is of a city doing the planning equivalent of stepping hard on the brake pedal with one foot, hard on the accelerator with the other.

96. Church Street South Housing, Tower One, and Tower East

Church Street South
MLTW / Charles Moore Associates, 1969
Tower One
MLTW / Charles Moore Associates, 1991
Tower East
Charles Moore Associates and Moore Grover Harper, 1982

Along with his own small house on Elm Street, these buildings constitute Charles Moore's New Haven legacy. Moore (1925–1995) was head of the Yale School of Architecture during the late 1960s and early 1970s, and some of the odd combination of seriousness and whimsicality that made him so appealing to many— and drove others furious—is still visible in the set of buildings here. New Haven Mayor Richard Lee wanted Moore, with the Church Street South public housing project, to rehabilitate a category of building then often despised alike by its occupants and by high-style architects. Moore returned to the conception of such housing as low-rise and predominantly street oriented, rather than high-rise and dependent on elevators. He gave the units stoops and garages (acknowledging the often resisted fact that the poor in America need cars, too). Any blank walls became supergraphic billboards and different concrete block textures made reverse "quoining" and other cutely historicizing details vaguely recalling palazzi; conceived in desperation because of the low budget, such things went on to become hallmarks of Moore's and of postmodernism generally. Moore conceived the project as having both public and private aspects, and took far more care than was characteristic of the period with the design of the public piazza areas, including the one supposed to be lined with shops facing the Railroad Station. In the 1990s, Church Street South is not in good shape, but then neither is virtually any other subsidized housing. It is an open question whether Moore's care and attention made this project's deterioration proceed at a slower pace.

Standing closer to the Connector, across a wide, usually weedy tract of cul-de-sac parking from the Church Street South project, is a building ensemble Moore designed slightly later. This one is a two-tower elderly high-rise, for which the local Jewish Community Council was client. The communal spaces on the ground floor exhibit some of the stage-set spatial games for which Moore was then becoming known. The two towers are markedly different from each other. One, slightly lower and of red brick, steps quirkily up and away from the Connector. The other consciously pokes rude fun at the heroic Knights of Columbus Tower, with its great, dark, cylindrical corner piers, just across the highway; Moore used to speak of his tower, conspicuously pierless by contrast, as a "neutered K of C."

Yale Psychiatric Institute

97. Yale Psychiatric Institute
Frank Gehry and Allan Dehar, 1990

The Yale Psychiatric Institute (YPI), like many of Gehry's buildings, is frankly odd.
It has an out-of-kilter combination of angles, materials, and facades that look
unfriendly, uninteresting, or just plain klutzy. But the unusual qualities in Gehry's
buildings often prove to be the result of his talent for seeing the familiar in a new
and often stimulating way. YPI is no Guggenheim/Bilbao (thank goodness), but a
conscientious attempt to deal with an uncomfortable program on a transitional
site, near a campus with architecture so strong as to be intimidating even to
world-class architects.

The Institute built this structure to house sixty-plus adolescent schizophrenics
in treatment, a residential college for psychiatric patients. Basically it is a near-
symmetrical scheme of center and wing pavilions, like something abstracted from
Vitruvius Britannicus, dropped accidentally, then picked back up and rearranged
more or less square with three faces of the angular block, on which it is the only
building. The fourth side is to the south; there Gehry has created another sun-
facing courtyard in the old Yale tradition. The pavilions, at three or four stories,
are the size and have the mundane windows (abstracted into squares) of an
ordinary apartment house in the Hill neighborhood. It is an unexpected recurrence,
but appropriate to the treatment going on within, of Yale's subliminal interest in
domesticity (see Walk Four).

Gehry shows himself an astute observer of historic New Haven patterns at a scale larger than the individual building. The Nine Squares, with streets that break off at angles at the edge, create by that geometry prominent sites just beyond the Plan limits. Many architects, presented with such sites, have responded with prominent or unusual roof lines. Gehry placed a low, metal-roofed dome, covering a gym, atop the central pavilion of his closet-neoclassical building; it stands, distantly answering SSS, just off the centerline of College Street when looking south.

The Yale Psychiatric Institute is not open to visitors at any time. Please do not take photographs when people are visible in the building or on the grounds.

98. 100 Church Street South, Knights of Columbus, and Temple Street Garage

100 Church Street South (former Richard C. Lee High School)
Kevin Roche, John Dinkeloo and Associates, 1964
Knights of Columbus
Roche–Dinkeloo, 1967
Temple Street Garage
Paul Rudolph, 1961

The 1960s witnessed the apogee of New Haven's reputation on the world architectural scene and the national political one. The city powered up into visibility on the strength of its urban renewal program, of its drastic, resolute highway construction, and of a vision of a new, modern-all-over-again architecture sculpted and scaled to the American reality of mass movement by car. The international talent that produced these designs was locally based; Paul Rudolph had his office in New Haven for the duration of his Yale Architecture chairmanship, and the partnership of Kevin Roche and John Dinkeloo, successor firm to Eero Saarinen, occupied an old castellated mansion in Hamden, just north of New Haven. Four of their works are close by the medical campus.

The earliest is the parking garage Rudolph designed, which opened two years before his A&A Building was dedicated in 1963. It is an enormous structure, 700 feet long, designed to hold 1,300 cars for two adjacent shopping blocks. In 1998, the city knocked down one of the blocks, long derelict, exposing a view of the rear of the garage that shows its sculptural and urbanistic ambitions all over again. Even though the rhythmic march of the garage's paired piers is impressive, seen from street level the real architectural thrill here is on the structure's top level, where under the sky, with concrete cobra lights and the church towers on the Green competing for attention, it is like being on the deck of an aircraft carrier ploughed into the heart of the city in some exhilarating disaster. Visions aside, it is more to

Rudolph's credit that commercial space was provided on the ground level of most of the garage, since every driver at some point becomes a pedestrian with the desire to see things more interesting than the rhythms of concrete formwork.

Concrete galore was what the students at Roche and Dinkeloo's Lee High School got on its opening in 1964—concrete, little daylight, and winds across fields of fire cleared by urban renewal and highway construction. Adolescence is hard enough without having to spend some years of it in a lost piece of the Maginot Line, and the city eventually divested itself of the building named after its urban-renewal mayor and sold it to Yale. It is now the nation's most defensible School of Nursing.

If the High School was simply conceived against the grain of common sense, the New Haven Coliseum, built in 1969, was a magnificent, Piranesian ruin that showed the results of logical design that proceeded with great technical facility from a premise that was proven to be mistaken. The premise was that, given the Oak Street Connector as the new entrance to the city, nothing could be a better than to locate a municipal arena at the gateway as an emblem of community and civic pride. The premise was maintained even when it was determined that the site was perhaps unsuitable; located just at the point where East and West creeks once entered New Haven harbor, it had a ground water level so high that parking could not be put below the arena. Roche and Dinkeloo solved the difficulty with bridge construction technology, simply lifting the four-level, 2,400-car garage six stories or so into the air. Two problems were thereby solved at once, for what better advertisement is there than the visible presence of large quantities of parking? Unfortunately the drive down the spiraling open-air access ramps for the garage, while within standard technical parameters, proved to be too much of a wintertime adventure for many drivers. Other difficulties showed up that were not simply psychological, foremost among them problems with the special variety of structural steel employed in the construction. Parts of the garage had to be disassembled, others blocked off, for safety. The architectural problems compounded the misperception that New Haven is not anywhere one wants to go, and resulted in an on-again, off-again ability of the Coliseum to draw crowds. The Coliseum was demolished in 2007.

Kevin Roche and John Dinkeloo also designed the Knights of Columbus Headquarters, next to the Coliseum. It was built in 1967, accidentally but appropriately on a site that puts it on center of the view down Hillhouse Avenue, on the other side of the Nine Squares; the Knights (a Catholic fraternal organization) were founded in St. Mary's Church on the Avenue. It stands as a brooding, 320-foot-high sentinel and a beacon at night. Its floors are strikingly open—a fact clearly apparent when the Tower is seen at night—as a result of the fact that they span the entire 80-foot distance between the four slip-formed concrete corner piers.

99. Union Station and New Haven Civic Commission Report

Union Station
Cass Gilbert, 1918; Skidmore, Owings & Merrill and Herbert S. Newman, 1990

New Haven Civic Commission Report
Cass Gilbert and Frederick Law Olmsted Jr., 1910

New Haven's railroad station, dating from 1918, is a solid and hard-serving building, which stands nonetheless as an emblem for a chain of much better might-have-beens. Cass Gilbert, who had just finished the New Haven Free Public Library, clearly intended the five pairs of tall windows on the central block, visible from the street and lighting the high waiting room within, to be symbolic gateway arches. They fail as such in two ways. First, the arches misdirect the passenger to the trains, for one does not go straight ahead but instead left down a stair and then out in a tunnel to the tracks; this was necessary because the tracks are parallel to the station and on the same level, rather than perpendicular to it and a level below, as is the case at New York's Grand Central and Penn Stations, and many others around the country. New Haven's first train station, built by Henry Austin in 1849 at the intersection of State and Chapel streets, in fact had an over-the-track arrangement. It is interesting to imagine Gilbert's station in that location; would a closer connection to the city center have made any difference either to railroad finances or to New Haven? The decision to move the train station away from downtown was certainly made in part because of problems with soot and noise, and in the confidence that the requisite sense of connection to the Green and civic buildings could still be had by the creation of a grand avenue.

But the grand boulevard is the second broken promise implicit in Gilbert's arches, and it is much the more serious of the two. In their 1910 Report, which a private group commissioned, Gilbert and Olmsted wanted Temple Street to pivot at a grand new city square located where it crossed old Oak Street, then continue as a 120-foot wide, tree-lined boulevard to the front of the new Union Station. The Plan contained much more, noting opportunities and proposing solutions for a range of technical, social, and aesthetic concerns. Perhaps it was its very comprehensiveness that prevented its formal adoption by a New Haven already operating at the level of factional power-brokering, with a greater sense of the short-term political deal than of the city's design and longer-term future. It is sometimes interesting to speculate on might-have-beens: if the Temple Street civic square at the foot of Oak Street had been built, would traffic planners and politicians have swept it away as lightly as they did the Oak Street neighborhood? Would New Haven, in the 1950s and 1960s, have become quite the intense experimental laboratory for urban renewal that it did?

WALK TEN: YALE BOWL AND THE NATURAL CITY

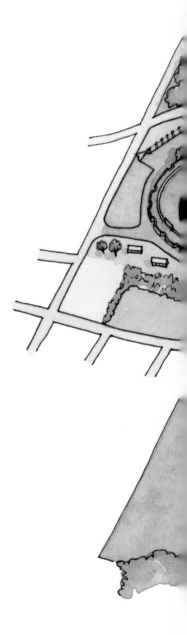

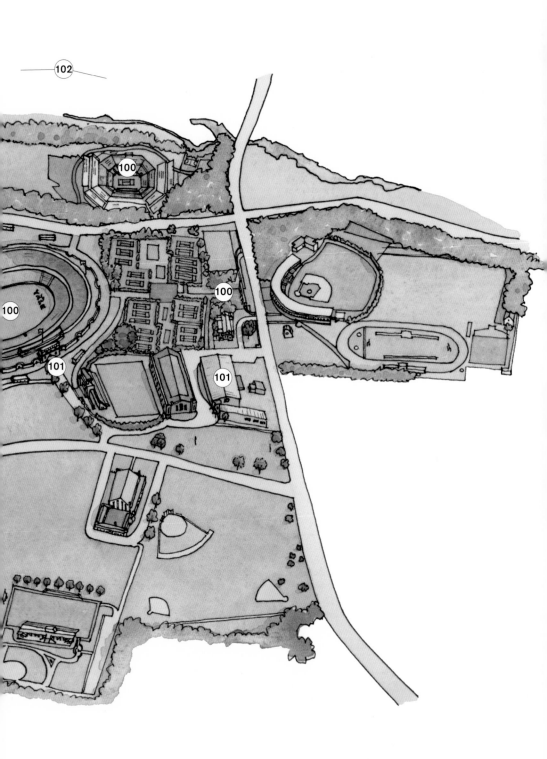

The long history of outdoor athletics at Yale began at the center of New Haven and culminated at its edge, an outward movement created by forces of repulsion but continued by others of attraction. A full map of the trajectory would set specific athletic facilities and events into a history of what was thought to make a healthy, well-ordered, and moral human body in a city possessing the same qualities. Since that would be a book in itself, two generalizations and a few details will have to suffice. First, looked at over the whole history of Yale, athletic activity at the College went from being pursued during the leftover bits of students' highly controlled scholastic lives, in games played on neglected patches of ground, to being a dominant force in Yale life, central to the University's self-conception and played out in enormous, specially designed structures located on a campus of their own. Along the way—second generalization—games went from being regarded as unwelcome intrusions on the city's goals of spiritual redemption, physical beauty, and economic order, to being thought of as a powerful mechanism for achieving them.

A College Law of 1765 forbade ballplaying in the Yard because of damage to windows and students' concentration. Students took their games across the street to the Green. As the Green's development and standards of maintenance advanced, with the addition of elms, a fence, new churches, and a proud new State Capitol building, the games increasingly came into conflict with ideals of civic dignity and with those charged with the care-taking of them, the firemen and police. In the late 1850s College and town authorities again expelled students athletes, this time from the Green. Rudimentary exercise facilities were provided at the rear of the College, but space for baseball and football was found ad hoc, often at locations left empty because of their unattractive real estate qualities; next to the Grove Street Cemetery, and beyond New Haven Hospital, for instance. After the Civil War, with the sudden rise of student appetite for athletic competition, coinciding with a surge of affluence and with the beginnings of a public transit system in New Haven, games began to be played on fields laid out on the undeveloped wetlands and farmlands alongside the West River, previously considered too distant from the College. Now, however, two related ideals began to compete for the same land. Americans sought the green suburban refuge from the city and admired the manly, disciplined, team-playing collegiate patriot. In 1881, after the city sold Hamilton Park, site of many an epic Yale game, for residential development, an association of students and graduates bought thirty acres on the west bank of West River. This was immediately "improved" by clearing and grading, and provided, in addition to fields for Yale, a useful example for the linked sequence of parks and cemeteries that emerged along West River under the guidance of Donald Grant Mitchell in the 1890s. The park system with the Yale fields and augmented by the lands for the Bowl and the Golf Course, proved to be an attractive, stable asset around which suburban development could occur. (Ironically, Mitchell's own Edgewood became one of the developed properties.)

The classical ideal of balance, "sound mind in healthy body," has proven to be quite complex in interpretation and achievement for Yale in New Haven. The changing values assigned to each half of the ideal, and consequently to the places in which their perfection is pursued, are what lie behind the location and character of the places in this walk.

100. Yale Bowl and Athletic Complex

Walter Camp Gateway
John W. Cross, 1928
Yale Bowl
Charles A. Ferry, with Edward G. Williams and Donn Barber, 1914;
renovation: Vincent Benic Architect, 2006
Charles E. Coxe Gymnasium (Coxe Cage)
Lockwood, Greene & Company, 1927
Connecticut Tennis Center at Yale
Edward Larrabee Barnes with John M. Y. Lee, 1991

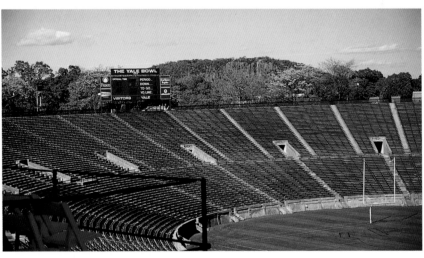

Yale Bowl

Yale maintains a large set of buildings and athletic fields a mile and a half west of the campus, just beyond the western boundary of New Haven. Clustering around the venerable Yale Bowl, these facilities form what really is a campus in itself, or perhaps two, since the Golf Course is separate and another mile beyond the Bowl. Excluding the Golf Course, the athletic fields aggregate to about 150 acres, very nearly the area of the Yale campus proper. There have been times when the image of Yale held by the outside world was formed as much or more by what went on here as by the work done in its lecture halls and libraries.

The Yale Bowl, completed in 1914, culminated a half century during which college life at Yale and many other American universities came to revolve around activities outside of classrooms and libraries, the "Extracurriculum," as one historian named it. College sports were the most prominent of them, and Yale's crew, track men, and baseball and football teams captured national titles and attention. In football, in particular, Yale was a national power. In a little under a quarter century following the organization of its Football Association in 1872, interest in the games grew to the point that, in 1896, it was necessary to build permanent seats to accommodate spectators. The 1896 stands held 18,000, and even that capacity soon became inadequate. Various additions then pumped the number up beyond 33,000, the largest set of wooden stands the world had ever seen.

The fact that the structure was of wood was both a maintenance problem and a hair-raising fire threat. The Yale Corporation appointed a well-heeled "Committee of Twenty-One" to solve the problem; it bought 87 acres just the other side of Derby Avenue from the older Yale Field, then turned to the question of what form the new stadium should take. One proposal considered a steel structure with wheeled pieces able to be moved to fit either baseball or football, while the other idea initially considered was a reinforced concrete recreation of the Colosseum in Rome, to hold only football. In the end a third, very original strategy won out, originating not in bridge construction technology, like the first proposal, or in updating a historical building type, as with the second, but in the engineering of water system reservoirs.

A Sheffield Scientific graduate, Charles Addison Ferry (1852–1924) proposed the third strategy. It brilliantly solved not only the need to accommodate large crowds

Coxe Cage

(the Bowl has held over 70,000) but did so in a way that let them get in and out easily and safely, and also minimized trucking quantities of materials on and off site during construction. Work began in August 1913, with Ferry as engineer. His solution essentially was to make a crater or reservoir shape, digging out earth to a depth of twenty-seven and a half feet in the center and pulling it back up around the edge to form an ovoid mound twenty-six feet high. Thirty tunnels, entered at ground level, penetrated the crater rim at equal intervals, with low concrete steps, to hold the seats, poured on top of the sloping earth. It was finished for the ever-important Yale-Harvard game on November 21, 1914. A memorial plaque honoring Ferry hangs above the southernmost portal.

The Bowl has become one of the national treasures of American sports. But in its reinvention of the stadium type by, in essence, crossbreeding a classical colosseum with hydrology and geology, it can also be interpreted as peculiarly Yale-ish, an unexpected continuation of old themes from back on the campus. A classical form is recalled but given a contemporary interpretation based on fitting into a site; Jeremiah Day's *Faculty Report* of 1828 meets Benjamin Silliman's geology texts. As if in reminder of the genius loci, East and West Rocks come rising into view from the topmost seats of the Bowl.

If one is inclined to criticism, the comment could be offered that the very nature of the Bowl's conception rendered it impressive within but almost invisible from without. That lack of a suitably monumental entrance was supplied by the erection of the Walter Camp Memorial Gateway on Derby Avenue in 1927–28. Camp (1859–1925), Yale's de facto football coach from 1886 until 1910, rule-giver to that sport and promoter of intercollegiate athletics generally, was venerated nationally. Over

Walter Camp Gateway

five hundred schools and colleges contributed to the construction fund. The architect was John W. Cross of New York, who also designed the pedestal for the Nathan Hale statue on the Old Campus. With its mixture of Doric and Ionic characteristics, the Gateway wished to suggest in the coded forms of classicism that the *memorialée*–and the game he regulated–possessed both strength and refinement.

Of the several other structures in the athletic area, two buildings deserve mention. Coxe Cage was built in 1927 by Lockwood, Greene & Company for track and indoor baseball practice.

Connecticut Tennis Center

West of the axis from Camp Gateway to the Bowl, its classic minimalist brick envelope covers a spectacular skylit interior volume. The Connecticut Tennis Center, by Edward L. Barnes and John M. Y. Lee, east on the same cross axis and just the other side of Yale Avenue, piles 15,000 seats up into the sky from a sloped and wooded embankment; upon construction it was the second largest tennis stadium in America and the third largest worldwide.

As the 2014 celebration of its centennial approaches, the Yale Bowl is looking better than it has in several decades. Vincent Benic Architect, a New York firm with an extensive preservationist record, oversaw a substantial renovation. Spalled concrete that made the Bowl entry gates resemble fish tank grottos was repaired; the thirty access tunnels had their leached-lime stalactites removed; all the old wooden seats were replaced, repaired, or repainted; and two new VIP terraces were added below the press box.

101. Kenney Center
Centerbrook Architects, 2009

Jensen Plaza
Centerbrook Architects, 2009
Cullman-Heyman Tennis Center addition and renovation
Centerbrook Architects, 2008
Reese Stadium
Centerbrook Architects, 2011

Since Centerbrook Architects did a master plan for Yale's Derby Avenue athletic facilities, the firm has been the architect of choice for its subsequent projects. It has designed a number of improvements to existing fields and buildings, each with its own definite character. Kenney Center is a chunky new entrance building for the Bowl, lightened by arched windows, a deep overhanging cornice, and decorative railings, and inserted neatly between two of the old portals. It also has rooms for use by the football team and a top floor with panoramic views east and west. Jensen Plaza leads to it through arched gates and brick piers, with granite benches lining its sides. The plaza has the names of all the men who have received the varsity *Y* since 1872 carved into its paving.

At the Cullman-Heyman Tennis Center, Centerbrook added a new wing, matched in size to the original, to the renovated 1972 metal building designed

Kenney Center and Jensen Plaza

Reese Stadium

by Herbert S. Newman. Cranked at an angle to the older structure, Centerbrook's addition parallels Central Avenue to the west. The crank makes room for a swoopy entrance canopy like a topspin lob, supported by decoratively capped columns, with a large yellow tennis ball emblem visible through the entry vestibule glass. It's an exuberant introduction to the joined buildings, and has the air of the 1970s work of Charles Moore, teacher and mentor of Centerbrook's founding principals.

Reese Stadium, for the soccer and lacrosse teams, is the newest Centerbrook work in the Bowl complex. It replaces nondescript bleachers adjacent to an existing playing field with a substantial permanent structure containing team rooms, concessions, and the other paraphernalia of successful contemporary athletic programs. The exterior has a massed gang of eleven arches, reminiscent of the Bowl portals, subtly arcing down from the building's center axis. With its broad central stair and slightly recessed arches, Reese has an appealing sort of WPA Art Deco spirit to it.

102. Edgewood, Edgewood Park, and West River Park

Edgewood
Donald Grant Mitchell and David R. Brown, circa 1870

Edgewood Farmhouse
Donald Grant Mitchell and David R. Brown, circa 1860

Edgewood Park
Donald Grant Mitchell, circa 1889

West River Park
Frederick Law Olmsted Jr., 1925

"Ik Marvel" is not now one of the more remembered of nineteenth-century pen names. In its day, though, the name under which Donald Grant Mitchell (1822–1908) published became not only famous and influential but, eventually, revered. Mitchell was the first editor of *Harper's Magazine* and wrote voluminously on art, literature, landscape gardening, and urban and rural aesthetics. He was a Yale graduate and an exact contemporary of the great journalist and landscape architect Frederick Law Olmsted (1822–1903). Mitchell finished his degree in 1841, just before Olmsted's short spell at Yale. The interests and careers of the two men were in fact very similar, and though today it may seem easy to rate Olmsted's legacy the more important–Central Park and the Fenway are famous, and his projects span the country–at the time Mitchell's writings were highly influential.

Mitchell bought himself and his family a farm on the outskirts of New Haven in 1855, named it Edgewood, and over the next half century used it as his laboratory and favorite source of subject material. Such books as *Rural Studies, My Farm of Edgewood,* and *Wet Days at Edgewood* contained aesthetic musings, character sketches, and practical advice on running a farm. These treatises did not advocate

Edgewood Farmhouse

rural retreat from urban problems, but the possibility of healthy interpenetration of rural and urban scenes to the benefit of both; it would be quite wrong to read Mitchell as foreshadowing suburban escapism of the post–World War II variety, and more accurate to see him as an heir to the work of the Hillhouses. (See Grove Street Cemetery and Hillhouse Avenue.)

Ik Marvel's 1884 essay on "Highways and Parks" reads as though it described an idealized version of the Hillhouses' New Haven:

> Indeed, an ideal city–when we have one–from a sanitary point of view, should have its little nucleus of business quarters upon a bay, or a river…and this business nucleus crystallizing there under the compression of an outlying circle of green, jealously guarded, would project its rays, or avenues of traffic athwart this circle; and those avenues of traffic, by their accretions of lesser and lighter business, would demand zebra-like cross-bars of space and greenness and foliage, to be flanked with files of houses–in such sort that a man could not go to his business without sight of trees, or a chance to put his foot to the live earth; while all schools and courts and hospitals should have their setting of green.

Mitchell suited action to words, and between 1885 and 1895 was instrumental in designing New Haven's park system. One chain of parks begins at the foot of the red mass of West Rock and follows the course of the West River down to New Haven Harbor. It includes the Bowl and the Yale athletic fields in "an outlying circle of green" exactly as Mitchell envisioned, writing from his house overlooking it. Frederick Law Olmsted Jr., son of Mitchell's contemporary, designed the last link to the chain in 1925.

Much of Mitchell's Edgewood farm was developed for a better sort of suburban housing after his death in 1908. Edgewood Avenue pays homage to Ik Marvel, his home, and his ideas, not only in its name but in its green connection of the parks to the center city. The house and at least one outbuilding still stand (just up Edgewood Way, past Forest Road)–in private hands and deteriorated condition.

103. Yale Golf Course at Ray Tompkins Memorial
Charles Blair Macdonald, 1926

The Yale Golf Course is situated on a 700-acre tract on the west side of the same hill from which Donald G. Mitchell's Edgewood property faces east. The land was given to Yale in 1924 by Sarah Wey Tompkins in memory of her husband Ray, football captain of the 1882 team, which first played the game according to Walter Camp's newly invented system of downs gained on a gridded field. That fact is not irrelevant to understanding the Yale Golf Course, its designer, and their significance. Charles Blair Macdonald (1856–1939), like Camp and at exactly the same time, systematized, theorized, and publicized his sport. Both took long-existing and

Yale Golf Course

loosely structured games and subjected them to rigorous scrutiny, discipline, and quantification. In particular, the settings for play—stadium or golf course—were newly seen as improvable by science and subject to history. In spirit and methods then, if not at all in forms, the Bowl and the Golf Course are the precise equivalents of James

Gamble Rogers's buildings for the central campus.

The Yale course, built between 1924 and 1926, is still regarded by golfers as one of the world's greatest, and many think it the best collegiate course in the country. The terrain Macdonald was presented with was a wooded wilderness of characteristic New England aspect: hilly, rocky, and cut by many streams. Upon completion, the landscape had become a technically masterful, seamless assembly of quotations from the history of golf worldwide. The course includes, according to one golf writer, "a Redan par-3, a Cape-style par-4, versions of the two par-3s at St. Andrews, the 8th ('Short') and the 11th ('Eden'), and a 'Biarritz' style par-3."

Contemporary golfers probably recognize such references as much and as little as contemporary users of Memorial Quadrangle do James Gamble Rogers's architectural and patronymic allusions. In neither case does it matter much. Both designers produced highly crafted, well-wearing, characterful results. The Golf Course is a beautiful walk even, or especially, if one is not a golfer.

104. Gilder Boathouse
Turner Brooks Architect, 2000

Adroitly inserted onto a narrow sliver of sloping land between the Housatonic River and the road along its edge, Gilder Boathouse makes slight angles, warm wood, and a large, slightly folded metal roof into a composition echoing the lean, low, strong, highly evolved lines of racing shells. Turner Brooks used the slope to slide in an angled ramp so crews can carry boats to and from the five-bay boat storage facility at river level. The upper floor, higher than the street, shelters a deck and large clear-span interior spectator space, anchored by a fireplace, at the building's south end "prow." Adjacent to it is a monumental stair, clerestory-lit, covered but not enclosed, down to dock level. The north side of the second level, the other side of the stair, contains coaches' offices and locker rooms. Gilder's wood and metal structure, simply but thoughtfully detailed, is left visible. Located in Derby, about ten miles west of New Haven, the boathouse is certainly worth a special trip from campus for a visit.

105. Lewis Walpole Library Renovation and Addition
Centerbrook Architects, 2007

Even further afield but similarly worth the trip—up to Farmington, in the vicinity of Hartford—is the Lewis Walpole Library. Wilmarth Sheldon "Lefty" Lewis (1895–1979), a 1918 Yale graduate and lifelong bibliophile, and his wife Annie Burr Lewis left their collections and historic house to the University to form a research library for eighteenth-century studies. Principal focus of the collection is the English author and eccentric Horace Walpole, designer (for himself) of one of the first examples of a house in Gothic Revival style, Strawberry Hill. In 2007

Lewis Walpole Library

Centerbrook renovated a portion of the Lewis's house and added a library in the form of a big, red barn with a side lean-to, cleverly sited to be visible but nonintrusive. Given the survival of many barns along Main Street in this scenic village center, the disguise is completely plausible and justified. The collections and the architectural ensemble add up to a place warming the heart and brain of anyone with even a hint of scholar in her or him. Throw in the many historic connections of Farmington to Yale—Noah Porter Jr., Yale president from 1871 to 1886, was the son of Farmington's congregational minister, for one—and this becomes an obligatory field trip for those interested in Yale and architecture.

ACKNOWLEDGMENTS

This book owes its greatest debt to Vincent Scully Jr. In several ways it would not have been written without him. In the narrowest sense, the book came about because he suggested to Princeton Architectural Press that I was the right person to write it, a referral for which I am deeply grateful. I hope only that the book aids in some way Vince's lifelong crusade for recognition that Yale's architectural heritage and that of New Haven, in which the University lives, are of first-rate importance and should be treated as such. Second, I would not have been able to try to understand and write about the ever-changing overall constellation of Yale buildings, the forces that connect each structure with the others and tie them specially to their sites, without his example; the theme of the importance of "place," of grasping the ways buildings stand with each other within the shape of their landscape, ties his diverse writings together. It therefore has become the theme that unites the generations, including my own, who have been his students. Third, I could not have written some of the things I have were I not an architect, and therefore possessed of the perhaps arrogant confidence that as a maker of buildings I can see choices faced and choices made by the architects of the buildings written about here. I made the decision to become an architect as a direct result of Vince's History of Modern Architecture course, taken during my junior year at Yale College. Beyond the role my profession has played in forming this book, I am thankful to Vince, most of all, for having started me toward it.

I also feel this book owes something to the late Bart Giamatti, whom I first knew when he was Master of Ezra Stiles, my undergraduate residential college, and I an English major, Master's Aide, and babysitter for his kids. It is a paradoxical debt, because Bart, with his deep love for Yale (abiding even when the place was showing extreme silliness or stupidity), always believed that the University really resided in, and for its own protection had better really reside in, the heads and hearts of its people. Buildings were necessary but secondary. I carry with me, because of him, the constant question of how a building, or set of buildings, affects the real University, which is not the architecture. That said, I have come to the conviction that buildings are truly as much the patrimony of an institution or a culture as its books, even though one must find their lessons by different routes. It would have been great fun to argue that with him now—during a change of pitchers, maybe, looking out at the Green Monster.

My students at Yale and elsewhere have taught me a lot, the Yalies in particular about campus locations, which I've picked for them to study as sites for design studio projects. Every hypothetical proposal subtly shifted the perception of the existing buildings around it, illuminating the place with a differently angled light. In a more focused, literal way, the research done by a number of students in various seminar classes has contributed factually and conceptually to this volume. I would like to single out Ben de Rubertis for his work on the Old Library, now Dwight Hall. Most of all, in the last year and a half I have been privileged to work with Erik Vogt, whose research will certainly lead to a book that, far better and more completely than this one can, will argue the case for the typological continuities of New Haven and Yale, their uniqueness, and national significance.

A number of Yale people have provided assistance both directly and as a result of their own work. Judith Schiff, the Chief Research Archivist at Manuscripts and Archives in Sterling Library, has been more than hospitable both to me and to the parade of students I have sent her way. As well, her invaluable, long-running series of articles for the *Yale Alumni Magazine*, covering all aspects of Yale's history, has provided both information used here and the stimulus to consider the buildings from a variety of perspectives. I very much hope, as do many others, that her articles will someday be collected into a book. Val Woods, Senior Architect and Planner in the University's Facilities Office, was kind enough to allow me to dig into the mountain of information on Yale buildings and plans—drawings, clippings, documents—which she has systematically accumulated (sometimes by saving from dumpsters) over decades, during several periods of which she was one of very few people who judged such things worth saving. I would like to thank, as well, Val's patient colleagues Pam Delphenich, University Planner, and Bob Dincecco, also Senior Architect and Planner, for bearing with me while I halted writing detailed histories of various buildings for their use in order to complete this book. Gus Kellogg, now retired from the position of Director of Campus Finance at the School of Medicine, provided information on the Medical Campus's history, as well as much good conversation on that and related University-wide topics.

I have enjoyed many discussions about the campus and its buildings with some of my former colleagues on the School of Architecture faculty. Peter de Bretteville has a wide knowledge of campus planning, which he has generously shared; there is no one better in the world with whom to discuss architectural ornament than Kent Bloomer; Alec Purves is a quiet source of real insight into building types; Harold Roth is the cheerful, informative veteran of a number of Yale building campaigns dating back to his time in Eero Saarinen's office; and Martin Gehner was not only selflessly concerned with integrating handicap accessibility into Yale's buildings well, but the most cordial of office mates. Others on the School of Architecture faculty, whom I would name if I thought they had the sense to be embarrassed by it, provided this book a negative impetus, or perhaps better to say, a certain case-hardening. Their incomprehension, verging on disdain, of an interest in Yale and New Haven—but not such "real places" as New York City and Boston—was a source of resolve on my part. The nadir of this attitude was reached when a seminar on the history of architectural education at Yale (and elsewhere) was judged unworthy of credit toward a Yale School of Architecture degree, an opinion from which the deans' offices did not dissent. The School, fortunately, is now under different leadership.

Great thanks and best wishes for the entire series go to the editor and publisher of this guide and its future sibling volumes. Jan Cigliano Hartman, series editor of The Campus Guides, and Kevin Lippert, founder of Princeton Architectural Press, deserve kudos for conceiving the series and, from my perspective, even more so for bearing with their endlessly belated Yale author.

My wife, the architectural historian Kathleen Curran, contributed to this book both with specific facts, with her pioneering work and publication on J. C. Cady, and the *Rundbogenstil* in Europe and America, and even more by many, many acts of spousal consideration, both of omission and commission, in the course of its writing.

Hartford, Connecticut, 1999

Preparation of the revised edition of this book was wonderfully aided by the Yale Facilities Office. I am grateful to Laura Cruickshank, University Planner, for her discussions of campus strategies and tactics; to Steve Brown, Director of University Planning Administration and Space Planning (and a fine photographer), for his insights; and to David Kula, my facilities information Virgil through the intricate architectural information circles of what was long ago simply the Plan Room. Carobe Hart, in particular, took time away from her real duties to find answers to all of my many arcane requests, track down photographs appropriate to my building descriptions, and make sure photographers were properly credited. All were knowledgeable, fast, and cheerful. It is genuinely good to see Yale in the care of such people, and I thank them even more for doing that work than for assisting this new edition.

Patrick L. Pinnell
Chester, Connecticut, October 2011

INTRODUCTION

1. See Erik Vogt's chapters in Vincent Scully, et al., *Yale in New Haven: Architecture and Urbanism*, (New Haven: Yale University Press, 2004).

2. Cotton Mather, *Magnalia III* (1684), 55, quoted by Edmund S. Morgan in *Visible Saints* (New York: New York University Press, 1963), 108.

WALK ONE

1. In his standard history, *Campus, An American Planning Tradition*, Paul Turner writes, "The form of this Yale Row was repeated at many other schools. These included Dartmouth in New Hampshire, Brown in Rhode Island, Amherst College in Massachusetts, Colby and Bowdoin colleges in Maine, Hamilton and Hobart college in New York, Washington (later Trinity) College and Wesleyan University in Connecticut, St. John's and Washington colleges in Maryland, Middlebury College in Vermont, the University of Vermont, and Ohio Wesleyan, Marietta, and Western Reserve colleges in Ohio. Many of these schools even copied Yale's A-B-A-B-A pattern of alternating the flat sides of buildings with the gabled ends of buildings, producing a rhythm of long and narrow facades."

2. I am indebted to Lila Freedman, Judith Ann Schiff, and Ben de Rubertis for their work on Dwight Hall. See, among other publications, Lila Freedman, "Yale's First Library, 1842–44–46: A Hundred and Fiftyish Anniversary," *Journal of the New Haven Colony Historical Society* 41, 1: 17–36; and Judith Ann Schiff, "Old Yale: The Original Temple of Learning," *Yale Alumni Magazine*, December 1994, 80. Ben de Rubertis, unpublished manuscript, 1996.

3. Louise L. Stevenson, *Scholarly Means to Evangelical Ends: The New Haven Scholars and the Transformation of Higher Learning in America*, 1830–1890 (Baltimore and London: Johns Hopkins University Press, 1986).

WALK TWO

1. Goethe died on March 22, 1832 (3/22/32). Skull and Bones, with a mysterious "322" on its emblem, was founded in 1832–33.

WALK THREE

1. For those equipped with binoculars or a good telephoto lens, and considerable patience, here is a low-to-high listing of major figures. They begin more or less halfway up, at the level of the clock faces on the belfry, with eight corner-buttress niches occupied (beginning at the southeast corner) by Elihu Yale, Jonathan Edwards, Nathan Hale, Noah Webster, James Fenimore Cooper (who was never graduated), John C. Calhoun, Samuel F. B. Morse, and Eli Whitney. A little higher than the center of the clock faces, out from 10 and 2, on the center mullions of the eight belfry openings, stand typifications of the arts and sciences in figures of Phidias, Homer, Aristotle and Euclid. Up further still, on the clock-face centerline, where the square belfry overlaps with the lower octagon or lantern, are freestanding figures symbolizing Business, Law, Medicine and the Ministry. At the same level but tied into the structure behind them, three figures at each of the four buttressed corners as they turn into pinnacles, are the twelve figures of Life, Progress, and so on, mentioned above. Even with the pinnacle tops, back on the octagonal lantern, are eight representations of the characteristic soldiery of America's wars from the Revolution to the First World War. Immediately higher than those serious figures are eight water-spitting student gargoyles, tiny but readily identifiable because they are the only horizontal elements on the Tower. As if to make immediate recompense, the Tower offers at just the same level masks of Homer, Virgil, Dante and Shakespeare, each centered on a face of the octagon. In its topmost or crown segment, the Tower is given over to a stalagmite forest of pure ornament.

SELECTED BIBLIOGRAPHY

The history of Yale University cannot be understood without reference to the history, the fortunes, and conditions of the city of New Haven. The reverse has not always been true, important as the University has sometimes been to the city, and certainly is today. Fortunately for both entities, the fact of interdependence is today more widely appreciated and acknowledged than it has been at other times past. Those in search of further information about the buildings, situations, and people touched upon in this guide ought to keep this well in mind as they encounter publications that, written about either the city or the educational institution, exhibit different degrees of resistance to recognizing the existence of the other. The best procedure is to consult "Yale" and "New Haven" sources interchangeably and equally.

Another sort of division encountered in the literature is the tendency to discuss buildings separately from policy, curriculum, and other aspects of educational management; and both without much reference to where on campus or in the city the buildings or the activities were happening. No institution, be it a small one like a family or one as large as a university, makes its real-life daily decisions with that kind of segregation of attention if it wants to survive. Nor has it ever been otherwise. One of the tasks this guide set for itself was to recall attention often to the spatial chess game integral to the operating life of a university within a city. Those who would look further into the historical patterns written about here would do well to equip themselves with the appropraite campus and New Haven maps.

Since the University sponsored a number of publications in connection with its Tercentenary Celebration in 2001, and the anniversary itself no doubt prompted many others, the following short and highly unsystematic list of books (and no articles) will perforce be outdated almost from the moment of its publication. The reader is advised, in particular, to look to Yale in *New Haven: Architecture and Urbanism* (2004) by Vincent Scully and Catherine Lynn, with contributions by Erik Vogt and Paul Goldberger. In addition, several sections of Scully's classic survey, *American Architecture and Urbanism* (1969), refer to Yale and New Haven in the course of developing an overall American argument.

The second edition includes additional new photography by Yale's University Photographer, Michael Marsland (53, 55, 63, 69 bottom, 89, 111, 133, 141, 142, 143, 145, 147, 151, 168, 169, 176, 178, 179, 182, 201, 211 bottom, 217), Stephen M. Brown (141, 177, 183, 193 bottom, 205, 207, 211 top, 212) William K.Sacco (67 bottom), and Phil Handler (65, 67 top, 68, 113, 125, 134, 193 top, 198 bottom, 208, 226, 241). New llustrations were provided by Robert A.M. Stern Architects (186) and Foster & Partners (191).

PRIMARY SOURCES

Department of Manuscripts and Archives, Sterling Memorial Library
(many listings of documents and drawings are publicly available online)
New Haven Colony Historical Society
New Haven Free Public Library
Detroit Publishing Company Collection (http://rs6.loc.gov/detroit/dethome.html)

PUBLISHED SOURCES: GENERAL HISTORY, NEW HAVEN, AND YALE UNIVERSITY

Balmori, Diana, Diane Kostial McGuire, and Eleanor M. McPeck. *Beatrix Farrand's American Landscapes: Her Gardens and Campuses.* Sagaponack, N.Y.: Sagapress, Inc., 1985.
Bedford, Steven McLeod. *John Russell Pope, Architect of Empire.* New York: Rizzoli, 1998.

Betsky, Aaron. *James Gamble Rogers and the Architecture of Pragmatism*. New York: Architectural History Foundation, and Cambridge, Mass.: MIT Press, 1994.

Brown, Elizabeth Mills. *New Haven: A Guide to Architecture and Urban Design*. New Haven, Conn.: Yale University Press, 1976.

Carroll, Richard C., ed. *Buildings and Grounds of Yale University*. New Haven, Conn.: Yale University Printing Service, September 1979.

Chesson, Frederick W., ed. *New Haven: From the Collection of Charles Rufus Harte*. Dover, N.H.: Arcadia Publishing, 1995.

Curran, Kathleen A. *A Forgotten architect of the Gilded Age: Josiah Cleaveland Cady's Legacy*. Hartford, Conn.: Watkinson Library and Department of Fine Arts, Trinity College, 1993.

Decrow, W. E. *Yale and "The City of Elms."* Boston: W. E. Decrow, 1882.

French, Robert Dudley. *The Memorial Quadrangle: A Book about Yale*. New Haven, Conn.: Yale University Press, 1929.

Holden, Reuben A. *Yale: A Pictorial History*. New Haven, Conn.: Yale University Press, 1967.

Kelley, Brooks Mather. *Yale: A History*. New Haven, Conn.: Yale University Press, 1974.

Kingsley, William Lathrop. *Yale College, A Sketch of Its History with Notices of Its Several Departments, Instructors and Benefactors, Together with Some Account of Student Life and Amusements*. New York: Henry Holt & Co., 1879.

Landau, Sarah Bradford. *P. B. Wight: Architect, Contractor, and Critic, 1838–1925*. Chicago: Art Institute of Chicago, 1981.

Morgan, Edmund S. *The Gentle Puritan: A Life of Ezra Stiles, 1727–1795*. New Haven, Conn.: Yale University Press, 1962.

Nettleton, George Henry, ed. *The Book of the Yale Pageant, 21 October 1916, In Commemoration of the Two Hundredth Anniversary of the Removal of Yale College to New Haven*. New Haven, Conn.: Yale University Press, 1916.

Osterweis, Rollin G. *Three Centuries of New Haven, 1638–1938*. New Haven, Conn.: Yale University Press, 1962.

Oviatt, Edwin. *The Beginnings of Yale (1701–1726)*. New Haven, Conn.: Yale University Press, 1916.

Peck, Amelia, ed. *Alexander Jackson Davis, American Architect 1803–1892*. New York: Rizzoli, 1992.

Pierson, George Wilson. *Yale: College and University, 1871–1937*. 2 vols. New Haven, Conn.: Yale University Press, 1952.

———. *Yale: A Short History*. New Haven, Conn.: Office of the Secretary, Yale University, 1976. Reprint, 1991.

Scully, Vincent. *American Architecture and Urbanism*. New York: Praeger Publications, 1969.

Seymour, George Dudley. *A book recording the varied activities of the author in his efforts over many years to promote the welfare of the city of his adoption since 1883, together with some researches into its storied past and many illustrations*. New Haven, Conn.: privately printed for the author, 1942.

Shumway, Floyd, and Richard Hegel, eds. *New Haven: An Illustrated History*. New Haven, Conn.: New Haven Colony Historical Society, 1981.

Stevenson, Louise L. *Scholarly Means to Evangelical Ends: The New Haven Scholars and the Transformation of Higher Learning in America, 1830–1890*. Baltimore, Md.: Johns Hopkins University Press, 1986.

Tucker, Louis Leonard. *Puritan Protaganist: President Thomas Clap of Yale College*. Chapel Hill, N.C.: University of North Carolina Press, 1962.

Warch, Richard. *School of the Prophets: Yale College, 1701–1740*. New Haven, Conn.: Yale University Press, 1973.

Welch, Lewis Sheldon, and Walter Camp. *Yale, Her Campus, Class-Rooms, and Athletics*. Boston: L. C. Page and Company, 1899.

INDEX